The Rag
and Bone Shop
of the Heart

The Rag and Bone Shop of the Heart

POEMS FOR MEN

Robert Bly, James Hillman,
and Michael Meade
EDITORS

HarperPerennial
A Division of HarperCollinsPublishers

THE LIBRARY OF CONGRESS HAS CATALOGUED
THE HARDCOVER EDITION AS FOLLOWS:

The Rag and bone shop of the heart : poems for men / edited by
Robert Bly, James Hillman, and Michael Meade. — 1st ed.
p. cm.
Includes index.
ISBN 0-06-092420-9 (pbk.)
I. Poetry. I. Bly, Robert. II. Hillman, James.
III. Meade, Michael, 1944– . IV. Title: Poems for men.
PN6101.R28 1992
808.81'0081—dc20   91-50460

10 DT/RRD 31

CONTENTS

TWO
FATHERS' PRAYERS FOR SONS AND DAUGHTERS
31

THREE
WAR
63

Contents

FOUR
I KNOW THE EARTH, AND I AM SAD
93

FIVE
THE HOUSE OF FATHERS AND TITANS
117

Contents

SIX

LANGUAGE:
SPEAKING WELL AND SPEAKING OUT
153

SEVEN
MAKING A HOLE IN DENIAL
193

Contents

EIGHT
LOVING THE COMMUNITY AND WORK
227

NINE
THE NAÏVE MALE
259

Contents

TEN
THE SECOND LAYER:
ANGER, HATRED, OUTRAGE
283

Contents

xi

ELEVEN
EARTHLY LOVE
313

Contents

THIRTEEN
MOTHER AND GREAT MOTHER
383

Contents
xiii

FOURTEEN
THE SPINDRIFT GAZE TOWARD PARADISE
415

Contents

xiv

FIFTEEN
ZANINESS
447

SIXTEEN
LOVING THE WORLD ANYWAY
471

Contents

Contents
xvi

Those masterful images because complete
Grew in pure mind, but out of what began?
A mound of refuse or the sweeping of a street,
Old kettles, old bottles, and a broken can,
Old iron, old bones, old rags, that raving slut
Who keeps the till. Now that my ladder's gone,
I must lie down where all the ladders start,
In the foul rag-and-bone shop of the heart.

—WILLIAM BUTLER YEATS

from *The Circus Animals' Desertion*

FOREWORD

How does the work of men connect to poetry? To this day in Kazakhstan roomfuls of men sit listening to a poet chant long narratives. We recall the importance of poetry in the lives of Norse farmers, Icelandic sheepherders, Greek olive growers and fishermen. Their attention cannot be explained in terms of literacy or electricity—that they can't read or watch television. Rather, the question becomes how do the life of men and the life of a culture connect to poetry?

The relation of poetry to culture has been debated as far back as Plato's attack on Homer, through the Renaissance and the Puritan's Reformation, and continuing with the Romantic Shelley's *Defense of Poetry* and today's arguments for a core curriculum of great books. While our European-American tradition questions and argues, and has to teach poetry to sullen students in English classes, other cultures, speaking Spanish, Russian, Arabic, to say nothing of the many tongues of Africa and the Indian subcontinent, grow up inside poems, drenched through with poetic metaphors and rhythms. As we learn to criticize, to take a poem apart, to get its meaning, they learn to listen and to recite.

By drawing this sharp contrast with other cultures, we are pointing to a defect in ours. We live in a poetically underdeveloped nation. Men blame their own lives for a deficiency in the culture. For, without the fanciful delicacy and the powerful truths that poems convey, emotions and imagination flatten out.

There's a lack of spirit, of vision. The loss in the heart appears as a loss of heart to take up the great cultural challenges that are part of every man's citizenship. It is in this sense that we have come to think that working in poetry and myth with men is a therapy of the culture at its psychic roots.

It is said that the poets of Ireland gathered together once to see if in company they could recall the old epic of the Tain. Each of them knew a part, no poet knew the whole poem, and in some spots masses of lines were missing altogether. One of the young poets went to the gravestone of Fergus and chanted to the spirit of the old hero. The spirit responded, and Fergus recited the epic for three days to the poet who put it all to memory in his heart. When the poets gathered again, the young man was able to supply the missing lines, and the poem was complete.

For years we have opened and closed the gatherings of men with poems. Through the collaboration of everyone involved, the diversity and number of poems have grown. A question painfully put in one poem is answered in another. Sometimes the answering poem came from a man in the audience, so that listeners became tellers and the speakers heard lines forgotten or never heard before; it was as if we were at the old man's gravestone, and were remembering the community of men joined together by poems still held in someone's memory.

Because this is America, there are many ancestral voices, and diverse gravestones carved in many languages. Our epic cannot be single like the Tain and must be composed only in a wide-ranging and ongoing fashion. No matter how many poets and poems, it can never be complete. And so, essential to that American soul is the feeling that something is not here, something is forgotten, and there's a longing in the heart for yet another line, another verse.

These poems have been argued over, repeated, mixed with tears and laughter, and required to end events that didn't want to close. We have collected the poems which moved men the most in gatherings over the last ten years. We hope it's clear that we are talking of spoken poetry, not poetry confined to the page. When one reads poetry that is "all on the page," one is alone. When poetry is spoken, particularly when the larnyx is opened and the voice can come from the midriff, people feel in company, in joy, in community. Depths of grief are reached, and flights of inspiration. So it might be well to let your own voice sound when coming upon a poem that particularly strikes you or one that seems remote and cold on the page.

Blake spoken aloud is always great in a company of men. Yeats is tremendous—his rhetoric penetrates to the bone. James Wright and Anna Akhmatova move the heart in such simple words when said quietly aloud. When David Ignatow's poems of ordinary office and working life are spoken, men say "unbelievable." D. H. Lawrence, William Carlos Williams, Etheridge Knight, Sharon Olds, Theodore Roethke, Marianne Moore, César Vallejo—much great poetry has been written in this century.

By calling it *Poems for Men* we don't mean that this collection is not to be read by women; we would rejoice if women read it.

As editors, each of us has our sources, our favorite poets, but our range is limited, and it's clear that there are many lines in our collection that are still missing.

R.B., J.H., M.J.M.

ONE

Approach
to Wildness

B oys feel wild; they love their tree houses, their wild spots in the woods, they all want to go down to the river, with Huck, away from domesticating aunts. Boys love to see some wildness in their fathers, to see their fathers dancing or carrying on. Some boys are so afraid that they will become domestic that they become savage, not wild.

The marks of wildness are love of nature, especially its silence, a voice box free to say spontaneous things, an exuberance, a love of "the edge," the willingness to admit the "three strange angels" that Lawrence speaks of. Yeats realized searching Roman and Greek texts that even Cicero, considered middle of the road, was much wilder than any of his friends; the wild man is not mad like a criminal or mad like a psychotic, but "Mad as the mist and snow."

> How many years ago
> Were you and I unlettered lads
> Mad as the mist and snow?

This question does not mean that wildness is restricted to childishness, or is dominated by so-called primitive emotions, or amounts to atavism. The wildness of nature is highly sophisticated.

Jung remarked, "It is difficult to say to anybody, you should . . . become acquainted with your animal, because people think it is a sort of lunatic asylum, they think the animal is jumping over walls and raising hell all over town. Yet the animal . . . is pious, it follows the path with great regularity. . . . Only man is extravagant . . ." (Visions Seminar I, p. 282).

Thoreau says, "In literature it is only the wild that attracts us." King Lear attracts us, the dervish, the Zen laugher. The civilized eye of man has become dulled, unable to take in the natural wildness of the planet. Blake says, "The roaring of lions, the howling of wolves, the raging of the stormy sea, and the destructive sword, are portions of eternity, too great for the eye of man."

Each of us wants to get in touch not so much with the harsh rebel, the self-destroying outsider, as with the beauty of what the Sufis call "Joseph," the round-faced troublemaker.

> Pharaoh and the whole Egyptian world
>   collapsed for such a Joseph.
> I'd gladly spend years getting word
>   of him, even third or fourth hand.

One of the great preservers of wildness is the Sufi poet Rumi, who founded the whirling dervishes. When he says wine, he doesn't mean physical wine, but the feeling of ecstasy that unites people after midnight and encourages them to "be thrown into the fire":

> Two strong impulses: One
> to drink long and deep,
> the other,
> not to sober up too soon.

One can keep one's job and still be wild; one can remain married and still be wild; one can live in cities and remain wild. What is needed is a soul discipline that Gary Snyder calls "practice of the wild"—Wendell Berry understands it well. García Lorca practices it by the way he leaps from one image to the next, surefooted as a cat. "What is the knocking?" Lawrence says.

> What is the knocking at the door in the night?
> It is somebody wants to do us harm.
>
> No, no, it is the three strange angels.
> Admit them, admit them.

The practice is a secret that not all understand, but many blues musicians and jazz soloists and lovers understand it. "Whoever's not killed for love is dead meat."

R.B.

DANSE RUSSE

If when my wife is sleeping
and the baby and Kathleen
are sleeping
and the sun is a flame-white disc
in silken mists
above shining trees,—
if I in my north room
dance naked, grotesquely
before my mirror
waving my shirt round my head
and singing softly to myself:
"I am lonely, lonely.
I was born to be lonely,
I am best so!"
If I admire my arms, my face,
my shoulders, flanks, buttocks
against the yellow drawn shades,—

Who shall say I am not
the happy genius of my household?

WILLIAM CARLOS WILLIAMS

SMELL!

Oh strong-ridged and deeply hollowed
nose of mine! what will you not be smelling?
What tactless asses we are, you and I boney nose
always indiscriminate, always unashamed,
and now it is the souring flowers of the bedraggled
poplars: a festering pulp on the wet earth
beneath them. With what deep thirst
we quicken our desires
to that rank odor of a passing springtime!
Can you not be decent? Can you not reserve your ardors
for something less unlovely? What girl will care
for us, do you think, if we continue in these ways?
Must you taste everything? Must you know everything?
Must you have a part in everything?

WILLIAM CARLOS WILLIAMS

CRAZY DOG EVENTS
Crow Indian

1. Act like a crazy dog. Wear sashes & other fine clothes, carry a rattle, & dance along the roads singing crazy dog songs after everybody else has gone to bed.

2. Talk crosswise: say the opposite of what you mean & make others say the opposite of what they mean in return.

3. Fight like a fool by rushing up to an enemy & offering to be killed. Dig a hole near an enemy, & when the enemy surrounds it, leap out at them & drive them back.

4. Paint yourself white, mount a white horse, cover its eyes & make it jump down a steep & rocky bank, until both of you are crushed.

arranged: 12-11-70

JEROME ROTHENBERG

FOUR QUATRAINS

1

Where is a foot worthy to walk a garden,
or any eye that deserves to look at trees?

Show me a man willing to be
thrown in the fire.

2

In the shambles of love, they kill only the best,
none of the weak or deformed.
Don't run away from this dying.
Whoever's not killed for love is dead meat.

3

Tonight with wine being poured
and instruments singing among themselves,
one thing is forbidden,
one thing: Sleep.

4

Two strong impulses: One
to drink long and deep,
the other,
not to sober up too soon.

RUMI
translated by Coleman Barks and
John Moyne

MUCH MADNESS
IS DIVINEST SENSE

Much Madness is divinest Sense—
To a discerning Eye—
Much Sense—the starkest Madness—
'Tis the Majority
In this, as All, prevail—
Assent—and you are sane—
Demur—you're straightway dangerous—
And handled with a Chain—

EMILY DICKINSON

from
NOTEBOOK OF A RETURN
TO THE NATIVE LAND

I would rediscover the secret of great communications and
great combustions. I would say storm. I would say river.
I would say tornado. I would say leaf. I would say tree.
I would be drenched by all rains, moistened by all dews.
I would roll like frenetic blood on the slow current of
the eye of words turned into mad horses into fresh children
into clots into vestiges of temples into precious stones
remote enough to discourage miners. Whoever would not
  understand
me would not understand any better the roaring of a tiger.

AIMÉ CÉSAIRE
translated by Clayton Eshleman and Annette Smith

BREAD AND WINE
Part 7

Oh friend, we arrived too late. The divine energies
  Are still alive, but isolated above us, in the archetypal
    world.
They keep on going there, and, apparently, don't bother if
  Humans live or not . . . that is a heavenly mercy.
Sometimes a human's clay is not strong enough to take the
    water;
  Human beings can carry the divine only sometimes.
What is living now? Night dreams of them. But craziness
  Helps, so does sleep. Grief and Night toughen us,
Until people capable of sacrifice once more rock
  In the iron cradle, desire people, like the ancients, strong
    enough for water.
In thunderstorms it will arrive. I have the feeling often,
    meanwhile,
  It is better to sleep, since the Guest comes so seldom;
We waste our life waiting, and I haven't the faintest idea
  How to act or talk . . . in the lean years who needs
    poets?
But poets as you say are like the holy disciple of the Wild
    One
  Who used to stroll over the fields through the whole
    divine night.

FRIEDRICH HÖLDERLIN
translated by R.B.

HAS ANYONE SEEN THE BOY?

Has anyone seen the boy who used to come here?
Round-faced trouble-maker, quick to find a joke,
      slow to be serious, red shirt,
      perfect coordination, sly, strong muscled,
      with things always in his pocket: reed flute,
      worn pick, polished and ready for his Talent
         you know that one.
Have you heard stories about him?
Pharaoh and the whole Egyptian world
      collapsed for such a Joseph.
I'd gladly spend years getting word
      of him, even third or fourth hand.

RUMI
version by Coleman Barks and John Moyne

from
THE WILL TO BELIEVE
on Extravagant Desires

Man's chief difference from the brutes lies in the exuberant excess of his subjective propensities,—his pre-eminence over them simply and solely in the number and in the fantastic and unnecessary character of his wants, physical, moral, aesthetic, and intellectual. Had his whole life not been a quest for the superfluous, he would never have established himself as inexpugnably as he has done in the necessary. And from the consciousness of this he should draw the lesson that his wants are to be trusted; that even when their gratification seems farthest off, the uneasiness they occasion is still the best guide of his life, and will lead him to issues entirely beyond his present powers of reckoning. Prune down his extravagance, sober him, and you undo him.

WILLIAM JAMES

from
PROVERBS FROM HELL

The pride of the peacock is the glory of God.
The lust of the goat is the bounty of God.
The wrath of the lion is the wisdom of God.
The nakedness of woman is the work of God.

The roaring of lions, the howling of wolves, the raging of the stormy sea, and the destructive sword, are portions of eternity, too great for the eye of man.

The tygers of wrath are wiser than the horses of instruction.

You never know what is enough unless you know what is more than enough.

What is now proved was once only imagin'd.

Improvement makes straight roads; but the crooked roads without improvements are roads of Genius.
Sooner murder an infant in its cradle than nurse unacted desires.

The road of excess leads to the palace of wisdom.

He who desires but acts not, breeds pestilence.

Eternity is in love with the productions of time.

No bird soars too high, if he soars with his own wings.

If the fool would persist in his folly he would become wise.

Exuberance is Beauty.

WILLIAM BLAKE

MIDDLE OF THE WAY

3

The coals go out,
The last smoke weaves up
Losing itself in the stars.
This is my first night to lie
In the uncreating dark.

In the heart of a man
There sleeps a green worm
That has spun the heart about itself,
And that shall dream itself black wings
One day to break free into the beautiful black sky.

I leave my eyes open,
I lie here and forget our life,
All I see is we float out
Into the emptiness, among the great stars,
On this little vessel without lights.

I know that I love the day,
The sun on the mountain, the Pacific
Shiny and accomplishing itself in breakers,
But I know I live half alive in the world,
Half my life belongs to the wild darkness.

GALWAY KINNELL

THE WILD MALLARD THOUGHT

In literature it is only the wild that attracts us. Dullness is but another name for tameness. It is the uncivilized free and wild thinking in Hamlet and the Iliad, in all the scriptures and mythologies, not learned in the schools, that delights us. As the wild duck is more swift and beautiful than the tame, so is the wild—the mallard—thought, which 'mid falling dews wings its way above the fens. A truly good book is something as natural, and as unexpectedly and unaccountably fair and perfect, as a wild-flower discovered on the prairies of the West or in the jungles of the East. Genius is a light which makes the darkness visible, like the lightning's flash, which perchance shatters the temple of knowledge itself,—and not a taper lighted at the hearth-stone of the race, which pales before the light of common day.

HENRY DAVID THOREAU

THE WILD MAN
COMES TO THE MONASTERY

. . . There was a time when I thought sweeter than the quiet converse of monks, the cooing of the ringdove flitting about the pool.

There was a time when I thought sweeter than the sound of a little bell beside me, the warbling of the blackbird from the gable and the belling of the stag in the storm.

There was a time when I thought sweeter than the voice of a lovely woman beside me, to hear at matins the cry of the heath-hen of the moor.

There was a time when I thought sweeter the howling of wolves, than the voice of a priest indoors, baa-ing and bleating.

Though you like your ale with ceremony in the drinking-halls, I like better to snatch a drink of water in my palm from a spring.

Though you think sweet, yonder in your church, the gentle talk of your students, sweeter I think the splendid talking the wolves make in Glenn mBolcáin.

Though you like the fat and meat which are eaten in the drinking-halls, I like better to eat a head of clean water-cress in a place without sorrow . . .

Irish; author unknown; twelfth century

from
SONG OF A MAN
WHO HAS COME THROUGH

Not I, not I, but the wind that blows through me!
A fine wind is blowing the new direction of Time.
If only I let it bear me, carry me, if only it carry me! . . .

If only I am keen and hard like the sheer tip of a wedge
Driven by invisible blows,
The rock will split, we shall come at the wonder, we
   shall find the Hesperides. . . .

What is the knocking?
What is the knocking at the door in the night?
It is somebody wants to do us harm.

No, no, it is the three strange angels.
Admit them, admit them.

D. H. LAWRENCE

KNOWING NOTHING
SHUTS THE IRON GATES

Knowing nothing shuts the iron gates; the new love opens
them.

The sound of the gates opening wakes the beautiful woman
asleep.

Kabir says: Fantastic! Don't let a chance like this go by!

KABIR
version by R.B.

from
IN A DARK TIME

In a dark time, the eye begins to see,
I meet my shadow in the deepening shade;
I hear my echo in the echoing wood—
A lord of nature weeping to a tree.
I live between the heron and the wren,
Beasts of the hill and serpents of the den.

What's madness but nobility of soul
At odds with circumstance? The day's on fire!
I know the purity of pure despair,
My shadow pinned against a sweating wall.
That place among the rocks—is it a cave,
Or winding path? The edge is what I have . . .

THEODORE ROETHKE

LITTLE INFINITE POEM

For Luis Cardoza y Aragón

To take the wrong road
is to arrive at the snow.
and to arrive at the snow
is to get down on all fours for twenty centuries and eat the
    grasses of the cemeteries.

To take the wrong road
is to arrive at woman,
woman who isn't afraid of light,
woman who murders two roosters in one second,
light which isn't afraid of roosters,
and roosters who don't know how to sing on top of the
    snow.

But if the snow truly takes the wrong road,
then it might meet the southern wind,
and since the air cares nothing for groans,
we will have to get down on all fours again and eat the
    grasses of the cemeteries.

I saw two mournful wheatheads made of wax
burying a countryside of volcanoes;
and I saw two insane little boys who wept as they leaned on
    a murderer's eyeballs.

But two has never been a number—
because it's only an anguish and its shadow,
it's only a guitar where love feels how hopeless it is,
it's the proof of someone else's infinity,
and the walls around a dead man,
and the scourging of a new resurrection that will never end.
Dead people hate the number two,

but the number two makes women drop off to sleep,
and since women are afraid of light,
light shudders when it has to face the roosters,
and since all roosters know is how to fly over the snow
we will have to get down on all fours and eat the grasses of
    the cemeteries forever.

January 10, 1930. New York.

FEDERICO GARCÍA LORCA
translated by R.B.

"Because I am mad about women
I am mad about the hills,"
Said that wild old wicked man
Who travels where God wills.
"Not to die on the straw at home,
Those hands to close these eyes,
That is all I ask, my dear,
From the old man in the skies.
                    Daybreak and a candle-end.

"Kind are all your words, my dear,
Do not the rest withhold.
Who can know the year, my dear,
When an old man's blood grows cold?
I have what no young man can have
Because he loves too much.
Words I have that can pierce the heart,
But what can he do but touch?"
                    Daybreak and a candle-end.

Then said she to that wild old man,
His stout stick under his hand,
"Love to give or to withhold
Is not at my command.
I gave it all to an older man:
That old man in the skies.
Hands that are busy with His beads
Can never close those eyes."
                    Daybreak and a candle-end.

"Go your ways, O go your ways,
I choose another mark,
Girls down on the seashore
Who understand the dark;

Bawdy talk for the fishermen;
A dance for the fisher-lads;
When dark hangs upon the water
They turn down their beds.

Daybreak and a candle-end.

"A young man in the dark am I,
But a wild old man in the light,
That can make a cat laugh, or
Can touch by mother wit
Things hid in their marrow-bones
From time long passed away,
Hid from all those warty lads
That by their bodies lay.

Daybreak and a candle-end.

"All men live in suffering,
I know as few can know,
Whether they take the upper road
Or stay content on the low,
Rower bent in his row-boat
Or weaver bent at his loom,
Horseman erect upon horseback
Or child hid in the womb.

Daybreak and a candle-end.

"That some stream of lightning
From the old man in the skies
Can burn out that suffering
No right-taught man denies.
But a coarse old man am I,
I choose the second-best,
I forget it all awhile
Upon a woman's breast."

Daybreak and a candle-end.

WILLIAM BUTLER YEATS

The Rag and Bone Shop of the Heart

MAD AS THE MIST AND SNOW

Bolt and bar the shutter,
For the foul winds blow:
Our minds are at their best this night,
And I seem to know
That everything outside us is
Mad as the mist and snow.

Horace there by Homer stands,
Plato stands below,
And here is Tully's open page.
How many years ago
Were you and I unlettered lads
Mad as the mist and snow?

You ask what makes me sigh, old friend,
What makes me shudder so?
I shudder and I sigh to think
That even Cicero
And many-minded Homer were
Mad as the mist and snow.

WILLIAM BUTLER YEATS

When the full moon comes
I'll go to Santiago in Cuba.
I'll go to Santiago
in a carriage of black water.
I'll go to Santiago.
Palm-thatching will start to sing.
I'll go to Santiago.
When the palm trees want to turn into storks,
I'll go to Santiago.
When the banana trees want to turn into jellyfish,
I'll go to Santiago.
With the golden head of Fonseca.
I'll go to Santiago
And with the rose of Romeo and Juliet
I'll go to Santiago.
Oh Cuba! Oh rhythm of dry seeds!
I'll go to Santiago.
Oh warm waist, and a drop of wood!
I'll go to Santiago.
Harp of living trees. Crocodile. Tobacco blossom!
I'll go to Santiago.
I always said I would go to Santiago
in a carriage of black water.
I'll go to Santiago.
Wind and alcohol in the wheels,
I'll go to Santiago.
My coral in the darkness,
I'll go to Santiago.
The ocean drowned in the sand,
I'll go to Santiago.
White head and dead fruit,

I'll go to Santiago.
Oh wonderful freshness of the cane fields!
Oh Cuba! Arc of sighs and mud!
I'll go to Santiago.

FEDERICO GARCÍA LORCA
translated by R.B.

ADVICE

Someone dancing inside us
learned only a few steps:
the "Do-Your-Work" in 4/4 time,
the "What-Do-You-Expect" waltz.
He hasn't noticed yet the woman
standing away from the lamp,
the one with black eyes
who knows the rhumba,
and strange steps in jumpy rhythms
from the mountains in Bulgaria.
If they dance together,
something unexpected will happen.
If they don't, the next world
will be a lot like this one.

BILL HOLM

TWO

Fathers' Prayers for Sons and Daughters

Protecting, till the danger past,
With human love.

—WILLIAM BUTLER YEATS

We call them prayers because each poem carries some blessing, even if hidden. We call them daughters and sons because they are being held and protected, because a blessing is trying to form around them. Not all the writers are parents through births, but all are doing that awkward praying that mothers and fathers a child into life. "[W]hat would you tell your child?" asks William Stafford in the first poem. Father and daughter are staring at the storming ocean from a dune. The child wants to know, standing in the mutual gaze over oceans, over time: "How far could you swim, Daddy, / in such a storm?" How far will the father go for the child; how far does my father's heart reach out into the world? The child is seven and needs to hear an emotional truth spoken, needs to hear the shape of the father's heart. The world has become an "absolute vista" and her father has pulled her up to view the great storms of life. Now her question pulls him into the wave-torn sea. In that moment he knows the answer in his heart:

> "As far as was needed," I said,
> and as I talked, I swam.

The blessing is partly in the father's capacity to hear the real question, partly in the heart-willingness of his answer.

But the conversation could go very differently. On another day the father might not hear the child's true question or might lack an answer. In "A Story," by Li-Young Lee, a son asks his father for a new story and the father can't come up with one. An entire history of father and son is lived out in that moment.

> . . . *Are you a god,*
> the man screams, *that I sit mute before you?*
> *Am I a god that I should never disappoint?*

No matter what, the son will live out his story, and, short or long, it will include disappointment with his father. It will include emptiness within which the father's love will pray. The father's story has silences in it; that's where the prayers rise from.

> Because of the great gloom that is in my mind.

> I have walked and prayed for this young child an hour.
> And heard the sea-wind scream upon the tower,

So says Yeats in that pacing prayer all parents know. It's as if he were walking with James Joyce, incanting against the threatening seas of life, for Joyce is saying of his son:

> From whining wind and colder
> Grey sea I wrap him warm . . .

> Around us fear, descending
> Darkness of fear above
> And in my heart how deep unending
> Ache of love!

I would stop it there, the father's arm around him warm, his voice dispelling fears. But a deeper voice speaks in these father's prayers. When the fears come fully down and the "crazy pierstakes groan," when fate takes the child's life before the father's own. "Oh, could I lose all father now!" says Ben Jonson.

And David Ray in "In the Third Month" after his son's death says how the poet and family will pray:

> . . . The tears pour down
> as I think how much he wanted to be a man,

It's our knowledge of death that makes us pray. Every path a child takes looks precarious to the parent's eye. And it is, and *precarious* is an old word that means "full of prayers."

The dangers that attend the birth of each child draw prayers and ritual acts from mothers and fathers. Women pray while breathing through labor. A father-to-be rhythmically wraps and unwraps a strip of cloth or string. Throughout history the fathers assisted the birthing ritually, symbolically, physically. Haki Madhubuti invites them to it again in "Men and Birth,"

> welcome to new seasons of wisdom. . . .
> to urging life onward quietly &
> magnificently.

The father's hands unwinding cloth mimics ancient rituals of unbinding everything tied up in the vicinity of the birth so the infant is not caught in the womb. It is the work of the father, as Haki says, that "unlocks cultural strangulation" and begins the blessing of his child with "smiles occasional tears and undying commitment." In "Changing Diapers," Gary Snyder urges life and the noble intensity of the child onward. He wipes away cultural and historical differences and wraps himself and his son into what is brave in all men:

> No trouble, friend,
> you and me and Geronimo
> are men.

The poems we've included aren't formulas or standards for prayer. Rather, they are instinctive, intuitive calls to a third area that is neither parent nor child. They call on earth, animals, and ancient images as James Joyce calls on the wildness hidden in the rose to sustain a daughter born to frailness. They are stories that bring something that is not of the parent next to the child. The blessing requires something of the "other worlds" or else it may miss the delicate accuracy of anointing a life. And the father cannot himself be in the position of the child nor caught in his own "inner child" if he is to bless. The one who prays must give the space of the child up or else a swamp of sentimentality will come in. If there is no bear or king or temple involved, the ritual of blessing will stop and a need of the parent or a moral lesson will rush into the gap.

As William Stafford tells it in "A Story That Could Be True," the child that needs prayer and blessing is already standing in "the robberies of the rain." At the moment of danger the "real mother died," the "father is lost," and no one knows the child's name. The one who would pray must, for a moment, know the child's true name.

M.J.M.

WITH KIT, AGE 7, AT THE BEACH

We would climb the highest dune,
from there to gaze and come down:
the ocean was performing;
we contributed our climb.

Waves leapfrogged and came
straight out of the storm.
What should our gaze mean?
Kit waited for me to decide.

Standing on such a hill,
what would you tell your child?
That was an absolute vista.
Those waves raced far, and cold.

"How far could you swim, Daddy,
in such a storm?"
"As far as was needed," I said,
and as I talked, I swam.

WILLIAM STAFFORD

A STORY

Sad is the man who is asked for a story
and can't come up with one.

His five-year-old son waits in his lap.
Not the same story, Baba. A new one.
The man rubs his chin, scratches his ear.

In a room full of books in a world
of stories, he can recall
not one, and soon, he thinks, the boy
will give up on his father.

Already the man lives far ahead, he sees
the day this boy will go. *Don't go!*
Hear the alligator story! The angel story once more!
You love the spider story. You laugh at the spider.
Let me tell it!

But the boy is packing his shirts,
he is looking for his keys. *Are you a god,*
the man screams, *that I sit mute before you?*
Am I a god that I should never disappoint?

But the boy is here. *Please, Baba, a story?*
It is an emotional rather than logical equation,
an earthly rather than heavenly one,
which posits that a boy's supplications
and a father's love add up to silence.

LI-YOUNG LEE

A PRAYER
FOR MY SON

Bid a strong ghost stand at the head
That my Michael may sleep sound,
Nor cry, not turn in the bed
Till his morning meal come round;
And may departing twilight keep
All dread afar till morning's back,
That his mother may not lack
Her fill of sleep.

Bid the ghost have sword in fist:
Some there are, for I avow
Such devilish things exist,
Who have planned his murder, for they know
Of some most haughty deed or thought
That awaits upon his future days,
And would through hatred of the bays
Bring that to nought.

Though You can fashion everything
From nothing every day, and teach
The morning stars to sing,
You have lacked articulate speech
To tell Your simplest want, and known,
Wailing upon a woman's knee,
All of that worst ignominy
Of flesh and bone;

And when through all the town there ran
The servants of Your enemy,
A woman and a man,
Unless the Holy Writings lie,

Hurried through the smooth and rough
And through the fertile and waste,
Protecting, till the danger past,
With human love.

WILLIAM BUTLER YEATS

ON THE BEACH AT FONTANA

Wind whines and whines the shingle,
The crazy pierstakes groan;
A senile sea numbers each single
Slimesilvered stone.

From whining wind and colder
Grey sea I wrap him warm
And touch his trembling fineboned shoulder
And boyish arm.

Around us fear, descending
Darkness of fear above
And in my heart how deep unending
Ache of love!

Trieste, 1914

JAMES JOYCE

IN THE THIRD MONTH

First snow wet against the windshield.
I drive by the storefront where we found
his blue Toyota. How he loved that car—
put fur upon the dashboard to cover cracks—
then he and his girl devotedly stretched leather
across the back seat making a love nest.
And they went out to Western Auto and bought
a little fan, the kind bus drivers use,
and mounted it to blow down upon them
when they made love, parked by a roadside
or perhaps in one of those shadowed drive-ins.
It's a weekend and I'm about my errands,
Bach's *Sleepers Awake* on FM. The tears pour down
as I think how much he wanted to be a man,
simply a man with his woman and his car, later
his fireside books, those I still have,
saved too long to pass on—*The Way
of All Flesh, A Shropshire Lad, Don Quixote,*
and one stamped in gold but with all pages blank.

DAVID RAY

ON MY FIRST SON

Farewell, thou child of my right hand, and joy;
　　My sin was too much hope of thee, loved boy.
Seven years thou wert lent to me, and I thee pay,
　　Exacted by thy fate, on the just day.
Oh, could I lose all father now! for why
　　Will man lament the state he should envy?
To have so soon 'scaped world's and flesh's rage,
　　And, if no other misery, yet age!
Rest in soft peace, and asked, say, here doth lie
　　Ben Jonson his best piece of poetry.
For whose sake henceforth all his vows be such,
　　As what he loves may never like too much.

BEN JONSON

THE IDEA OF ANCESTRY

1

Taped to the wall of my cell are 47 pictures: 47 black
faces: my father, mother, grandmothers (1 dead), grand-
fathers (both dead), brothers, sisters, uncles, aunts,
cousins (1st & 2nd), nieces and nephews. They stare
across the space at me sprawling on my bunk. I know
their dark eyes, they know mine. I know their style,
they know mine. I am all of them, they are all of me;
they are farmers, I am a thief, I am me, they are thee.

I have at one time or another been in love with my mother,
1 grandmother, 2 sisters, 2 aunts (1 went to the asylum),
and 5 cousins. I am now in love with a 7-yr-old niece
(she sends me letters written in large block print, and
her picture is the only one that smiles at me).

I have the same name as 1 grandfather, 3 cousins, 3 nephews,
and 1 uncle. The uncle disappeared when he was 15, just took
off and caught a freight (they say). He's discussed each year
when the family has a reunion, he causes uneasiness in
the clan, he is an empty space. My father's mother, who is 93
and who keeps the Family Bible with everybody's birth dates
(and death dates) in it, always mentions him. There is no
place in her Bible for "whereabouts unknown."

2

Each fall the graves of my grandfathers call me, the brown
hills and red gullies of mississippi send out their electric
messages, galvanizing my genes. Last yr / like a salmon
   quitting
the cold ocean-leaping and bucking up his birthstream / I
hitchhiked my way from LA with 16 caps in my pocket and a

monkey on my back. And I almost kicked it with the
   kinfolks.
I walked barefooted in my grandmother's backyard / I smelled
   the old
land and the woods / I sipped cornwhiskey from fruit jars
   with the men /
I flirted with the women / I had a ball till the caps ran out
and my habit came down. That night I looked at my
   grandmother
and split / my guts were screaming for junk / but I was almost
contented / I had almost caught up with me.
(The next day in Memphis I cracked a croaker's crib for a
   fix.)

This year there is a gray stone wall damming my stream, and
   when
the falling leaves stir my genes, I pace my cell or flop on my
   bunk
and stare at 47 black faces across the space. I am all of them,
they are all of me, I am me, they are thee, and I have no
   children
to float in the space between.

ETHERIDGE KNIGHT

malepractice and maleabsence issue is loneliness & limiting to-morrows. men need to experience rising screams, husbands, lov-ers, fathers, menfriends should be with their wives, women before. during & after. helping them weather labor and lonely storms. we, locating new climates & seasons working with mid-wives, doctors & wife allowing them to take you back to school. you, who thought that baby delivering was others' work, stranger's work.

welcome to new seasons of wisdom.
welcome to counting & breathing,
to pushing & contractions,
to urging life onward quietly &
magnificently.

muffled grunts interrupt sleep urging participation counting push pushing encouraging your mate to relax to breathe prop-erly, constantly setting the mental clock. in the bed at her rear pulling legs back enlarging womb creating unbelievable spaces wider urging life here. men viewing & aiding the unquestioned miracle on earth. sliding head first helpless struggling searching attacking life into waiting hands baby crying for mother & lov-ing touches. this is the drama, birth the maturing force that can transform males, making them men of conscious. making them bringers of life and partners in the fight to guarantee better better futures.

birth
unlocks cultural strangulation allowing
men to feel & touch & experience
a source of love that springs in
smiles occasional tears and   undying commitment.

HAKI R. MADHUBUTI

The Rag and Bone Shop of the Heart

LASTNESS
(Part 2)

A black bear sits alone
in the twilight, nodding from side
to side, turning slowly around and around
on himself, scuffing the four-footed
circle into the earth. He sniffs the sweat
in the breeze, he understands
a creature, a death-creature
watches from the fringe of the trees,
finally he understands
I am no longer here, he himself
from the fringe of the trees watches
a black bear
get up, eat a few flowers, trudge away,
all his fur glistening
in the rain.

And what glistening! Sancho Fergus,
my boychild, had such great shoulders,
when he was born his head
came out, the rest of him stuck. And he opened
his eyes: his head out there all alone
in the room, he squinted with pained,
barely unglued eyes at the ninth-month's
blood splashing beneath him
on the floor. And almost
smiled, I thought, almost forgave it all in advance.

When he came wholly forth
I took him up in my hands and bent
over and smelled
the black, glistening fur

Fathers' Prayers for Sons and Daughters
47

of his head, as empty space
must have bent
over the newborn planet
and smelled the grasslands and the ferns.

GALWAY KINNELL

CHANGING DIAPERS

How intelligent he looks!
    on his back
    both feet caught in my one hand
    his glance set sideways,
    on a giant poster of Geronimo
    with a Sharp's repeating rifle by his knee.

I open, wipe, he doesn't even notice
    nor do I.
Baby legs and knees
    toes like little peas
    little wrinkles, good-to-eat,
    eyes bright, shiny ears,
    chest swelling drawing air,

No trouble, friend,
    you and me and Geronimo
    are men.

GARY SNYDER

AT THE WASHING OF MY SON

I ran up and grabbed your arm, the way a man
On a battlefield would recognize a long-lost comrade.
You were still wrinkled, and had a hidden face,
Like a hedgehog or a mouse, and you crouched in
The black elbows of a Negro nurse. You were
Covered with your mother's blood, and I saw
That navel where you and I were joined to her.
I stood by the glass and watched you squeal.
Just twice in a man's life there's this
Scrubbing off of blood. And this holy
Rite that Mother Superior in her white starched hat
Was going to deny me. But I stood my ground.
And then went in where for the first time you felt
Your mother's face, and her open blouse.

DAVID RAY

from
A PRAYER
FOR MY DAUGHTER

Once more the storm is howling, and half hid
Under this cradle-hood and coverlid
My child sleeps on. There is no obstacle
But Gregory's wood and one bare hill
Whereby the haystack- and roof-levelling wind,
Bred on the Atlantic, can be stayed;
And for an hour I have walked and prayed
Because of the great gloom that is in my mind.

I have walked and prayed for this young child an hour
And heard the sea-wind scream upon the tower,
And under the arches of the bridge, and scream
In the elms above the flooded stream;
Imagining in excited reverie
That the future years had come,
Dancing to a frenzied drum,
Out of the murderous innocence of the sea.

May she be granted beauty and yet not
Beauty to make a stranger's eye distraught,
Or hers before a looking-glass, for such,
Being made beautiful overmuch,
Consider beauty a sufficient end,
Lose natural kindness and maybe
The heart-revealing intimacy
That chooses right, and never find a friend.

Helen being chosen found life flat and dull
And later had much trouble from a fool,
While that Great Queen, that rose out of the spray,
Being fatherless could have her way

Yet chose a bandy-leggèd smith for man.
It's certain that fine women eat
A crazy salad with their meat
Whereby the Horn of Plenty is undone.

WILLIAM BUTLER YEATS

A FLOWER
GIVEN TO MY DAUGHTER

Frail the white rose and frail are
Her hands that gave
Whose soul is sere and paler
Than time's wan wave.

Rosefrail and fair—yet frailest
A wonder wild
In gentle eyes thou veilest,
My blueveined child.

Trieste, 1913

JAMES JOYCE

AN ARK
FOR LAWRENCE DURRELL

If we are to cross the barriers of snow
into the cave-home of our childhood, dark
among darkend lights, telling our beads,
if we are to cross over the wheel of night
and dwell among the roots of sorrow—
let us take with us the fox,
for he is quicker than our sickness;
let us take the cock, for he remembers the day
and leaps for light. And let us take
the white-haird ass who is gentle
and bows his head.

The snake has his own way among us.

ROBERT DUNCAN

THE TURTLE

(For My Grandson)

Not because of his eyes,
>> the eyes of a bird,
>>>> but because he is beaked,
birdlike, to do an injury,
>> has the turtle attracted you.
>>>> He is your only pet.
When we are together
>> you talk of nothing else
>>>> ascribing all sorts
of murderous motives
>> to his least action.
>>>> You ask me
to write a poem,
>> should I have poems to write,
>>>> about a turtle.

The turtle lives in the mud
>> but is not mud-like,
>>>> you can tell it by his eyes
which are clear.
>> When he shall escape
>>>> his present confinement
he will stride about the world
>> destroying all
>>>> with his sharp beak.
Whatever opposes him
>> in the streets of the city
>>>> shall go down.
Cars will be overturned.
>> And upon his back
>>>> shall ride,

to his conquests,
        my Lord,
                you!

You shall be master!
        In the beginning
                there was a great tortoise
who supported the world.
        Upon him
                all ultimately
rests.
        Without him
                nothing will stand.
He is all wise
        and can outrun the hare.
                In the night
his eyes carry him
        to unknown places.
                He is your friend.

WILLIAM CARLOS WILLIAMS

BOY AT THE WINDOW

Seeing the snowman standing all alone
In the dusk and cold is more than he can bear.
The small boy weeps to hear the wind prepare
A night of gnashings and enormous moan.
His tearful sight can hardly reach to where
The pale-faced figure with bitumen eyes
Returns him such a god-forsaken stare
As outcast Adam gave to Paradise.

The man of snow is, nonetheless, content,
Having no wish to go inside and die.
Still, he is moved to see the youngster cry.
Though frozen water is his element,
He melts enough to drop from one soft eye
A trickle of the purest rain, a tear
For the child at the bright pane surrounded by
Such warmth, such light, such love, and so much fear.

RICHARD WILBUR

FOR MY SON, NOAH, TEN YEARS OLD

Night and day arrive, and day after day goes by,
and what is old remains old, and what is young remains
   young, and grows old,
and the lumber pile does not grow younger, nor the
   weathered two by fours lose their darkness,
but the old tree goes on, the barn stands without help so
   many years,
the advocate of darkness and night is not lost.

The horse swings around on one leg, steps, and turns,
the chicken flapping claws onto the roost, its wings whelping
   and whalloping,
but what is primitive is not to be shot out into the night and
   the dark.
And slowly the kind man comes closer, loses his rage, sits
   down at table.

So I am proud only of those days that we pass in undivided
   tenderness,
when you sit drawing, or making books, stapled, with
   messages to the world . . .
or coloring a man with fire coming out of his hair.
Or we sit at a table, with small tea carefully poured;
so we pass our time together, calm and delighted.

ROBERT BLY

AFTER MAKING LOVE
WE HEAR FOOTSTEPS

For I can snore like a bullhorn
or play loud music
or sit up talking with any reasonably sober Irishman
and Fergus will only sink deeper
into his dreamless sleep, which goes by all in one flash,
but let there be that heavy breathing
or a stifled come-cry anywhere in the house
and he will wrench himself awake
and make for it on the run—as now, we lie together,
after making love, quiet, touching along the length of our
    bodies,
familiar touch of the long-married,
and he appears—in his baseball pajamas, it happens,
the neck opening so small
he has to screw them on, which one day may make him
    wonder
about the mental capacity of baseball players—
and flops down between us and hugs us and snuggles himself
    to sleep,
his face gleaming with satisfaction at being this very child.

In the half darkness we look at each other
and smile
and touch arms across his little, startlingly muscled body—
this one whom habit of memory propels to the ground of his
    making,
sleeper only the mortal sounds can sing awake,
this blessing love gives again into our arms.

GALWAY KINNELL

SOMETIMES A MAN STANDS UP
DURING SUPPER

Sometimes a man stands up during supper
and walks outdoors, and keeps on walking,
because of a church that stands somewhere in the East.

And his children say blessings on him as if he were dead.

And another man, who remains inside his own house,
dies there, inside the dishes and in the glasses,
so that his children have to go far out into the world
toward that same church, which he forgot.

RAINER MARIA RILKE
translated by R.B.

A STORY THAT COULD BE TRUE

If you were exchanged in the cradle and
your real mother died
without ever telling the story
then no one knows your name,
and somewhere in the world
your father is lost and needs you
but you are far away.

He can never find
how true you are, how ready.
When the great wind comes
and the robberies of the rain
you stand in the corner shivering.
The people who go by—
you wonder at their calm.

They miss the whisper that runs
any day in your mind,
"Who are you really, wanderer?"—
and the answer you have to give
no matter how dark and cold
the world around you is:
"Maybe I'm a king."

WILLIAM STAFFORD

THREE

War

And the young ones?
In the coffins.

—MIGUEL HERNANDEZ

And the coffins rest on coffins in the worldwide fields of war. For all wars end in funerals, and only funerals end a war. Marching off to war also begins the funeral march. As every ear lifts to hear the rumors of war, the coffin-makers hear the call. Every battalion steps off under the two-sided banner: "Marching to death, marching to life?" The young ones, compelled from within to march into life, wanting to feel fully alive, don't see the death side of the banner. The young, filled with dreams of immortality, can't feel that the death side could claim them. The old know better, whether they say it or not. They've seen the other side of the banner; they've heard the other voice of the First World War:

Bent double, like old beggars under sacks,
Knock-kneed, coughing like hags, we cursed through sludge
Till on the haunting flares we turned our backs,
And towards our distant rest began to trudge.
Men marched asleep. Many had lost their boots,
But limped on, blood-shod. All went lame, all blind;
Drunk with fatigue; deaf even to the hoots
Of gas-shells dropping softly behind.

(Wilfred Owen)

The elders know of this blind, limping march of beggars who carry the banners back. When the elders don't speak what they know of their war, they simply grow old and the war begins calling the next generation. When the dead are given no voice, are no longer remembered to the society, the next generation is already side-stepping to the next war. When the "body count" in battles is changed or withheld, those bodies "don't count," and the marching orders for the next generation are being prepared.

Everything that can be said of war above the ground has been said. The screaming missiles are given play-by-play send-offs by TV commentators at launch sites, and fellow commentators describe their arrival in stricken lands. The nonstop chatter of justification and explanation from leaders and experts rattles on beyond human comprehension, and human decency. This great "white noise" is not the only voice of the war. After the generals, the tanks, the cameras, and the news teams have moved on to fresh fields, the voice of war roars and weeps from behind, from below. Below the victory speeches. The voice of war is speaking from the torn earth, from broken walls, from coffins, from mausoleum-bunkers in the deserts of the Middle East, from the basements of Dubrovnik is speaking. From the black wall in Washington, D.C., the voice of the Vietnam War is still speaking its litany of American dead. Names that descend into the ground as if to pull America down from the skies, away from TV monitors; as if to pull America deeper into the earth, as if to slow the haste of America through the weight of its war dead. The names of the young in their coffins no longer serve as a base to uphold war statues that rise in sad victories in disheveled city parks. The descending litany carries the names of families from the world over, now become Americans marching down where they finally meet in equality in the land below.

> It is equal to living in a tragic land
> To live in a tragic time.

> *(Wallace Stevens)*

The voice of war speaks from the families that lost sons and daughters:

> I had a son.
> He disappeared into the vaulted darkness one Friday of All
>   Souls.

> *(Federico García Lorca)*

And the war continues to speak in the nightmares of victors and vanquished alike. Now, it speaks from the homeless haunts of veterans returned from war, never finding home, each the sole witness of his own homecoming. Wandering, hearing ". . . in no metaphorical way, the awful chorus of Soeur Anicet's orphans writhing in their cribs."

When the awful chorus that attends the end of war is denied by the pretend parades of victory, when the chorus of lament is silenced in favor of forgetting, the war is calling to the next generation. These poems are the other voice of war; the chorus of laments, rages, warnings, cries, and prayers. These are the landmarks left behind, the shrapnel, the ruins, the unexploded bombs, and the unfinished sentences of war. Ultimately, poets must speak the truth. Even when no one listens, poets must speak some truth or lose their language. Here, the poets speak as old dirge mothers, as funeral fathers who remind the living, who don't forget the dead:

> . . . But, in another year,
> We will mourn you, whose fossil courage fills
> The limestone histories; brave; ignorant; amazed;
> Dead in the rice paddies, dead on the nameless hills.

> *(Thomas McGrath)*

M.J.M.

WAR

Old age in the towns.
The heart without an owner.
Love without any object.
Grass, dust, crow.
And the young ones?

In the coffins.

The tree alone and dry.
Women like a stick
of widowhood across the bed.
Hatred there is no cure for.
And the young ones?

In the coffins.

MIGUEL HERNANDEZ
translated by Hardie St. Martin

THE MAN FROM WASHINGTON

The end came easy for most of us.
Packed away in our crude beginnings
in some far corner of a flat world,
we didn't expect much more
than firewood and buffalo robes
to keep us warm. The man came down,
a slouching dwarf with rainwater eyes,
and spoke to us. He promised
that life would go on as usual,
that treaties would be signed, and everyone—
man, woman and child—would be inoculated
against a world in which we had no part,
a world of money, promise and disease.

JAMES WELCH

RUNDOWN CHURCH
(Ballad of the First World War)

I had a son and his name was John.
I had a son.
He disappeared into the vaulted darkness one Friday of All
    Souls.
I saw him playing on the highest steps of the Mass
throwing a little tin pail at the heart of the priest.
I knocked on the coffins. My son! My son! My son!
I drew out a chicken foot from behind the moon and then
I understood that my daughter was a fish
down which the carts vanish.
I had a daughter.
I had a fish dead under the ashes of the incense burner.
I had an ocean. Of what? Good Lord! An ocean!
I went up to ring the bells but the fruit was all wormy
and the blackened match-ends
were eating the spring wheat.
I saw the stork of alcohol you could see through
shaving the black heads of the dying soldiers
and I saw the rubber booths
where the goblets full of tears were whirling.
In the anemones of the offertory I will find you, my love!
when the priest with his strong arms raises up the mule and
    the ox
to scare the nighttime toads that roam in the icy landscapes
    of the chalice.
I had a son who was a giant,
but the dead are stronger and know how to gobble down
    pieces of the sky.
If my son had only been a bear,
I wouldn't fear the secrecy of the crocodiles
and I wouldn't have seen the ocean roped to the trees
to be raped and wounded by the mobs from the regiment.
If my son had only been a bear!

I'll roll myself in this rough canvas so as not to feel the chill
   of the mosses.
I know very well they will give me a sleeve or a necktie,
but in the innermost part of the Mass I'll smash the rudder
   and then
the insanity of the penguins and seagulls will come to the
   rock
and will make the people sleeping and the people singing on
   the street-corners say:
he had a son.
A son! A son! A son
and it was no one else's, because it was his son!
His son! His son! His son!

FEDERICO GARCÍA LORCA
translated by R.B.

DULCE ET DECORUM EST

Bent double, like old beggars under sacks,
Knock-kneed, coughing like hags, we cursed through sludge
Till on the haunting flares we turned our backs,
And towards our distant rest began to trudge.
Men marched asleep. Many had lost their boots,
But limped on, blood-shod. All went lame, all blind;
Drunk with fatigue; deaf even to the hoots
Of gas-shells dropping softly behind.

Gas! GAS! Quick, boys!—An ecstasy of fumbling,
Fitting the clumsy helmets just in time,
But someone still was yelling out and stumbling
And floundering like a man in fire or lime.—
Dim through the misty panes and thick green light,
As under the green sea, I saw him drowning.
In all my dreams before my helpless sight
He plunges at me, guttering, choking, drowning.

If in some smothering dreams, you too could pace
Behind the wagon that we flung him in,
and watch the white eyes writhing in his face,
His hanging face, like a devil's sick of sin;
If you could hear, at every jolt, the blood
Come gargling from the froth-corrupted lungs,
Bitter as the cud
Of vile, incurable sores on innocent tongues,—
My friend, you would not tell with such high zest
To children ardent for some desperate glory,
The old Lie: Dulce et decorum est
Pro patria mori.

WILFRED OWEN

POSTCARD
(found on his body after he was killed by the Nazis)

I fell next to him. His body rolled over.
It was tight as a string before it snaps.
Shot in the back of the head—"This is how
you'll end. Just lie quietly," I said to myself.
Patience flowers into death now.
"Der springt noch auf,"* I heard above me.
Dark filthy blood was drying on my ear.

Szentkiralyszabadja
October 31, 1944

MIKLÓS RADNÓTI
translation by Steven Polgar, Stephen Berg, and S. J. Marks

* *"Der springt noch auf"*: He's getting up again.

DRY LOAF

It is equal to living in a tragic land
To live in a tragic time.
Regard now the sloping, mountainous rocks
And the river that batters its way over stones,
Regard the hovels of those that live in this land.

That was what I painted behind the loaf,
The rocks not even touched by snow,
The pines along the river and the dry men blown
Brown as the bread, thinking of birds
Flying from burning countries and brown sand shores,

Birds that came like dirty water in waves
Flowing above the rocks, flowing over the sky,
As if the sky was a current that bore them along,
Spreading them as waves spread flat on the shore,
One after another washing the mountains bare.

It was the battering of drums I heard.
It was hunger, it was the hungry that cried
And the waves, the waves were soldiers moving,
Marching and marching in a tragic time
Below me, on the asphalt, under the trees.

It was soldiers went marching over the rocks
And still the birds came, came in watery flocks,
Because it was spring and the birds had to come.
No doubt that soldiers had to be marching
And that drums had to be rolling, rolling, rolling.

WALLACE STEVENS

ODE FOR THE AMERICAN DEAD
IN ASIA

1

God love you now, if no one else will ever,
Corpse in the paddy, or dead on a high hill
In the fine and ruinous summer of a war
You never wanted. All your false flags were
Of bravery and ignorance, like grade school maps:
Colors of countries you would never see—
Until that weekend in eternity
When, laughing, well armed, perfectly ready to kill
The world and your brother, the safe commanders sent
You into your future. Oh, dead on a hill,
Dead in a paddy, leeched and tumbled to
A tomb of footnotes. We mourn a changeling: you;
Handselled to poverty and drummed to war
By distinguished masters whom you never knew.

2

The bee that spins his metal from the sun,
The shy mole drifting like a miner ghost
Through midnight earth—all happy creatures run
As strict as trains on rails the circuits of
Blind instinct. Happy in your summer follies,
You mined a culture that was mined for war:
The state to mold you, church to bless, and always
The elders to confirm you in your ignorance.
No scholar put your thinking cap on nor
Warned that in dead seas fishes died in schools
Before inventing legs to walk the land.
The rulers stuck a tennis racket in your hand,
An Ark against the flood. In time of change

Courage is not enough: the blind mole dies,
And you on your hill, who did not know the rules.

3

Wet in the windy counties of the dawn
The lone crow skirls his draggled passage home:
And God (whose sparrows fall aslant his gaze.
Like grace or confetti) blinks and he is gone,
And you are gone. Your scarecrow valor grows
And rusts like early lilac while the rose
Blooms in Dakota and the stock exchange
Flowers. Roses, rents, all things conspire
To crown your death with wreaths of living fire.
And the public mourners come: the politic tear
Is cast in the Forum. But, in another year,
We will mourn you, whose fossil courage fills
The limestone histories; brave; ignorant; amazed;
Dead in the rice paddies, dead on the nameless hills.

THOMAS MCGRATH

WORDS FOR MY DAUGHTER

About eight of us were nailing up forts
in the mulberry grove behind Reds' house
when his mother started screeching and
all of us froze except Reds—fourteen, huge
as a hippo—who sprang out of the tree so fast
the branch nearly bobbed me off. So fast,
he hit the ground running, hammer in hand,
and seconds after he got in the house
we heard thumps like someone beating a tire
off a rim   his dad's howls the screen door
banging open   Saw   Reds barreling out
through the tall weeds towards the highway
the father stumbling after his fat son
who never looked back across the thick swale
of teasel and black-eyed Susans until it was safe
to yell fuck you at the skinny drunk
stamping around barefoot and holding his ribs.

Another time, the Connelly kid came home to find
his alcoholic mother getting fucked by the milkman.
Bobby broke a milk bottle and jabbed the guy
humping on his mom. I think it really happened
because none of us would loosely mention that
wraith of a woman who slippered around her house
and never talked to anyone, not even her kids.

Once a girl ran past my porch
with a dart in her back, her open mouth
pumping like a guppy's, her eyes wild.
Later that summer, or maybe the next,
the kids hung her brother from an oak.
Before they hoisted him, yowling and heavy
on the clothesline, they made him claw the creekbank
and eat worms. I don't know why his neck didn't snap.

Reds had another nickname you couldn't say
or he'd beat you up: "Honeybun."
His dad called him that when Reds was little.

So, these were my playmates. I love them still
for their justice and valor and desperate loves
twisted in shapes of hammer and shard.
I want you to know about their pain
and about the pain they could loose on others.
If you're reading this, I hope you will think,
Well, my dad had it rough as a kid, so what?
If you're reading this, you can read the news
and you know that children suffer worse.

Worse for me is a cloud of memories
still drifting off the South China Sea,
like the nine-year-old boy, naked and lacerated,
thrashing in his pee on a steel operating table
and yelling "Dau. Dau," while I, trying to translate
in the mayhem of Tet for surgeons who didn't know
who this boy was or what happened to him, kept asking
"Where? Where's the pain?" until a surgeon
said "Forget it. His ears are blown."

I remember your first Halloween
when I held you on my chest and rocked you,
so small your toes didn't touch my lap
as I smelled your fragrant peony head
and cried because I was so happy and because
I heard, in no metaphorical way, the awful chorus
of Soeur Anicet's orphans writhing in their cribs.
Then the doorbell rang and a tiny Green Beret
was saying trick or treat and I thought *oh oh*
but remembered it was Halloween and where I was.
I smiled at the evil midget, his map light and night
paint, his toy knife for slitting throats, said,

"How ya doin', soldier?" and, still holding you asleep
in my arms, gave him a Mars bar. To his father
waiting outside in fatigues I hissed, "You shit,"
and saw us, child, in a pose I know too well.

I want you to know the worst and be free from it.
I want you to know the worst and still find good.
Day by day, as you play nearby or laugh
with the ladies at People's Bank as we go around town
and I find myself beaming like a fool,
I suspect I am here less for your protection
than you are here for mine, as if you were sent
to call me back into our helpless tribe.

JOHN BALABAN

TO PRESIDENT BUSH
AT THE START OF THE GULF WAR

This thin-lipped king with his helmeted head
Remembers the quirky fits of light
That tempt the cobra. No, the temper of the dove
Does not fit him; and nothing in the world
Can bring him to bless. He will not feed,
Nourish or help; and his rabbity hand
Lifted in the fading light of the hemlocks
Waves to them, gestures to the young to die.

ROBERT BLY

BECOMING MILTON

Milton, the airport driver, retired now
from trucking, who ferried me
from the Greenville-Spartanburg airport
to Athens last Sunday midnight to 2:30 A.M.,
tells me about his son, Tom, just back
from the Gulf war. "He's at Fort Stewart
with the 102nd Mechanized, the first tank unit
over the line, not a shot fired at them.
His job was to check the Iraqi tanks
that the airstrikes hit, hundreds of them.
The boy had never even come up on a car accident
here at home, twenty-four years old. Can you
imagine what he lifted the lid to find?
Three helmets with heads in them staring
from the floor, and that's just one tank.
He has screaming flashbacks, can't talk about it
anymore. I just told him to be strong
and put it out of his mind. With time,
if you stay strong, those things'll go away.
Or they'd find a bunker, one of those holes
they hid in, and yell something in American,
and wait a minute, and then roll grenades in
and check it and find nineteen freshly killed guys,
some sixty, some fourteen, real thin.
They were just too scared to move.
He feels pretty bad about it, truthfully,
all this yellow ribbon celebrating.
It wasn't a war really. I mean, he says
it was just piles and piles of their bodies.
Some of his friends got sick, started vomiting,
and had to be walked back to the rear.
Looks like to me it could have been worked
some other way. My boy came through OK,
but he won't go back, I'll tell you that.

War
81

He's getting out as soon as he can.
First chance comes, he'll be in Greenville
selling cars, or fixing them. He's good at both.
Pretty good carpenter too, you know how I know?
He'll tear the whole thing out if it's not right
and start over. There's some that'll look
at a board that's not flush and say *shit,
nail it,* but he can't do that, Tom."

COLEMAN BARKS

from
THE HOMERIC HYMN TO ARES

Hear me,
helper of mankind,
dispenser of youth's sweet courage,
beam down from up there
your gentle light
on our lives,
and your martial power,
so that I can shake off
cruel cowardice
from my head,
and diminish that deceptive rush
of my spirit, and restrain
that shrill voice in my heart
that provokes me
to enter the chilling din of battle.
You, happy god,
give me courage,
let me linger
in the safe laws of peace,
and thus escape
from battles with enemies
and the fate of a violent death.

translated by Charles Boer

THE SECRET OF VICTORY

Despite the impossibility of physically detecting the soul, its existence is proven by its tangible reflection in acts and thoughts. So with war, beyond its physical aspect of armed hosts there hovers an impalpable something which dominates the material. ... [T]o understand this "something" we should seek it in a manner analogous to our search for the soul.

GEORGE PATTON

LESSONS OF THE WAR
Naming of Parts

To Alan Michell

*Vixi duellis nuper idoneus
Et militavi non sine gloria*

Today we have naming of parts. Yesterday,
We had daily cleaning. And tomorrow morning,
We shall have what to do after firing. But today,
Today we have naming of parts. Japonica
Glistens like coral in all of the neighboring gardens,
    And today we have naming of parts.

This is the lower sling swivel. And this
Is the upper sling swivel, whose use you will see,
When you are given your slings. And this is the piling swivel,
Which in your case you have not got. The branches
Hold in the gardens their silent, eloquent gestures,
    Which in our case we have not got.

This is the safety-catch, which is always released
With an easy flick of the thumb. And please do not let me
See anyone using his finger. You can do it quite easy
If you have any strength in your thumb. The blossoms
Are fragile and motionless, never letting anyone see
    Any of them using their finger.

And this you can see is the bolt. The purpose of this
Is to open the breech, as you see. We can slide it
Rapidly backwards and forwards: we call this
Easing the spring. And rapidly backwards and forwards
The early bees are assaulting and fumbling the flowers:
    They call it easing the Spring.

They call it easing the Spring: it is perfectly easy
If you have any strength in your thumb: like the bolt,
And the breech, and the cocking-piece, and the point of
    balance,
Which in our case we have not got; and the almond-blossom
Silent in all of the gardens and the bees going backwards and
    forwards
    For today we have naming of parts.

HENRY REED

BIG DREAM, LITTLE DREAM

The Elgonyi say, there are big dreams and little dreams.
The little dream is just personal . . .
Sitting in a plane that is flying
too close to the ground. There are wires . . .
on either side there's a wall.

The big dream feels significant.
The big dream is the kind the president has.
He wakes and tells it to the secretary,
together they tell it to the cabinet,
and before you know there is war.

LOUIS SIMPSON

DO NOT WEEP, MAIDEN,
FOR WAR IS KIND

Do not weep, maiden, for war is kind.
Because your lover threw wild hands toward the sky
And the affrighted steed ran on alone,
Do not weep.
War is kind.

Hoarse, booming drums of the regiment,
Little souls who thirst for fight,
These men were born to drill and die.
The unexplained glory flies above them,
Great is the Battle-God, great, and his Kingdom—
A field where a thousand corpses lie.

Do not weep, babe, for war is kind.
Because your father tumbled in the yellow trenches,
Raged at his breast, gulped and died,
Do not weep.
War is kind.

Swift blazing flag of the regiment,
Eagle with crest of red and gold.
These men were born to drill and die.
Point for them the virtue of slaughter,
Make plain to them the excellence of killing
And a field where a thousand corpses lie.

Mother whose heart hung humble as a button
On the bright splendid shroud of your son,
Do not weep.
War is kind.

STEPHEN CRANE

THE COLONEL

What you have heard is true. I was in his house. His wife carried a tray of coffee and sugar. His daughter filed her nails, his son went out for the night. There were daily papers, pet dogs, a pistol on the cushion beside him. The moon swung bare on its black cord over the house. On the television was a cop show. It was in English. Broken bottles were embedded in the walls around the house to scoop the kneecaps from a man's legs or cut his hands to lace. On the windows there were gratings like those in liquor stores. We had dinner, rack of lamb, good wine, a gold bell was on the table for calling the maid. The maid brought green mangoes, salt, a type of bread. I was asked how I enjoy the country. There was a brief commercial in Spanish. His wife took everything away. There was some talk then of how difficult it had become to govern. The parrot said hello on the terrace. The colonel told it to shut up, and pushed himself from the table. My friend said to me with his eyes: say nothing. The colonel returned with a sack used to bring groceries home. He spilled many human ears on the table. They were like dried peach halves. There is no other way to say this. He took one of them in his hands, shook it in our faces, dropped it into a water glass. It came alive there. I am tired of fooling around he said. As for the rights of anyone, tell your people they can go fuck themselves. He swept the ears to the floor with his arm and held the last of his wine in the air. Something for your poetry, no? he said. Some of the ears on the floor caught this scrap of his voice. Some of the ears on the floor were pressed to the ground.

May 1978

CAROLYN FORCHÉ

"KEEPING THEIR WORLD LARGE"

All too literally, their flesh and their spirit are our shield.
New York Times, June 7, 1944

I should like to see that country's tiles, bedrooms,
stone patios
          and ancient wells: Rinaldo
Caramonica's the cobbler's, Frank Sblendorio's
          and Dominick Angelastro's country—
               the grocer's, the iceman's, the dancer's—the
beautiful Miss Damiano's; wisdom's

          and all angels' Italy, this Christmas Day
this Christmas year,
          A noiseless piano, an
innocent war, the heart that can act against itself. Here,
               each unlike and all alike, could
               so many—stumbling, falling, multiplied
               till bodies lay as ground to walk on—

          "If Christ and the apostles died in vain,
I'll die in vain with them"
               against this way of victory.
That forest of white crosses!
          My eyes won't close to it.

          All laid like animals for sacrifice—
like Isaac on the mount,
               were their own sacrifice.

          Marching to death, marching to life?
"Keeping their world large,"
               whose spirits and whose bodies
all too literally were our shield,
          are still our shield.

They fought the enemy,
we fight fat living and self-pity.
  Shine, o shine,
unfalsifying sun, on this sick scene.

MARIANNE MOORE

PASSING AN ORCHARD BY TRAIN

Grass high under apple trees,
The bark of the trees rough and sexual,
the grass growing heavy and uneven.

We cannot bear disaster, like
the rocks—
swaying nakedly
in open fields.

One slight bruise and we die!
I know no one on this train.
A man comes walking down the aisle.
I want to tell him
that I forgive him, that I want him
to forgive me.

ROBERT BLY

FOUR

I Know the Earth, and I Am Sad

My pain comes from the north wind and from the
south wind, like those neuter eggs certain rare
birds lay in the wind.

—CÉSAR VALLEJO

A man often follows or flies on an ascending arc, headed toward brilliance, inner power, authority, leadership in community, and that arc is very beautiful. But many ancient stories declare that in the midst of a man's beautiful ascending arc, the time will come naturally when he will find himself falling; he will find himself on the road of ashes, and discover at night that he is holding the ashy hand of the Lord of Death or the Lord of Divorce. He will find himself noticing the tears inside brooms or old boards; noticing how much grief the whales carry in their skulls. He realizes how much he has already lost in the reasonable way he chose to live, and how much he could easily lose in the next week. For some men, it is a time of crying in airports. "For two years, all I did, it seems to me, was cry in airports." The ashes he gets on his palm from holding hands with the Lord of Loss at night he puts on his face, and the ashes he wears will be darker than an ashy fingerprint on the forehead, even though that Catholic ritual on Ash Wednesday is so beautiful.

The greatest masculine art has always had what the Romans called *gravitas*—soberness, weight, and grief. We can feel gravity when we see great art; we remember the word *grave;* and *gravid* in French remembers pregnancy. We naturally honor *gravitas* in Rembrandt, in Goya, in Turner, particularly in his sea paintings, and we honor it as well in certain twentieth-century painters such as Max Ernst and the German artist Anselm Kiefer. We could say each of these artists has accomplished, before he made the paintings, a descent, a fall, a drop through the floor; he has honored an agreement he could not resist to go into grief, into *katabasis* as the ancient Greeks called it, a drop into the underworld, that which the elevated hero such as Oedipus found himself undergoing. Tragedies, then, are not so much about personality flaws as about the depths that call up to certain men and insist that they descend.

In our century the Spanish and South American poets have been the masters of descent. Neruda says that he is sad because he "knows the earth." That implies that the earth itself is in grief. We can feel the sadness in the northern pines; the South Americans feel it in the rain forest, in the little towns where nothing happens.

> But above all there is a terrifying,
> a terrifying deserted dining room . . .
> and around it there are expanses,
> sunken factories, pieces of timber
> which I alone know,
> because I am sad, and because I travel,
> and I know the earth, and I am sad.

> *(Pablo Neruda)*

A few years ago in Romania archaeologists found a small basalt statue, very elegant in its blackness, of a man seated. It is the oldest Sorrowing Male so far found. It hints that grief has been for thousands of years a masculine emotion; men's sorrow seems unusual in that it seems inexplicable. Perhaps that sorrow goes back to the million or so years when men were primarily hunters: they felt the sorrow of the animal whose life they took; or perhaps they felt the sadness of the forest. The Mediterranean world still believed at the time of Christ that there is such a thing as *lacrimae rerum,* that is, tears inside things, or tears inside nature itself. Perhaps whales and bears and oceans bear grief inside them. Ancient man lived for so many thousands of years outdoors, hunting, running, watching; and he lived in such intimate contact with animals that we can still feel in the Dordogne paintings how thin the veil was between men and creatures. The sorrow of animals passed directly into men. This may be the unexplainable grief that César Vallejo says comes "from the north wind and from the south wind" and is neither father nor son.

Perhaps that is why for men depression is sometimes the entrance to soul, melancholy a wide road to God, and ordinary grief a door that when swung wide opens into feeling. Men often enter genuine feeling for the first time when in deep grief, after cheerfulness and excitement have failed for years to bring them there. Private grief can lead them to feel "the sorrow of the world."

Masculine sadness, then, is a holy thing. Some men in middle age labor to find the holy stair "right to the bottom of the night." It is the old god, Saturn, who presides over this dive, and it is he who knows the sadness of the huge cliffs, and the melancholy that animals feel in having to eat each other dawn after dawn, and the puzzled grief we all feel at being appointed to do mysterious tasks here, on this planet, among mountain meadows and falling stars.

> Let the young rain of tears come.
> Let the calm hands of grief come.
> It's not all as evil as you think.
>
> *(Rolf Jacobsen)*

The growth of a man can be imagined as a power that gradually expands downward: the voice expands downward into the open vowels that carry emotion, and into the rough consonants that are like gates holding that water; the hurt feelings expand downward into compassion; the intelligence expands with awe into the great arguments or antinomies men have debated for centuries; and the mood-man expands downward into those vast rooms of melancholy under the earth, where we are more alive the older we get, more in tune with the earth and the great roots.

R.B.

THE WIND, ONE BRILLIANT DAY

The wind, one brilliant day, called
to my soul with an odor of jasmine.

"In return for the odor of my jasmine,
I'd like all the odor of your roses."

"I have no roses; all the flowers
in my garden are dead."

"Well then, I'll take the withered petals
and the yellow leaves and the waters of the fountain."

The wind left. And I wept. And I said to myself:
"What have you done with the garden that was entrusted
   to you?"

ANTONIO MACHADO
translated by R.B.

SONNETS TO ORPHEUS IV

O you lovers that are so gentle, step occasionally
into the breath of the sufferers not meant for you,
let it be parted by your cheeks,
it will tremble, joined again, behind you.

You have been chosen, you are sound and whole,
you are like the very first beat of the heart,
you are the bow that shoots the arrows, and also their target,
in tears your smile would glow forever.

Do not be afraid to suffer, give
the heaviness back to the weight of the earth;
mountains are heavy, seas are heavy.

Even those trees you planted as children
became too heavy long ago—you couldn't carry them now.
But you can carry the winds . . . and the open spaces . . .

RAINER MARIA RILKE
translated by R.B.

THE NEGRO SPEAKS OF RIVERS

I've known rivers:
I've known rivers ancient as the world and older than the
    flow of human blood in human veins.

My soul has grown deep like the rivers.

I bathed in the Euphrates when dawns were young.
I built my hut near the Congo and it lulled me to sleep.
I looked upon the Nile and raised the pyramids above it.
I heard the singing of the Mississippi when Abe Lincoln
    went down to New Orleans, and I've seen its muddy
    bosom turn all golden in the sunset.

I've known rivers:
Ancient, dusky rivers.

My soul has grown deep like the rivers.

LANGSTON HUGHES

RAIN

Each storm-soaked flower has a beautiful eye.
And this is the voice of the stone-cold sky:
"Only boys keep their cheeks dry.
Only boys are afraid to cry.
Men thank God for tears
Alone with the memory of their dead,
Alone with lost years."

VACHEL LINDSAY

MELANCHOLY INSIDE FAMILIES

I keep a blue bottle.
Inside it an ear and a portrait.
When the night dominates
the feathers of the owl,
when the hoarse cherry tree
rips out its lips and makes menacing gestures
with rinds which the oceans wind often perforates—
then I know that there are immense expanses hidden from us,
quartz in slugs,
ooze,
blue waters for a battle,
much silence, many ore-veins
of withdrawals and camphor,
fallen things, medallions, kindnesses,
parachutes, kisses.

It is only the passage from one day to another,
a single bottle moving over the seas,
and a dining room where roses arrive,
a dining room deserted
as a fish-bone; I am speaking of
a smashed cup, a curtain, at the end
of a deserted room through which a river passes
dragging along the stones. It is a house
set on the foundations of the rain,
a house of two floors with the required number of windows,
and climbing vines faithful in every particular.

I walk through afternoons, I arrive
full of mud and death,
dragging along the earth and its roots,
and its indistinct stomach in which corpses
are sleeping with wheat,
metals, and pushed-over elephants.

But above all there is a terrifying,
a terrifying deserted dining room,
with its broken olive oil cruets,
and vinegar running under its chairs,
one ray of moonlight tied down,
something dark, and I look
for a comparison inside myself:
perhaps it is a grocery store surrounded by the sea
and torn clothing from which sea water is dripping.

It is only a deserted dining room,
and around it there are expanses,
sunken factories, pieces of timber
which I alone know,
because I am sad, and because I travel,
and I know the earth, and I am sad.

PABLO NERUDA
translated by R.B. and James Wright

WALKING AROUND

It so happens I am sick of being a man.
And it happens that I walk into tailorshops and movie
     houses
dried up, waterproof, like a swan made of felt
steering my way in a water of wombs and ashes.

The smell of barbershops makes me break into hoarse sobs.
The only thing I want is to lie still like stones or wool.
The only thing I want is to see no more stores, no gardens,
no more goods, no spectacles, no elevators.

It so happens I am sick of my feet and my nails
and my hair and my shadow.
It so happens I am sick of being a man.

Still it would be marvelous
to terrify a law clerk with a cut lily,
or kill a nun with a blow on the ear.
It would be great
to go through the streets with a green knife
letting out yells until I died of the cold.

I don't want to go on being a root in the dark,
insecure, stretched out, shivering with sleep,
going on down, into the moist guts of the earth,
taking in and thinking, eating every day.

I don't want so much misery.
I don't want to go on as a root and a tomb,
alone under the ground, a warehouse with corpses,
half frozen, dying of grief.

That's why Monday, when it sees me coming
with my convict face, blazes up like gasoline,

and it howls on its way like a wounded wheel,
and leaves tracks full of warm blood leading toward the
   night.

And it pushes me into certain corners, into some moist
   houses,
into hospitals where the bones fly out the window,
into shoeshops that smell like vinegar,
and certain streets hideous as cracks in the skin.

There are sulphur-colored birds, and hideous intestines
hanging over the doors of houses that I hate,
and there are false teeth forgotten in a coffeepot,
there are mirrors
that ought to have wept from shame and terror,
there are umbrellas everywhere, and venoms, and umbilical
   cords.

I stroll along serenely, with my eyes, my shoes,
my rage, forgetting everything,
I walk by, going through office buildings and orthopedic
   shops,
and courtyards with washing hanging from the line:
underwear, towels and shirts from which slow
dirty tears are falling.

PABLO NERUDA
translated by R.B.

NO MORE AUCTION BLOCK

No more auction block for me,
No more, no more,
No more auction block for me,
Many thousand gone.

No more peck of corn for me,
No more, no more,
No more peck of corn for me,
Many thousand gone.

No more pint of salt for me,
No more, no more,
No more pint of salt for me,
Many thousand gone.

No more driver's lash for me,
No more, no more,
No more driver's lash for me,
Many thousand gone.

Spiritual

I FELT A FUNERAL, IN MY BRAIN

I felt a Funeral, in my Brain,
And Mourners to and fro
Kept treading—treading—till it seemed
That Sense was breaking through—

And when they all were seated,
A Service, like a Drum—
Kept beating—beating—till I thought
My Mind was going numb—

And then I heard them lift a Box
And creak across my Soul
With those same Boots of Lead, again,
Then Space—began to toll.

As all the Heavens were a Bell,
And Being, but an Ear,
And I, and Silence, some strange Race
Wrecked, solitary, here—

And then a Plank in Reason, broke,
And I dropped down, and down—
And hit a World, at every plunge,
And Finished knowing—then—

EMILY DICKINSON

THE DAY LADY DIED

It is 12:20 in New York a Friday
three days after Bastille Day, yes
it is 1959 and I go get a shoeshine
because I will get off the 4:19 in Easthampton
at 7:15 and then go straight to dinner
and I don't know the people who will feed me

I walk up the muggy street beginning to sun
and have a hamburger and a malted and buy
an ugly NEW WORLD WRITING to see what the poets
in Ghana are doing these days
                          I go on to the bank
and Miss Stillwagon (first name Linda I once heard)
doesn't even look up my balance for once in her life
and in the GOLDEN GRIFFIN I get a little Verlaine
for Patsy with drawings by Bonnard although I do
think of Hesiod, trans. Richmond Lattimore or
Brendan Behan's new play or *Le Balcon* or *Les Nègres*
of Genet, but I don't, I stick with Verlaine
after practically going to sleep with quandariness

and for Mike I just stroll into the PARK LANE
Liquor Store and ask for a bottle of Strega and
then I go back where I came from to 6th Avenue
and the tobacconist in the Ziegfeld Theatre and
casually ask for a carton of Gauloises and a carton
of Picayunes, and a NEW YORK POST with her face on it

and I am sweating a lot by now and thinking of
leaning on the john door in the FIVE SPOT
while she whispered a song along the keyboard
to Mal Waldron and everyone and I stopped breathing

7/17/59

FRANK O'HARA

I Know the Earth, and I Am Sad

SONNETS TO ORPHEUS VIII

Where praise already is is the only place Grief
ought to go, that water spirit of the pools of tears;
she watches over our defeats to make sure
the water rises clear from the same rock

that holds up the huge doors and the altars.
You can see, around her motionless shoulders, a feeling
dawns—we sense more and more that she
is the youngest of the three sisters we have inside.

Rejoicing has lost her doubts, and Longing broods on her
    error,
only Grief still learns; she spends the whole night
counting up our evil inheritance with her small hands.

She is awkward, but all at once
she makes our voice rise, sideways, like a constellation
into the sky, not troubled by her breath.

RAINER MARIA RILKE
translated by R.B.

SUNFLOWER

What sower walked over earth,
which hands sowed
our inward seeds of fire?
They went out from his fists like rainbow curves
to frozen earth, young loam, hot sand,
they will sleep there
greedily, and drink up our lives
and explode it into pieces
for the sake of a sunflower that you haven't seen
or a thistle head or a chrysanthemum.

Let the young rain of tears come.
Let the calm hands of grief come.
It's not all as evil as you think.

ROLF JACOBSEN
translated by R.B.

SNOWBANKS NORTH OF THE HOUSE

Those great sweeps of snow that stop suddenly six feet from
    the house . . .
Thoughts that go so far.
The boy gets out of high school and reads no more books;
the son stops calling home.
The mother puts down her rolling pin and makes no more
    bread.
And the wife looks at her husband one night at a party, and
    loves him no more.
The energy leaves the wine, and the minister falls leaving the
    church.
It will not come closer—
the one inside moves back, and the hands touch nothing, and
    are safe.

The father grieves for his son, and will not leave the room
    where the coffin stands.
He turns away from his wife, and she sleeps alone.

And the sea lifts and falls all night, the moon goes on
    through the unattached heavens alone.
The toe of the shoe pivots
in the dust . . .
And the man in the black coat turns, and goes back down
    the hill.
No one knows why he came, or why he turned away, and
    did not climb the hill.

ROBERT BLY

HEALING

I am not a mechanism, an assembly of various sections.
And it is not because the mechanism is working wrongly,
   that I am ill.
I am ill because of wounds to the soul, to the deep emotional
   self
and the wounds to the soul take a long, long time, only time
   can help
and patience, and a certain difficult repentance,
long, difficult repentance, realisation of life's mistake, and the
   freeing oneself
from the endless repetition of the mistake
which mankind at large has chosen to sanctify.

D. H. LAWRENCE

COME IN

As I came to the edge of the woods,
Thrush music—hark!
Now if it was dusk outside,
Inside it was dark.

Too dark in the woods for a bird
By sleight of wing
To better its perch for the night,
Though it still could sing.

The last of the light of the sun
That had died in the west
Still lived for one song more
In a thrush's breast.

Far in the pillared dark
Thrush music went—
Almost like a call to come in
To the dark and lament.

But no, I was out for stars:
I would not come in.
I meant not even if asked,
And I hadn't been.

ROBERT FROST

I AM GOING TO SPEAK OF HOPE

I do not suffer this pain as César Vallejo. I do not ache now as an artist, as a man or even as a simple living being. I do not suffer this pain as a Catholic, as a Mohammedan or as an atheist. Today I am simply in pain. If my name were not César Vallejo, I would still suffer this very same pain. If I were not an artist, I would still suffer it. If I were not a man or even a living being, I would still suffer it. If I were not a Catholic, atheist or Mohammedan, I would still suffer it. Today I am in pain from further below. Today I am simply in pain.

I ache now without any explanation. My pain is so deep, that it never had a cause nor does it lack a cause now. What could have been its cause? Where is that thing so important, that it might stop being its cause? Its cause is nothing; nothing could have stopped being its cause. For what has this pain been born, for itself? My pain comes from the north wind and from the south wind, like those neuter eggs certain rare birds lay in the wind. If my bride were dead, my pain would be the same. If they had slashed my throat all the way through, my pain would be the same. If life were, in short, different, my pain would be the same. Today I suffer from further above. Today I am simply in pain.

I look at the hungry man's pain and see that his hunger is so far from my suffering, that if I were to fast unto death, at least a blade of grass would always sprout from my tomb. The same with the lover! How engendered his blood is, in contrast to mine without source or use!

I believed until now that all the things of the universe were, inevitably, parents or sons. But behold that my pain today is neither parent nor son. It lacks a back to darken, as well as having too much chest to dawn and if they put it in a dark room, it would not give light and if they put it in a brightly lit room, it would cast no shadow. Today I suffer no matter what happens. Today I am simply in pain.

CÉSAR VALLEJO
translated by Clayton Eshleman and José Rubia Barcia

AND WHAT IF AFTER SO MANY WORDS

And what if after so many words,
the word itself doesn't survive!
And what if after so many wings of birds
the stopped bird doesn't survive!
It would be better then, really,
if it were all swallowed up, and let's end it!

To have been born only to live off our own death!
To raise ourselves from the heavens toward the earth
carried up by our own bad luck,
always watching for the moment to put out our darkness
    with our shadow!
It would be better, frankly,
if it were all swallowed up, and the hell with it!

And what if after so much history, we succumb,
not to eternity,
but to these simple things, like being
at home, or starting to brood!
What if we discover later
all of a sudden, that we are living
to judge by the height of the stars
off a comb and off stains on a handkerchief!
It would be better, really,
if it were all swallowed up, right now!

They'll say that we have a lot
of grief in one eye, and a lot of grief
in the other also, and when they look
a lot of grief in both. . . .
Well then! . . . Wonderful! . . . Then . . . Don't say a word!

CÉSAR VALLEJO
translated by Douglas Lawder and R.B.

FIVE

The House of Fathers and Titans

Who is my father in this world, in this house, at the spirit's base?

—WALLACE STEVENS

Walking into the house of fathers means beginning in questions and entering into mysteries. Questions abound about our "real fathers." At the root our fathers connect us to a mysterious spark that flared between ancestors and two living people when we were conceived in this world. After that conception, walls stand between father and the child to be. When an infant comes struggling from the warm body of mother it begins to fall into the expanse of air and light and the world of innumerable things. And the infant falls also into a realm of questions: Is it a girl or a boy? Is it okay? Intact? What's its name? The child is leaving mother, falling in questions toward father.

Before the umbilical is cut, questions surround the newborn. Cutting the tie to mother increases the uncertainties that attend new life and begin the shaping of that life from outside. Father may be in the hands that catch that child and ease the fall, or nearby in eyes that alertly watch the entrance to this life, but father may be kept back by custom or fear. The father may be in question himself: Where is he? Is the father here? Who is the father, is the father known? Whether in the hands waiting or long gone, the father inevitably brings distance to the child's world. And sadness. He is somewhere beyond the falling, reaching, calling of the child. And later, whether the father moves closer through the efforts of love or disappears in some struggle, he will always be present in the distance between one thing and another.

So father must be sought in the world, in the wind between things, in whatever separates and distinguishes, in questions that penetrate the past, and in "distant footsteps" that we inevitably follow, not knowing where. Even in his own house a father presents a mystery. As Robert Bly says:

> His two-story house he turned
> into a forest,
> where both he and I are the hunters.

We are always hunting something of our father's, and he's hunting too, and we're sure we'll know more of ourselves if we can get to him. Father is absent even in his own house. Somehow the father must be reached, touched. And we must be touched by him to fully enter life, to feel held in the world and separate from mother. In some tribes the child was not fully born until held by the father overnight, sleeping against his skin and bathed in his sweat. The child is not fully born, except by the laboring and milk-giving by mother and the stopping of work and giving of sweat by father.

Seeking that touch, that blessing from the father can cause us to be as passive as an infant, or as eager for risk as a youth with a burning question. We will seek it in whatever gentleness we can find—in the tangle of his hair and beard, the stare of his eye, the nod of his head. But we will also endure the weight of his hand, the wreck of his rage, and the bitter ring of his words to learn his touch. And the father risks too, risks turning into an old Titan, a Kronos-Saturn giant who fears the touch of children and so eats them.

As Sharon Olds says:

> . . . no one knew
> my father was eating his children. . . .
> . . . and yet as he lay
> . . . snoring, our lives slowly
> disappeared down the hole of his life.

Something in every father is Titanic, ancient and huge as a cave or the depth of the sea. Something ancient awakens in a man when he becomes a father. Something that comes from those old Titans at the beginning of time. There's some of Prometheus in a father that again and again will steal fire from the "blue black cold" and warm the rooms of family and culture. There's some of Atlas there too, as new fathers heft great works and plan ideal futures for child and family. Also activated deep in the psychic roots are the titanic forces of the brooding underworld. And Kronos, with his will to devour everything. The Titans, once defeated, were pushed down into Tartaros and forced behind an iron wall and beneath the roots of earth and sea. Becoming a father opens the iron gates, and the Titans awaken and come striding up carrying our inheritance from the Iron Age.

The father of the Titans was Ouranos, the Father of fathers. He is the disappearing sky god who mated with great Gaia Earth. That started the whole thing. When Ouranos awakens, father disappears behind newspaper walls, floats off like a cloud of "ask your mother," or smolders in silence like a sky withholding a storm. Ascending like Ouranos, the human father rises above the Titanic errors of fatherhood. Instead of heavy-handedness and the sweat of mistakes made, the absent father offers disappearing acts and clouds of uncertainty. Father has become a distant god, a Holy Ghost that keeps everything mysterious and hidden behind vague generalities, or single-minded endeavors or metallic silences that haunt a child's life. The twentieth century has birthed great broods of children trying to reach him as ". . . father moves faster and farther ahead."

Each one returning to the house of the father must go through the door of uncertainty; who can foresee what knocking on the iron gate will call up? Once again will he be unreachable, not really home; or waiting, willing to sweat out the truths? Or will Saturn answer the call with a raging appetite that crushes the bones of children, steps on their hopes, eats through their ambitions with acid criticism, and slams the gate again. This time will my own anger and resentment diminish, and I'll find him in a room making fires ". . . with cracked hands that ached from labor in weekday weather . . ."; find him "steering through the vicious seas of those bitter times . . ."; find him attending some mystery I didn't know, didn't guess at; find him decently attending funerals; find him among ". . . the race of fathers: earth and air and sea."

M.J.M.

FOR, BROTHER, WHAT ARE WE?

For, brother, what are we?

We are the sons of our father,
Whose face we have never seen,
We are the sons of our father,
Whose voice we have never heard,
We are the sons of our father,
To whom we have cried for strength and comfort
In our agony,
We are the sons of our father,
Whose life like ours
Was lived in solitude and in the wilderness,
We are the sons of our father,
To whom only can we speak out
The strange, dark burden of our heart and spirit,
We are the sons of our father,
And we shall follow the print of his foot forever.

THOMAS WOLFE

from
DEMOCRACY IN AMERICA

It has been universally remarked that in our time the several members of the family stand upon an entirely new footing towards each other; that the distance which formerly separated a father from his sons has been lessened; and that paternal authority, if not destroyed, is at least impaired. . . .

When men live more for the remembrance of what has been than for the care of what is, and when they are more given to attend to what their ancestors thought than to think themselves, the father is the natural and necessary tie between the past and the present, the link by which the ends of these two chains are connected. In aristocracies, then, the father is not only the civil head of the family, but the organ of its traditions, the expounder of its customs, the arbiter of its manners. He is listened to with deference, he is addressed with respect, and the love that is felt for him is always tempered with fear.

When the condition of society becomes democratic and men adopt as their general principle that it is good and lawful to judge of all things for oneself, using former points of belief not as a rule of faith, but simply as a means of information, the power which the opinions of a father exercise over those of his sons diminishes as well as his legal power.

ALEXIS DE TOCQUEVILLE

THE BONES OF MY FATHER

1

There are no dry bones
here in this valley. The skull
of my father grins
at the Mississippi moon
from the bottom
of the Tallahatchie,
the bones of my father
are buried in the mud
of these creeks and brooks that twist
and flow their secrets to the sea.
but the wind sings to me
here the sun speaks to me
of the dry bones of my father.

2

There are no dry bones
in the northern valleys, in the Harlem alleys
young/black/men with knees bent
nod on the stoops of the tenements
and dream
of the dry bones of my father.

And young white longhairs who flee
their homes, and bend their minds
and sing their songs of brotherhood
and no more wars are searching for
my father's bones.

3

There are no dry bones
here, my brothers. We hide from the sun.

The House of Fathers and Titans

No more do we take the long straight strides.
Our steps have been shaped by the cages
that kept us. We glide sideways
like crabs across the sand.
We perch on green lilies, we search
beneath white rocks. . . .
THERE ARE NO DRY BONES HERE

The skull of my father
grins at the Mississippi moon
from the bottom
of the Tallahatchie.

Conn.—Feb. 21, 1971

ETHERIDGE KNIGHT

from
THEOGONY
The Great Father
Eating His Children

Rheia, submissive in love to Kronos,
  bore glorious children,
Hestia and Demeter,
  Hera of the golden sandals,
and strong Hades, who under the ground
  lives in his palace
and has a heart without pity;
  the deep-thunderous Earthshaker,
and Zeus of the counsels,
  who is the father of gods and of mortals,
and underneath whose thunder
  the whole wide earth shudders;
but, as each of these children
  came from the womb of its mother
to her knees, great Kronos swallowed it down,
  with the intention
that no other of the proud children
  of the line of Ouranos
should ever hold the king's position
  among the immortals . . .
Therefore he kept watch, and did not sleep,
  but waited
for his children, and swallowed them,
  and Rheia's sorrow was beyond forgetting.

HESIOD
translated by Richmond Lattimore

SATURN

He lay on the couch night after night,
mouth open, the darkness of the room
filling his mouth, and no one knew
my father was eating his children. He seemed to
rest so quietly, vast body
inert on the sofa, big hand
fallen away from the glass.
What could be more passive than a man
passed out every night—and yet as he lay
on his back, snoring, our lives slowly
disappeared down the hole of his life.
My brother's arm went in up to the shoulder
and he bit it off, and sucked at the wound
as one sucks at the sockets of lobster. He took
my brother's head between his lips
and snapped it like a cherry off the stem. You would have
    seen
only a large, handsome man
heavily asleep, unconscious. And yet
somewhere in his head his soil-colored eyes
were open, the circles of the whites glittering
as he crunched the torso of his child between his jaws,
crushed the bones like the soft shells of crabs
and the delicacies of the genitals
rolled back along his tongue. In the nerves of his gums and
bowels he knew what he was doing and he could not
stop himself, like orgasm, his
boy's feet crackling like two raw fish
between his teeth. This is what he wanted,
to take that life into his mouth
and show what a man could do—show his son
what a man's life was.

SHARON OLDS

THE GUILD

Every night, as my grandfather sat
in the darkened room in front of the fire,
the liquor like fire in his hand, his eye
glittering meaninglessly in the light
from the flames, his glass eye baleful and stony,
a young man sat with him
in silence and darkness, a college boy with
white skin, unlined, a narrow
beautiful face, a broad domed
forehead, and eyes amber as the resin from
trees too young to be cut yet.
This was his son, who sat, an apprentice,
night after night, his glass of coals
next to the old man's glass of coals,
and he drank when the old man drank, and he learned
the craft of oblivion—that young man
not yet cruel, his hair dark as the
soil that feeds the tree's roots,
that son who would come to be in his turn
better at this than the teacher, the apprentice
who would pass his master in cruelty and oblivion,
drinking steadily by the flames in the blackness,
that young man my father.

SHARON OLDS

MY PAPA'S WALTZ

The whiskey on your breath
Could make a small boy dizzy;
But I hung on like death:
Such waltzing was not easy.

We romped until the pans
Slid from the kitchen shelf;
My mother's countenance
Could not unfrown itself.

The hand that held my wrist
Was battered on one knuckle;
At every step you missed
My right ear scraped a buckle.

You beat time on my head
With a palm caked hard by dirt,
Then waltzed me off to bed
Still clinging to your shirt.

THEODORE ROETHKE

AMERICAN PRIMITIVE

Look at him there in his stovepipe hat,
His high-top shoes, and his handsome collar;
Only my Daddy could look like that,
And I love my Daddy like he loves his Dollar.

The screen door bangs, and it sounds so funny—
There he is in a shower of gold;
His pockets are stuffed with folding money,
His lips are blue, and his hands feel cold.

He hangs in the hall by his black cravat,
The ladies faint, and the children holler:
Only my Daddy could look like that,
And I love my Daddy like he loves his Dollar.

WILLIAM JAY SMITH

MY FATHER'S WEDDING
1924

Today, lonely for my father, I saw
a log, or branch,
long, bent, ragged, bark gone.
I felt lonely for my father when I saw it.
It was the log
that lay near my uncle's old milk wagon.

Some men live with a limp they don't hide,
stagger, or drag
a leg. Their sons often are angry.
Only recently I thought:
Doing what you want . . .
Is that like limping? Tracks of it show in sand.

Have you seen those giant bird-
men of Bhutan?
Men in bird masks, with pig noses, dancing,
teeth like a dog's, sometimes
dancing on one bad leg!
They do what they want, the dog's teeth say that.

But I grew up without dog's teeth,
showed a whole body,
left only clear tracks in sand.
I learned to walk swiftly, easily,
no trace of a limp.
I even leaped a little. Guess where my defect is!

Then what? If a man, cautious,
hides his limp,
somebody has to limp it. Things
do it; the surroundings limp.
House walls get scars,
the car breaks down; matter, in drudgery, takes it up.

On my father's wedding day,
no one was there
to hold him. Noble loneliness
held him. Since he never asked for pity
his friends thought he
was whole. Walking alone he could carry it.

He came in limping. It was a simple
wedding, three
or four people. The man in black,
lifting the book, called for order.
And the invisible bride
stepped forward, before his own bride.

He married the invisible bride, not his own.
In her left
breast she carried the three drops
that wound and kill. He already had
his bark-like skin then,
made rough especially to repel the sympathy

he longed for, didn't need, and wouldn't accept.
So the Bible's
words are read. The man in black
speaks the sentence. When the service
is over, I hold him
in my arms for the first time and the last.

After that he was alone
and I was alone.
Few friends came; he invited few.
His two-story house he turned
into a forest,
where both he and I are the hunters.

ROBERT BLY

The House of Fathers and Titans

THE PORTRAIT

My mother never forgave my father
for killing himself,
especially at such an awkward time
and in a public park,
that spring
when I was waiting to be born.
She locked his name
in her deepest cabinet
and would not let him out,
though I could hear him thumping.
When I came down from the attic
with the pastel portrait in my hand
of a long-lipped stranger
with a brave moustache
and deep brown level eyes,
she ripped it into shreds
without a single word
and slapped me hard.
In my sixty-fourth year
I can feel my cheek
still burning.

STANLEY KUNITZ

THE CORE OF MASCULINITY

The core of masculinity does not derive from being male,
nor friendliness from those who console.

Your old grandmother says,
"Maybe you shouldn't to school.
You look a little pale."

Run when you hear that.
A father's stern slaps are better.

Your bodily soul wants comforting.
The severe father wants spiritual clarity.
He scolds, but eventually
leads you into the open.

Pray for a tough instructor
to hear and act and stay within you.

We have been busy accumulating solace.
Make us afraid of how we were.

(*Mathnawi, VI, 1430–1445*)

RUMI
translated by Coleman Barks

THE GIFT

To pull the metal splinter from my palm
my father recited a story in a low voice.
I watched his lovely face and not the blade.
Before the story ended, he'd removed
the iron sliver I thought I'd die from.

I can't remember the tale,
but hear his voice still, a well
of dark water, a prayer.
And I recall his hands,
two measures of tenderness
he laid against my face,
the flames of discipline
he raised above my head.

Had you entered that afternoon
you would have thought you saw a man
planting something in a boy's palm,
a silver tear, a tiny flame.
Had you followed that boy
you would have arrived here,
where I bend over my wife's right hand.

Look how I shave her thumbnail down
so carefully she feels no pain.
Watch as I lift the splinter out.
I was seven when my father
took my hand like this,
and I did not hold that shard
between my fingers and think,
Metal that will bury me,
christen it Little Assassin,
Ore Going Deep for My Heart.
And I did not lift up my wound and cry,

Death visited here!
I did what a child does
when he's given something to keep.
I kissed my father.

                                        LI-YOUNG LEE

THE WEIGHT OF SWEETNESS

No easy thing to bear, the weight of sweetness.

Song, wisdom, sadness, joy: sweetness
equals three of any of these gravities.

See a peach bend
the branch and strain the stem until
it snaps.
Hold the peach, try the weight, sweetness
and death so round and snug
in your palm.
And, so, there is
the weight of memory:

Windblown, a rain-soaked
bough shakes, showering
the man and the boy.
They shiver in delight,
and the father lifts from his son's cheek
one green leaf
fallen like a kiss.

The good boy hugs a bag of peaches
his father has entrusted
to him.
Now he follows
his father, who carries a bagful in each arm.
See the look on the boy's face
as his father moves
faster and farther ahead, while his own steps
flag, and his arms grow weak, as he labors
under the weight
of peaches.

LI-YOUNG LEE

ONLY
WHEN MY HEART
FREEZES

Only when my heart freezes
do I covet the power
to hurt an enemy
as you and I can hurt
each other, my son:
with a thoughtless word,
a careless glance,
an unexpected departure.

You crush your tears
in your fists.
Every door in the house
bangs shut.

And I too am afflicted
like the refugee orphan
who leaves a full table
with breadcrusts
to hide in her pillow.

We understand why
Johnson gave
that terrible shout
when Boswell left him,
without a word,
and galloped ahead
to search out an inn.

"If you had not come back,
I had never spoken to you again,"
the old man said.

The House of Fathers and Titans
139

The pair of them,
half-mad,
like you and me,
and night falling
in a strange, wild country.

ALDEN NOWLAN

THOSE WINTER SUNDAYS

Sundays too my father got up early
and put his clothes on in the blueblack cold,
then with cracked hands that ached
from labor in the weekday weather made
banked fires blaze. No one ever thanked him.

I'd wake and hear the cold splintering, breaking.
When the rooms were warm, he'd call,
and slowly I would rise and dress,
fearing the chronic angers of that house,

Speaking indifferently to him,
who had driven out the cold
and polished my good shoes as well.
What did I know, what did I know
of love's austere and lonely offices?

ROBERT HAYDEN

MY FATHER WENT TO FUNERALS

What could my father do?
I realized when I was still small
that he couldn't build or fix anything,
and later it occurred to me
that he had no original thoughts.
He could tell jokes that made people laugh,
keep track of money, mainly other people's,
and serve on committees.
Not what a boy could care much about.
And another thing: he went to funerals.
Often in the evening, after the commute
into the city and back from the city,
he went out again, mildly against his will,
to the lodge or some church committee,
and often enough it was a funeral he attended.
It was a decency he had. I knew that,
maybe. But I would not have thought
he tended any mystery.
I have learned, only lately,
that when you sit in the front row
in the eternal weather of the funeral parlor,
it is surprising, and a relief,
to see the faces that appear before you
and pass by, not far from where he lies.
It is a mystery. Maybe
the decency itself is the mystery,
or maybe we cross from the one to the other
only on a bridge of grief.
My father's father died
when my father was twenty-three.
My father was a man who held the cables.
And I have begun to go to funerals.

HOWARD NELSON

OFFERING

Father, you must have been,
Like now—
On a tiny raft while the big ship went down.

You had taken our mother aboard
While the decks were still awash.
Then, for a little time, it must have seemed almost like
    heaven—
Though you've never said that
In words.
Nor has she
            but I saw it
In both your eyes when you thought
We were not watching.

Heaven, then.
Even on the dark and shoreless waters.
Other rafts went down. Around you cries
Went up—
            agonies—
Sharks clouding and clotting in the sea—
Heaven.

Then our mother began
Presenting us to you:
One, every couple of years,
Was conjured out of the gypsy tent of her black skirts.
And you fed us:
Fishing all night in the hungry waters,
Giving your clothing to warm us,
And you naked, shivering in the cold,
                            enduring—
Why didn't you drown us like a litter of sick cats?

But . . . didn't.
You have your freedom for our mother's fulfillment.
And you gave us
All the lost honey of a young man's years—
Steering through the vicious seas of those bitter times . . .
Ah . . . dearest father, dear
Helmsman!

THOMAS MCGRATH

THE DISTANT FOOTSTEPS

My father is sleeping. His noble face
suggests a mild heart;
he is so sweet now . . .
if anything bitter is in him, I must be the bitterness.

There is loneliness in the parlor; they are praying;
and there is no news of the children today.
My father wakes, he listens
for the flight into Egypt, the good-bye that dresses wounds.
Now he is so near;
if anything distant is in him, I must be the distance.

And my mother walks past in the orchard,
savoring a taste already without savor.
Now she is so gentle,
so much wing, so much farewell, so much love.

There is loneliness in the parlor with no sound,
no news, no greenness, no childhood.
And if something is broken this afternoon,
and if something descends or creaks,
it is two old roads, curving and white.
Down them my heart is walking on foot.

CÉSAR VALLEJO
translated by James Wright and John Knoepfle

YESTERDAY

My friend says I was not a good son
you understand
I say yes I understand

he says I did not go
to see my parents very often you know
and I say yes I know

even when I was living in the same city he says
maybe I would go there once
a month or maybe even less
I say oh yes

he says the last time I went to see my father
I say the last time I saw my father

he says the last time I saw my father
he was asking me about my life
how I was making out and he
went into the next room
to get something to give me

oh I say
feeling again the cold
of my father's hand the last time

he says and my father turned
in the doorway and saw me
look at my wristwatch and he
said you know I would like you to stay
and talk with me

oh yes I say

he says my father
said maybe
you have important work you are doing
or maybe you should be seeing
somebody I don't want to keep you

I look out the window
my friend is older than I am
he says and I told my father it was so
and I got up and left him then
you know

though there was nowhere I had to go
and nothing I had to do

W. S. MERWIN

from
MEMORIES OF MY FATHER

When I come back to my father's house,
it will be in any month, though I have loved
fall, and August, and the august moon,
and the moonstruck flagstones going to the door.
When I come back someone will be singing
in an upstairs room, and I will stop
just inside the door to hear who it is,
or is it someone I don't know, singing,
in my father's house, when I come back?

GALWAY KINNELL

THE RACE

When I got to the airport I rushed up to the desk
and they told me the flight was cancelled. The doctors had
said my father would not live through the night
and the flight was cancelled. A young man with a
dark blond mustache told me
another airline had a non-stop
leaving in seven minutes—see that
elevator over there well go
down to the first floor, make a right you'll
see a yellow bus, get off at the
second Pan Am terminal—I
ran, I who have no sense of direction
raced exactly where he'd told me, like a fish
slipping upstream deftly against the
flow of the river. I jumped off that bus with my
heavy bags and ran, the bags
wagged me from side to side as if to
prove I was under the claims of the material, I
ran up to a man with a white flower on his breast,
I who always go to the end of the line, I said
Help me. He looked at my ticket, he said make a
left and then a right go up the moving stairs and then
run. I raced up the moving stairs
two at a time, at the top I saw the
long hollow corridor and
then I took a deep breath, I said
goodbye to my body, goodbye to comfort, I
used my legs and heart as if I would
gladly use them up for this, to
touch him again in this life. I ran and the
big heavy dark bags
banged me, wheeled and swam around me like
planets in wild orbits—I have seen
pictures of women running down roads with their

belongings tied in black scarves
grasped in their fists, running under serious
gray historical skies—I blessed my
long legs he gave me, my strong
heart I abandoned to its own purpose, I
ran to Gate 17 and they were
just lifting the thick white
lozenge of the door to fit it into the
socket of the plane. Like the man who is not
too rich, I turned to the side and
slipped through the needle's eye, and then I
walked down the aisle toward my father. The jet was
full and people's hair was shining, they were
smiling, the interior of the plane was filled with a
mist of gold endorphin light,
I wept as people weep when they enter heaven,
in massive relief. We lifted up
gently from one tip of the continent and
did not stop until we set down lightly on the
other edge, I walked into his room and
watched his chest rise slowly and
sink again, all night
I watched him breathe.

SHARON OLDS

THE IRISH CLIFFS OF MOHER

Who is my father in this world, in this house,
At the spirit's base?

My father's father, his father's father, his—
Shadows like winds

Go back to a parent before thought, before speech,
At the head of the past.

They go to the cliffs of Moher rising out of the mist,
Above the real,

Rising out of present time and place, above
The wet, green grass.

This is not landscape, full of the somnambulations
Of poetry

And the sea. This is my father or, maybe,
It is as he was,

A likeness, one of the race of fathers: earth
And sea and air.

WALLACE STEVENS

SIX

Language: Speaking Well and Speaking Out

Form your letters carefully and well.
Making things carefully
Is more important than making them.

—ANTONIO MACHADO
translated by R.B.

Confucius supposedly said that the rectification of society starts with the rectification of its language. This suggests that a careful use of words comes before new laws, new programs, and new leaders. Laws and programs begin in words, and if the words of our leaders are entangled in garbled speech, intoned as nasal whining, bereft of inspiration and wit, and flatter than the commercials that surround them, then we can't expect the society to prosper.

Yet as late as the 1930s and '40s Senate debates and presidential campaigns demanded strong oratorical ability. In the last century you paid a compliment to the young man who was a-courtin' your daughter or was hired for a job by describing him as "well-spoken." A man's word was his honor because in his word was his spirit. Schools used to teach elocution; colleges, public speaking. Rhetoric, once upon a time, was an educational necessity alongside math and logic. We learned poetry in elementary grades by heart, with heart. As Dylan Thomas says, his magical ways with words began with listening to the incantations of nursery rhymes, the playful power of language.

These older ways with speech have devolved into "language skills," "information access and delivery," "communication." Language has mainly become a tool for sending communiqués "in no uncertain terms." Or for a sales pitch. Exuberant exaggeration, hellfire sermons, boasting, swearing and cursing, talking dirty (Rabelais), fantastic alliterations, skip rope and nonsense

155

rhymes, ethnic dialects and regional accents, to say nothing of simply beautiful poems, all fade in the electronic light of the TV screen. Yet as the Trobrianders say: "The force of magic . . . resides within man and can escape only through his voice."

The people of Russia, Eastern Europe, Latin America, the Muslim cultures, and traditional Africa still recognize this magic. Poetry and common speech keep close company. Poetry is not intended for an in-group of elite specialists. (In Iran, when I was there some years ago, classical poems were broadcast over radio loudspeakers in the bazaar.) The public of these other cultures honors poets, reads them, goes to hear them. Poetry is a respectable occupation; writers are appointed to government office. But here at home poetry is kept away from life. Whoever invites a poet to speak to current issues on TV? Would any of the talk shows ever devote one of their controversial afternoon sessions to language? We have "talk shows" that never reflect upon the nature of talk, and we have the "talking cure," as Freud first called his method of psychoanalysis, whose own talk needs cure of its inflated jargon. We have become a culture that has let its most basic infrastructure—our words, their ordering in rhythms, the magic of their beauty, and the voices that speak them—decay into disheveled neglect.

When the magic of language withers, we are left in the desolate condition Charles Darwin at the end of this section describes as a "loss of happiness," and our minds become, as he says, "a kind of machine for grinding general laws out of large collections of fact." He here refers to the literal level of language which gives accurate accounts, such as the length of a board or how to put up a folding cot. When Frost speaks of a dreary kind of "grammatical prose" and Thoreau, of the language of "common sense," they are warning about the deadening effect of literal language. This literal style is also the "ordinary speech" that no longer suffices when people are moved by "great forces" of fear, joy, and sorrow (Orpingalik). In fact, Thoreau insists, to stay only with this restricted language produces "brain-rot."

But the notion of ordinary, only literal speech can be questioned, since words cannot be cut free from their primordial messages. As Gerhart Hauptmann says, "Poetry is the art of letting the primordial word resound through the common word." All words have roots, histories, families, genders, offspring. They reach back through centuries to the dead tongues of ancient peoples, and they go on accumulating wealth and shedding outworn baggage as they travel from region to region. They bring blessings—like a long-awaited letter from your son or your father; and they bring curses so that even the most soberly abstract term can fix us in spells that last for years, like a psychiatric diagnosis. Because words are so laden with hidden messages, they cannot help but be metaphors, by nature "poetic," opening beyond their commonsense definitions into mystery and myth. In fact, the Italian philosopher Giambattista Vico wrote, "a metaphor is a myth in brief."

Thoreau recommends extravagance for breaking through usual language. "I am convinced that I cannot exaggerate enough even to lay the foundation of a true expression." J. M. Cohen's translation of the incredible exaggerations by the classic French writer Rabelais and a contemporary version of "Amergin and Cessair," an ancient Celtic incantation, show the power of extravagance. Bombast, scurrility, farfetched similes and startlingly sensuous images, and the humongous immensity of their vocabularies enchant the eye as it reads, the ear as it hears. We are charmed out of the ordinary by the riches of words.

Besides richness—deepness. Something else lurks in the language of a poem. It is a ". . . sullen art / Exercised in the still night / When only the moon rages . . . ," says Dylan Thomas. Wallace Stevens says poetry is: "A lion, an ox in his breast . . . stout dog. / Young ox, bow-legged bear, / He tastes its blood." "Poetry Is a Destructive Force," says Stevens; "It can kill a man."

We have come to Lorca and what the Spanish tradition knows as the *duende,* a "spirit of the earth" "that has black tones." "The true struggle is with the duende," Lorca declares, which descends or arises into the body's gestures and voice, half scream of pain, half leaping exaltation, and wholly a creation of the blood soul. "The poet creates in a trance," writes Hernandez; and Orpingalik, the Eskimo, knows it too, "making his breath come in gasps and his heart throb." Poetry as seizure by the lion.

There is yet another element essential to poetic language: elegant intelligence or the edge of wit. When Amergin and Cessair compete, theirs is a battle of wit. They challenge each other to the farthest shores of imagery. How far "out" can you go and still stay sharply brilliant? How to find the fine line between sheer beauty and mere bravado? It takes effort, says Samuel Johnson; recollection in "tranquillity" says Wordsworth, "modesty," says Hernandez, and "tradition," says Pound, because, says Machado, a poem must be well made, as evidenced in the subtle rhythms and complex internal rhymes of Marianne Moore's "Rigorists."

Even Keats's gorgeously florid vision of the harvest goddess "sitting careless on a granary floor, / Thy hair soft-lifted by the winnowing wind . . . ," is exquisitely well made. Though it begins in a general mist and echoes with mournful premonitions of the poet's dying, the language, despite the romantic emotion, is elegantly composed of precise images—hazel shells, gnats, hedge-crickets, and twittering swallows, and sounds like the bees humming in those double *m*'s of the first stanza's last line: "For Summer has o'er-brimm'd their clammy cells."

What makes a poem's language work is the work in the language, and what makes it last is the love for this language work. All good poems are love poems—not because they tell of love and lovers, but because they reveal the poet's love of language. Not about love, the poem *is* love. So Pound writes, "What thou lovest well remains . . . / What thou lov'st well is thy true heritage . . ." Shakespeare imagines that the only truly lasting love resides in the miracle of the poet's "black ink."

If, as Nalungiaq says, "in the very earliest time . . . people and animals . . . spoke the same language," then the rectification of language requires closeness with our animal nature. Then the vitality of our language resides as much in the sound of our words and beat of their rhythms as in their meanings. That's why Lorca puts the poetry of *duende* together with song, dance, and bull-fighting, and that's why poems belong more to speaking than to reading, more to passionate declamation and ecstatic jubilation, keening, crying, and screaming and to the secret whispers of lovers' lips than to typed lines on bleached paper. Good language asks to be spoken aloud, mind to mind and heart to heart, by embodied voices that still retain the animal and by tongues that still delight in savoring vowels and the clipped spitting of explosive consonants.

Robert Frost insists that "Words in themselves do not convey meaning . . . the sound of them does." Dylan Thomas began to write because he had "fallen in love with words. . . . What the words stood for . . . was of very secondary importance. What mattered was the *sound* of them . . ." Because the sound of them is so crucial, we've learned from reading poems at men's gatherings that each poem puts the voice in a different place, demanding what the Trobrianders would call the intelligence of the larynx. As our reciting voices give body to the poem, the poem conversely works on the voice and its body, teaching it to dig for an animal substrate and find the strength and sensitivity of which any voice is always capable. Poems, beyond their human meanings, beyond their human feelings, enliven *nanola*, what Trobrianders call moral intelligence. By teaching men to speak well, men learn to speak up and out. Isn't this precisely what is needed, according to Confucius, to refound society?

J.H.

MAGIC WORDS

In the very earliest time,
when both people and animals lived on earth,
a person could become an animal if he wanted to
and an animal could become a human being.
Sometimes they were people
and sometimes animals
and there was no difference.
All spoke the same language.
That was the time when words were like magic.
The human mind had mysterious powers.
A word spoken by chance
might have strange consequences.
It would suddenly come alive
and what people wanted to happen could happen—
all you had to do was say it.
Nobody can explain this:
That's the way it was.

Eskimo

THE MIND

The mind, *nanola*, by which term intelligence, power of discrimination, capacity for learning magical formulae, and all forms of nonmanual skill are described, as well as moral qualities, resides somewhere in the larynx. . . . The memory, however, the store of formulae and traditions learned by heart, resides deeper, in the belly. . . . The force of magic, crystallized in the magical formulae, is carried by men of the present generation in their bodies. . . . The force of magic does not reside in the things; it resides within man and can escape only through his voice.

Trobriands, New Guinea

SONGS ARE THOUGHTS

Songs are thoughts, sung out with the breath when people are moved by great forces and ordinary speech no longer suffices. Man is moved just like the ice floe sailing here and there in the current. His thoughts are driven by a flowing force when he feels joy, when he feels fear, when he feels sorrow. Thoughts can wash over him like a flood, making his breath come in gasps and his heart throb. Something like an abatement in the weather will keep him thawed up. And then it will happen that we, who always think we are small, will feel still smaller. And we will fear to use words. But it will happen that the words we need will come of themselves. When the words we want to use shoot up of themselves—we get a new song.

ORPINGALIK
Netsilik Eskimo

ON BEING EXTRAVAGANT

I fear chiefly lest my expression may not be *extra-vagant* enough, may not wander far enough beyond the narrow limits of my daily experience, so as to be adequate to the truth of which I have been convinced. *Extra vagance!* it depends on how you are yarded. . . .

I am convinced that I cannot exaggerate enough even to lay the foundation of a true expression. . . .

Why level downward to our dullest perception always, and praise that as common sense? The commonest sense is the sense of men asleep, which they express by snoring. . . .

"They pretend," as I hear, "that the verses of Kabir have four different senses; illusion, spirit, intellect, and the exoteric doctrine of the Vedas"; but in this part of the world it is considered a ground for complaint if a man's writings admit of more than one interpretation. While England endeavors to cure the potato-rot, will not any endeavor to cure the brain-rot, which prevails so much more widely and fatally?

HENRY DAVID THOREAU

from
GARGANTUA

The cake-bakers, however, were not at all inclined to accede to this request and, what is worse, they heaped insults on the shepherds, calling them babblers, snaggle-teeth, crazy carrot-heads, scabs, shit-a-beds, boors, sly cheats, lazy louts, fancy fellows, drunkards, braggarts, good-for-nothings, dunderheads, nut-shellers, beggars, sneak-thieves, mincing milksops, apers of their betters, idlers, half-wits, gapers, hovel-dwellers, poor fish, cacklers, conceited monkeys, teeth-clatterers, dung-drovers, shitten shepherds, and other such abusive epithets.

"After that," said Gargantua, "I wiped myself with a kerchief, with a pillow, with a slipper, with a game-bag, with a basket—but what an unpleasant arse-wiper that was!—then with a hat. And note that some hats are smooth, some shaggy, some velvety, some of taffeta, and some of satin. The best of all are the shaggy ones, for they make a very good abstersion of the faccal matter. Then I wiped myself with a hen, a cock, and a chicken, with a calf's skin, a hare, a pigeon, and a cormorant, with a lawyer's bag, with a penitent's hood, with a coif, with an otter. But to conclude, I say and maintain that there is no arse-wiper like a well-downed goose, if you hold her neck between your legs. You must take my word for it, you really must. You get a miraculous sensation in your arse-hole, both from the softness of the down and from the temperate heat of the goose herself; and this is easily communicated to the bum-gut and the rest of the intestines, from which it reaches the heart and the brain. Do not imagine that the felicity of the heroes and demigods in the Elysian Fields arises from their asphodel, their ambrosia, or their nectar, as those ancients say. It comes, in my opinion, from their wiping their arses with the neck of a goose, . . .

FRANÇOIS RABELAIS
translated by J. M. Cohen

"Everything that has black tones has duende." And there is no truth greater.

These black tones are mystery itself whose roots are held fast in the mulch we all know and ignore, but whence we arrive at all that is substantial in art. Black tones, said the popular man from Spain and the contemporary of Goethe (who defines duende when speaking of Paganini), are a "mysterious power which everyone feels but which no philosopher can explain."

So then, the duende is a power and not a method, a struggle and not a thought. I have heard an old guitar teacher say that "the duende is not in the singer's throat, the duende rises inside from the very soles of one's feet." That is to say, it is not a question of ability or aptitude but a matter of possessing an authentic living style; that is to say of blood, of culture most ancient, of creation in act.

This "mysterious power which everyone feels and no philosopher can explain" is in short, the spirit of the earth.

The true struggle is with the duende.

The arrival of the duende always presupposes a radical transformation on every plane. It produces a feeling of totally unedited freshness. It bears the quality of a newly created rose, of a miracle that produces an almost religious enthusiasm.

All art is capable of duende. But the place that it naturally occurs is in music, dance, or spoken poetry because they require a living body for interpretation and because they are forms that perpetually live and die, their contours are raised upon an exact presence.

FEDERICO GARCÍA LORCA
translated by Stella Rodriquez

POETRY IS A DESTRUCTIVE FORCE

That's what misery is,
Nothing to have at heart.
It is to have or nothing.

It is a thing to have,
A lion, an ox in his breast,
To feel it breathing there.

Corazon, stout dog.
Young ox, bow-legged bear,
He tastes its blood, not spit.

He is like a man
In the body of a violent beast.
Its muscles are his own . . .

The lion sleeps in the sun.
Its nose is on its paws.
It can kill a man.

WALLACE STEVENS

IN MY CRAFT OR SULLEN ART

In my craft or sullen art
Exercised in the still night
When only the moon rages
And the lovers lie abed
With all their griefs in their arms,
I labor by singing light
Not for ambition or bread
Or the strut and trade of charms
On the ivory stages
But for the common wages
Of their most secret heart.

Not for the proud man apart
From the raging moon I write
On these spindrift pages
Nor for the towering dead
With their nightingales and psalms
But for the lovers, their arms
Round the griefs of the ages,
Who pay no praise or wages
Nor heed my craft or art.

DYLAN THOMAS

ON THE WORDS IN POETRY

You want to know why and how I just began to write poetry. . . .

To answer . . . this question, I should say I wanted to write poetry in the beginning because I had fallen in love with words. The first poems I knew were nursery rhymes, and before I could read them for myself I had come to love just the words of them, the words alone. What the words stood for, symbolized, or meant, was of very secondary importance. What mattered was the *sound* of them as I heard them for the first time on the lips of the remote and incomprehensible grown-ups who seemed, for some reason, to be living in my world. And these words were, to me, as the notes of bells, the sounds of musical instruments, the noises of wind, sea, and rain, the rattle of milkcarts, the clopping of hooves on cobbles, the fingering of branches on a window pane, might be to someone, deaf from birth, who has miraculously found his hearing. I did not care what the words said, overmuch, not what happened to Jack and Jill and the Mother Goose rest of them; I cared for the shapes of sound that their names, and the words describing their actions, made in my ears, I cared for the colors the words cast on my eyes. I realize that I may be, as I think back all that way, romanticizing my reactions to the simple and beautiful words of those pure poems; but that is all I can honestly remember, however much time might have falsified my memory. I fell in love—that is the only expression I can think of—at once, and am still at the mercy of words, though sometimes now, knowing a little of their behavior very well, I think I can influence them slightly and have even learned to beat them now and then, which they appear to enjoy. I tumbled for words at once. And, when I began to read the nursery rhymes for myself, and, later, to read other verses and ballads, I knew that I had discovered the most important things, to me, that could be ever. There they were, seemingly lifeless, made only of black and white, but out of them, out of their own being, came love and terror and pity and pain and wonder and all the other vague abstractions that make our ephemeral lives dangerous, great, and bearable.

DYLAN THOMAS

SOUND-POSTURE

What we do get in life and miss so often in literature is the sentence sounds that underlie the words. Words in themselves do not convey meaning, and to [. . . prove] this, which may seem entirely unreasonable to any one who does not understand the psychology of sound, let us take the example of two people who are talking on the other side of a closed door, whose voices can be heard but whose words cannot be distinguished. Even though the words do not carry, the sound of them does, and the listener can catch the meaning of the conversation. This is because every meaning has a particular sound posture. . . . You recognize the sentence sound in this: You, you . . . ! It is so strong that if you hear it as I do you have to pronounce the two yous differently. Just so many sentence sounds belong to man as just so many vocal runs belong to one kind of bird. We come into the world with them and create none of them. What we feel as creation is only selection and grouping. We summon them from Heaven knows where under excitement with the audile [audial] imagination. And unless we are in an imaginative mood it is no use trying to make them, they will not rise. We can only write the dreary kind of grammatical prose known as professorial.

ROBERT FROST

AMERGIN AND CESSAIR
A Battle of Poetic Incantation

AMERGIN: I plant my foot on this land.
For I am Amergin
Son of Mil
Son of the People of the Sea
Peoples of ships and barks
Prince of the White Cave
Son of the builder of the Spiral Castle.
Foetus of the Womb of the Earth
Son of the Hag of Beara
Builder of the Tower of Bregon
Climber through the Needle's Eye
Namer of names
Judge between combatants.

CESSAIR: Here I stand
Daughter of the moon
Cessair.
Poet of Arianrhod
Daughter of Danae, the Mother and Queen
Keeper of the house of Sidh
Daughter of the Northwest Wind; I am
Cessair.
Navigator on water
Mistress on shore
Fair as a flower
Daughter of Darkness
Daughter of the House of Arianrhod.

AMERGIN: Who fortells the ages of the moon?
Who brings the cattle from the sea and
segregates them?
For whom but me will the fish of the laughing
ocean make welcome?

Who but I knows the secret of the unhewn
    Dolmens?
Who shapes weapons from hill to hill?
Who but myself knows where the sun shall
    set?

CESSAIR: I am the flash of sun on water.
I am the clash of battle swords.
I am the teeth in the sea-shark's mouth.
I am the blood of wild beasts.
I am the fire in the witch's hearth.
I am the evening sky ablaze—
The red of serpents' tongues,
The black of deepest night.
I am a mare that knows no reins.

AMERGIN: I am the roar of the sea.
I am a bull of seven fights.
I am a hawk on a cliff.
I rove the hills, a ravening boar.
I am lightning that blasts the trees.
I am the point of weapons.
I am thunder on the mountains.
I am a God that fashions fire for a head.
I am a dragon that eats the sky.

CESSAIR: I thread the stars across the sky.
I am the kiss of lovers' lips.
I am the mortar and the stone.
I am the song of my homeland.

AMERGIN: I am the wind on the sea.

CESSAIR: I am the bow of every ship.

AMERGIN: I am ocean waves.

CESSAIR: I am the foam upon the sea.

AMERGIN: I am a lake on a plain.

CESSAIR: I am the green of the fairest hill.

AMERGIN: I am dewdrop, a tear of the sun.

CESSAIR: I am a lily on a still pond.

AMERGIN: I am the son of harmony.

CESSAIR: I am a word of skill.

AMERGIN: I am the silence of things secret.

Traditional

adapted by Michael Meade and Erica Helm Meade

NOTE: The early inhabitants of Ireland fended off invaders through magical, poetic incantations that caused the ocean waves to churn and batter invading ships before they could reach the shore. The poet Cessair attempted to defend her homeland by using powerful verse to halt the invasion of the poet-warrior Amergin. But Amergin used his own potent song to tame the sea and gain a foothold on Irish soil. Like the goddesses of old, giving way to newer religions, Cessair and her people yielded rule of the land to Amergin and his tribe. The words of Amergin are adapted and embellished by Michael Meade, from what remains of the ancient Song of Amergin. The words of Cessair were written by Erica Helm Meade. As none of Cessair's actual words have been preserved, Erica relied for her inspiration upon early myths of Irish goddesses.

What thou lovest well remains,
                              the rest is dross
What thou lov'st well shall not be reft from thee
What thou lov'st well is thy true heritage . . .

The ant's a centaur in his dragon world.
Pull down thy vanity, it is not man
Made courage, or made order, or made grace,
            Pull down thy vanity, I say pull down.
Learn of the green world what can be thy place
In scaled invention or true artistry.
Pull down thy vanity,
                      Paquin pull down!
The green casque has outdone your elegance.

"Master thyself, then others shall thee beare"
            Pull down thy vanity
Thou art a beaten dog beneath the hail,
A swollen magpie in a fitful sun,
Half black half white
Nor knowst'ou wing from tail
Pull down thy vanity
                  How mean thy hates
Fostered in falsity,
                  Pull down thy vanity,
Rathe to destroy, niggard in charity,
Pull down thy vanity,
                  I say pull down.

But to have done instead of not doing
                  this is not vanity
To have, with decency, knocked

That a Blunt should open
      To have gathered from the air a live tradition
or from a fine old eye the unconquered flame
This is not vanity.
      Here error is all in the not done,
all in the diffidence that faltered.

EZRA POUND

SONNET LXV

Since brass, nor stone, nor earth, nor boundless sea,
But sad mortality o'er-sways their power,
How with this rage shall beauty hold a plea,
Whose action is no stronger than a flower?
O, how shall summer's honey breath hold out
Against the wreckful siege of battering days,
When rocks impregnable are not so stout,
Nor gates of steel so strong, but Time decays?
O fearful meditation! where, alack!
Shall Time's best jewel from Time's chest lie hid?
Or what strong hand can hold his swift foot back?
Or who his spoil of beauty can forbid?
    O, none, unless this miracle have might,
    That in black ink my love may still shine bright.

WILLIAM SHAKESPEARE

The rigorous intricacy, like lace, of Marianne Moore's lines and rhymes shows what language can do with a subject as odd and seemingly simple as a reindeer's face.

RIGORISTS

"We saw reindeer
browsing," a friend who'd been in Lapland, said:
"finding their own food; they are adapted

to scant *reino*
or pasture, yet they can run eleven
miles in fifty minutes; the feet spread when

the snow is soft,
and act as snow-shoes. They are rigorists,
however handsomely cutwork artists

of Lapland and
Siberia elaborate the trace
or saddle-girth with saw-tooth leather lace.

One looked at us
with its firm face part brown, part white,—a queen
of alpine flowers. Santa Claus' reindeer, seen

at last, had grey-
brown fur, with a neck like edelweiss or
lion's foot,—*leontopodium* more

exactly." And
this candelabrum-headed ornament
for a place where ornaments are scarce, sent

to Alaska,
was a gift preventing the extinction
of the Esquimo. The battle was won

by a quiet man,
Sheldon Jackson, evangel to that race
whose reprieve he read in the reindeer's face.

MARIANNE MOORE

TO AUTUMN

1

Season of mists and mellow fruitfulness,
  Close bosom-friend of the maturing sun;
Conspiring with him how to load and bless
  With fruit the vines that round the thatch-eves run;
To bend with apples the moss'd cottage-trees,
  And fill all fruit with ripeness to the core;
    To swell the gourd, and plump the hazel shells
With a sweet kernel; to set budding more,
  And still more, later flowers for the bees,
  Until they think warm days will never cease,
    For Summer has o'er-brimm'd their clammy cells.

2

Who hath not seen thee oft amid thy store?
  Sometimes whoever seeks abroad may find
Thee sitting careless on a granary floor,
  Thy hair soft-lifted by the winnowing wind;
Or on a half-reap'd furrow sound asleep,
  Drows'd with the fume of poppies, while thy hook
    Spares the next swath and all its twined flowers:
And sometimes like a gleaner thou dost keep
  Steady thy laden head across a brook;
  Or by a cyder-press, with patient look,
    Thou watchest the last oozings hours by hours.

3

Where are the songs of Spring? Ay, where are they?
  Think not of them, thou hast thy music too,—
While barred clouds bloom the soft-dying day,
  And touch the stubble-plains with rosy hue;
Then in a wailful choir the small gnats mourn

Among the river sallows, borne aloft
  Or sinking as the light wind lives or dies;
And full-grown lambs loud bleat from hilly bourn;
  Hedge-crickets sing; and now with treble soft
  The red-breast whistles from a garden-croft;
  And gathering swallows twitter in the skies.

JOHN KEATS

ON THE WRITING OF POETRY

A writer is not so much someone who has something to say as he is someone who has found a process that will bring about new things he would not have thought of if he had started to say them. That is, he does not draw on a reservoir; instead, he engages in an activity that brings to him a whole succession of unforeseen stories, poems, essays, plays, laws, philosophies, religions, or—but wait!

Back in school, from the first when I began to try to write things, I felt this richness. One thing would lead to another; the world would give and give. Now, after twenty years or so of trying, I live by that certain richness, an idea hard to pin, difficult to say, and perhaps offensive to some. For there are strange implications in it.

One implication is the importance of just plain receptivity. When I write, I like to have an interval before me when I am not likely to be interrupted. For me, this means usually the early morning, before others are awake. I get pen and paper, take a glance out of the window (often it is dark out there), and wait. It is like fishing. But I do not wait very long, for there is always a nibble—and this is where receptivity comes in. To get started I will accept anything that occurs to me. Something always occurs, of course, to any of us. We can't keep from thinking. Maybe I have to settle for an immediate impression: it's cold, or hot, or dark, or bright, or in between! Or—well, the possibilities are endless. If I put down something, that thing will help the next thing come, and I'm off. If I let the process go on, things will occur to me that were not at all in my mind when I started. These things, odd or trivial as they may be, are somehow connected. And if I let them string out, surprising things will happen.

WILLIAM STAFFORD

THOUGHTS

Poetry is the art of letting the primordial word resound through the common word.

GERHART HAUPTMANN

What is written without effort is in general read without pleasure.

SAMUEL JOHNSON

Poetry is the spontaneous overflow of powerful feelings: it takes its origin from emotion recollected in tranquillity.

WILLIAM WORDSWORTH

SELECTIONS

The classical poet is one who finds the solution to his life and, therefore, to his work. The romantic, one who solves nothing, neither in his work nor in his life.

Lack of modesty is a romantic vice: it means speaking of the most intimate things, of what only belongs to a few loved persons. Publishing griefs, misfortunes, with too much freedom, is lack of foresight in a poet; he doesn't let any image or object alone that comes his way. . . .

The poet creates in trance as an angel, in moments of crisis as a man.

The lemon tree in my garden is a bigger influence on my work than all the poets together. . . .

MIGUEL HERNANDEZ
translated by Hardie St. Martin

THESE DAYS

whatever you have to say, leave
the roots on, let them
dangle

And the dirt

       Just to make clear
       where they come from

CHARLES OLSON

AMERICAN POETRY

Whatever it is, it must have
A stomach that can digest
Rubber, coal, uranium, moons, poems.

Like the shark, it contains a shoe.
It must swim for miles through the desert
Uttering cries that are almost human.

LOUIS SIMPSON

CATCH

Two boys uncoached are tossing a poem together,
Overhand, underhand, backhand, sleight of hand, every hand,
Teasing with attitudes, latitudes, interludes, altitudes,
High, make him fly off the ground for it, low, make him
    stoop,
Make him scoop it up, make him as-almost-as-possible miss it,
Fast, let him sting from it, now, now fool him slowly,
Anything, everything tricky, risky, nonchalant,
Anything under the sun to outwit the prosy,
Over the tree and the long sweet cadence down,
Over his head, make him scramble to pick up the meaning,
And now, like a posy, a pretty one plump in his hands.

ROBERT FRANCIS

PITCHER

His art is eccentricity, his aim
How not to hit the mark he seems to aim at,

His passion how to avoid the obvious,
His technique how to vary the avoidance.

The others throw to be comprehended. He
Throws to be a moment misunderstood.

Yet not too much. Not errant, arrant, wild,
But every seeming aberration willed.

Not to, yet still, still to communicate
Making the batter understand too late.

ROBERT FRANCIS

Whereas Robert Francis tells how the metaphorical fuses with actions, such as throwing a ball, this piece by Louis Jenkins and the next by Tomas Tranströmer keep one in all three places at once. Each literal description echoes with psychological insights and feelings and also becomes an extended metaphor with surprising implications.

LIBRARY

I sit down at a table and open a book of poems and move slowly into the shadows of tall trees. They are white pines I think. The ground is covered with soft brown needles and there are signs that animals have come here silently and vanished before I could catch sight of them. But here the trail edges into a cedar swamp; wet ground, deadfall, and rotting leaves. I move carefully but rapidly, pleased with myself.

Someone else comes and sits down at the table, a serious looking young man with a large stack of books. He takes a book from the top of the stack and opens it. The book is called *How to Get a High Paying Job*. He flips through it and lays it down and picks up another and pages through it quickly. It is titled *Moving Ahead*.

We are moving ahead very rapidly now, through a second growth of popple and birch, our faces scratched and our clothes torn by the underbrush. We are moving even faster now, marking the trail, followed closely by bulldozers and crews with chain saws and representatives of the paper company.

LOUIS JENKINS

from
STANDING UP

It's been a hard winter, but summer is here and the fields want us to walk upright. Every man unimpeded, but careful, as when you stand up in a small boat. I remember a day in Africa: on the banks of the Chari, there were many boats, an atmosphere positively friendly, the men almost blue-black in color with three parallel scars on each cheek (meaning the Sara tribe). I am welcomed on a boat—it's a canoe hollowed from a dark tree. The canoe is incredibly rocky, even when you sit on your heels. A balancing act. If you have the heart on the left side you have to lean a bit to the right, nothing in the pockets, no big arm movements, please, all rhetoric has to be left behind. It's necessary: rhetoric will ruin everything here. The canoe glides out over the water.

TOMAS TRANSTRÖMER
translated by R.B.

Events of the green day are transposed to another key by the blue instrument of imaginative language.

from
THE MAN WITH THE BLUE GUITAR

I

The man bent over his guitar,
A shearsman of sorts. The day was green.

They said, "You have a blue guitar,
You do not play things as they are."

The man replied, "Things as they are
Are changed upon the blue guitar."

And they said then, "But play, you must,
A tune beyond us, yet ourselves,

A tune upon the blue guitar
Of things exactly as they are."

II

I cannot bring a world quite round,
Although I patch it as I can.

I sing a hero's head, large eye
And bearded bronze, but not a man,

Although I patch him as I can
And reach through him almost to man.

If to serenade almost to man
Is to miss, by that, things as they are,

Say that it is the serenade
Of a man that plays a blue guitar.

WALLACE STEVENS

from
AUTOBIOGRAPHY OF CHARLES DARWIN

Poetry of many kinds . . . gave me great pleasure, and even as a schoolboy I took intense delight in Shakespeare, especially in the historical plays. I have also said that formerly pictures gave me considerable, and music very great, delight. But now for many years I cannot endure to read a line of poetry: I have tried lately to read Shakespeare, and found it so intolerably dull that it nauseated me. I have also lost almost any taste for pictures or music. . . . My mind seems to have become a kind of machine for grinding general laws out of large collections of fact, but why this should have caused the atrophy of that part of the brain alone, on which the higher tastes depend, I cannot conceive. . . . The loss of these tastes is a loss of happiness, and may possibly be injurious to the intellect, and more probably to the moral character, by enfeebling the emotional part of our nature.

SEVEN

Making a Hole in Denial

Denial ain't just a river in Egypt.

—*Rap song*

It's possible that the United States has achieved the first consistent culture of denial in the modern world. Denial can be considered as an extension—into all levels of society—of the naïve person's inability to face the harsh facts of life.

The health of any nation's soul depends on the capacity of adults to face the harsh facts of the time. But the covering up of painful emotions inside us and the blocking out of fearful images coming from outside have become in our country the national and private style. We have established, with awesome verve, the animal of denial as the guiding beast of the nation's life. The inner city collapses, and we build bad housing projects rather than face the bad education, lack of jobs, and persistent anger at black people. When the homeless increase, we build dangerous shelters rather than face the continuing decline in actual wages. Of course we know this beast lives in every country; we have been forced lately to look at our beast. As the rap song has it: "Denial ain't just a river in Egypt."

Ernest Becker says that denial begins with the refusal to admit that we will die. We don't want anyone to say that. Early on in the cradle, swans talk to us about immortality. Death is intolerable. To eat, shit, and rot is unthinkable for those of us brought up with our own bedrooms. We want special treatment, eternal life on other planets, toilets that will take away our shit and its smell. We love the immortality of metal, chromium implants, the fact that there are no bodily fluids in the machine, the precise memory the computer has, the fact that mathematics never gets colon cancer; and we are deeply satisfied that Disneyland can give us Germany, Spain, and Morocco without their messy, murderous, shit-filled histories. "All this the world well knows."

Some brain defect in human beings, assisted by the politics of oppression, allows this not-knowing to persist for years, decades, an entire life.

> in every language even deafanddumb
> thy sons acclaim your glorious name by gorry
> by jingo by gee by gosh by gum
> why talk of beauty what could be more beau-
> tiful than these heroic happy dead
> who rushed like lions to the roaring slaughter
> they did not stop to think they died instead

> (E. E. Cummings)

In Ibsen's *Wild Duck* a disgusting priest says, after the daughter has shot herself, "She is not dead, but sleepeth." Religion can fight denial, or give in to it. The pope gives in to denial when, standing in Mexico City, surrounded by three million people destroying the environment and their own children, he says that birth control is wrong. Each of us has the pope's brain defect, which is perfectly compatible with nobility, intelligence, courage, education.

We learned to lie about life early. Alice Miller in *Prisoners of Childhood* and *For Your Own Good* notes how fiercely children who have suffered abuse from parents will resist the truth. The child does not want to confront. The child will defend the parent, insisting that it deserved beating, and the abuse was done for "my own good." So we, as taxpayers and citizens, did not and do not confront Ronald Reagan. This habit of not-seeing, and lying about life, has been attached like a limpet to the American soul.

The mechanism of denial, once established by the longing not to see death, as Becker emphasizes, or by the need not to see parental cruelty, as Alice Miller emphasizes, becomes rooted in our whole way of being. We specialize in not seeing what the deficit and rapid use of oil will do to our grandchildren and great-grandchildren. Goethe in his poem "The Invisible King" declares that there are ominous and dangerous forces in the other world, both female and male in tone. When the rationalist European father refuses to see the horrors that mythology has talked of for centuries, the children—in this case the son—dies.

> In grief and fear at last the father got home.
> The boy lay dead in the father's arms.

Voznesensky says there is a power in the other world which he calls "Darkmotherscream." He says:

> Don't forget—Rome fell
> not having grasped the phrase: darkmotherscream.

In this situation, art and literature are more important than ever before. Essays, poetry, fiction, still relatively cheap to print, are the best hope in making headway against denial. The corporate deniers own television. We can forget about that. There's no hope in commercial television at all. The schools teach denial by not teaching, and the students' language is so poor that they can't do anything but deny. School boards forbid teachers in high school to teach conflict, questioning of authority, picking apart of arguments, mockery of news and corporate lies. A goodly supply of four-letter words doesn't help. César Vallejo is willing not only to say he is sick, but willing to take it all the way to God.

Well, on the day I was born,
God was sick.

The student needs to know great works of art that punch a hole in denial—Rembrandt's self-portraits, Mencken, Swift, Mark Twain's "The War Prayer," David Ignatow's poetry. Haki R. Madhubuti, Amiri Baraka, and Etheridge Knight write of harsh realities in the black community that the political candidates don't want to talk of. David Ignatow points out in "A First on TV" that one of the most popular forms of denial now is the agreement television anchors have not to become excited about anything. This coolness is spreading to the whole population.

This is the twentieth century,
you are there, preparing to skin
a human being alive. Your part
will be to remain calm

Our particular denial, the denial practiced in American culture, involves a protection of innocence. Mark Twain talked of "Innocents Abroad." France knows its history, England its, but we have a passionate dedication to not-knowing. Our wars are always noble, our bombing surgical, intended to make the patient better.

Great art and literature are the only models we have left to help us stop lying. The greater the art the less the denial. We don't need avant-garde art now, but great art. Breaking through the wall of denial helps us get rid of self-pity, and replaces self-pity with awe at the complicated misery of all living things.

A poem that confronts denial has a certain tone: it is dark but not pulled down by evil. It is intense but not hysterical; it feels weighty, and there is something bitter in it, as if the writer were fighting against great resistance when he or she writes the poem.

The anger that breaks the good down into doubts,
and doubt down into three matching arcs,
and the arc, then, into unimaginable tombs;
the anger of the poor
owns one piece of steel against two daggers.

(César Vallejo)

The writer could be said to be "eating his shadow"; in the Japanese martial arts tradition, it is called "eating bitter."

Eating bitter means to turn and face life. If we deny our animalness, our shit and death, if we refuse to see the cruelties and abuse by S&L executives, presidents, and sexual abusers, it means we have turned our backs on life. If we have turned our backs on life, don't be surprised if we kill the poor, the homeless, ourselves, and the earth. Getting rid of denial, then, means getting used to the flavor of "bitter," getting used to having that flavor of bitter truth in the mouth.

R.B.

THE INNER PART

When they had won the war
And for the first time in history
Americans were the most important people—

When the leading citizens no longer lived in their shirt
    sleeves,
and their wives did not scratch in public;
Just when they'd stopped saying "Gosh!"—

When their daughters seemed as sensitive
As the tip of a fly rod,
And their sons were as smooth as a V-8 engine—

Priests, examining the entrails of birds,
Found the heart misplaced, and seeds
As black as death, emitting a strange odor.

LOUIS SIMPSON

MINIVER CHEEVY

Miniver Cheevy, child of scorn,
　　Grew lean while he assailed the seasons;
He wept that he was ever born,
　　And he had reasons.

Miniver loved the days of old
　　When swords were bright and steeds were prancing;
The vision of a warrior bold
　　Would set him dancing.

Miniver sighed for what was not,
　　And dreamed, and rested from his labors;
He dreamed of Thebes and Camelot,
　　And Priam's neighbors.

Miniver mourned the ripe renown
　　That made so many a name so fragrant;
He mourned Romance, now on the town,
　　And Art, a vagrant.

Miniver loved the Medici,
　　Albeit he had never seen one;
He would have sinned incessantly
　　Could he have been one.

Miniver cursed the commonplace
　　And eyed a khaki suit with loathing;
He missed the medieval grace
　　Of iron clothing.

Miniver scorned the gold he sought,
　　But sore annoyed was he without it;
Miniver thought, and thought, and thought,
　　And thought about it.

Miniver Cheevy, born too late,
   Scratched his head and kept on thinking;
Miniver coughed, and called it fate,
   And kept on drinking.

EDWIN ARLINGTON ROBINSON

"next to of course god america i
love you land of the pilgrims' and so forth oh
say can you see by the dawn's early my
country 'tis of centuries come and go
and are no more what of it we should worry
in every language even deafanddumb
thy sons acclaim your glorious name by gorry
by jingo by gee by gosh by gum
why talk of beauty what could be more beau-
tiful than these heroic happy dead
who rushed like lions to the roaring slaughter
they did not stop to think they died instead
then shall the voice of liberty be mute?"

He spoke. And drank rapidly a glass of water

E. E. CUMMINGS

WE REAL COOL

The Pool Players.
Seven at the Golden Shovel.

We real cool. We
Left school. We

Lurk late. We
Strike straight. We

Sing sin. We
Thin gin. We

Jazz June. We
Die soon.

GWENDOLYN BROOKS

TWENTY-FIRST. NIGHT. MONDAY.

Twenty-first. Night. Monday.
Silhouette of the capitol in darkness.
Some good-for-nothing—who knows why—
made up the tale that love exists on earth.

People believe it, maybe from laziness
or boredom, and live accordingly:
they wait eagerly for meetings, fear parting,
and when they sing, they sing about love.

But the secret reveals itself to some,
and on them silence settles down . . .
I found this out by accident
and now it seems I'm sick all the time.

ANNA AKHMATOVA
translated by Jane Kenyon

The rationalist father denies, fanatically, any suggestion of "the other world" or the spiritual world, and the result is that his son dies. This poem is a miniature history of Europe.

THE INVISIBLE KING

Who rides at night, who rides so late?
The father rides on, his child in his arms.
His arms are curled and firm round the boy,
He keeps him from falling, he keeps him warm.

"My boy, why is it you hide your face?"
"Dad, over there do you see the King?
The Invisible King with ermine and staff?"
"Dear boy, what you see is a rolling mist."

"Hey there, my boy, come along with me!
I have the neatest games you'll ever see.
On the shore my daisies blow in a line.
My mother has shirts all golden and fine."

"Dad, is it true you don't hear at all
The little gifts the King is offering me?"
"Calm down, my boy, no need for all this—
It's a dry oak leaves making noise in the wind."

"Child, good child, do you want to go?
My daughters will care and wait on you so.
The great circle dance they do every night,
They'll sing and dance and tuck you in tight."

"Dad, it worries me that you don't see
The Daughters there at that ugly spot."
"I see the spot very clearly, my boy—
An old gray willow, that's all there is."

"Your body is slim, and I love you.
Come now, or seize you is what I'll do."
"Dad Listen, please Dad, he's got hold of me!
He's done something bad to me, he has!"

The terrified father rides wilder and wilder;
The boy is now groaning as he sits slumped over;
In grief and fear at last the father got home.
The boy lay dead in the father's arms.

GOETHE
translated by R.B.

*The various civilizations sometimes seem to be various ingenious ways to
deny the really terrible powers of life.*

DARKMOTHERSCREAM

Darkmotherscream is a Siberian dance,
cry from prison or a yell for help,
or, perhaps, God has another word for it—
ominous little grin—darkmotherscream.

Darkmotherscream is the ecstasy of the sexual gut;
We let the past sink into darkmotherscream also.
You, we—oooh with her eyes closed
woman moans in ecstasy—darkmother, darkmotherscream.

Darkmotherscream is the original mother of languages.
It is silly to trust mind, silly to argue against it.
Prognosticating by computers
We leave out darkmotherscream.

"How's it going?" Darkmotherscream.
"Motherscream! Motherscream!"
            "OK, we'll do it, we'll do it."

The teachers can't handle darkmotherscream.
That is why Lermontov is untranslatable.
When the storm sang in Yelabuga,
What did it say to her? Darkmotherscream.

Meanwhile go on dancing, drunker and drunker.
"Shagadam magadam—darkmotherscream."
Don't forget—Rome fell
not having grasped the phrase: darkmotherscream.

ANDREI VOZNESENSKY
translated by R.B. and Vera Dunham

The Rag and Bone Shop of the Heart

the men.
occupying bedrooms and unemployment lines, on corners, in
   bars,
stranded between middle management and bankruptcy,
   caught in
warped mindsets of "success in america," the kind taught to
first generation immigrants at local trade schools and jr.
colleges, taught to people lost and unaware of history or
future, ignorant of the middle passages.

the men,
occupying space with men and motives, in prisons, in safe
houses, shooting up with juice and junk, many with hairless
noses and needle-marked toes, searching for missing history,
searching for the when and how of "making it in america."

the men
escaped and taken, twice and three times absorbed in life and
   sharing,
absorbed in locating the mission and magic, the manner and
muscle, the answer and aims, walking the borders between
smiles and outrage.

HAKI R. MADHUBUTI

ON THE YARD

A slim
young fascist
fresh from the Hole
slid into me
murdered me
with his eyes
and said, "Man,
why ain't you
doing something?"

All night
I sat up
All night
Wrote 5,000 words
explaining how
I
was doing something

but the slim cat—
beautiful fascist
didn't buy
it—nor
did I
completely.

ETHERIDGE KNIGHT

Amiri Baraka says that for decades we have expected "knowledgeable workers" to come forward in North America. It has not happened.

A POEM
SOME PEOPLE WILL HAVE
TO UNDERSTAND

Dull unwashed windows of eyes
and buildings of industry. What
industry do I practice? A slick
colored boy, 12 miles from his
home. I practice no industry.
I am no longer a credit
to my race. I read a little,
scratch against silence slow spring
afternoons.

                I had thought, before, some years ago
that I'd come to the end of my life.

                Watercolor ego. Without the preciseness
a violent man could propose.

                But the wheel, and the wheels,
wont let us alone. All the fantasy
                and justice, and dry charcoal winters
All the pitifully intelligent citizens
                I've forced myself to love.

                We have awaited the coming of a natural
                phenomenon. Mystics and romantics,
  knowledgeable

      workers
      of the land.

But none has come.
(Repeat)
        but none has come.

Will the machinegunners please step forward?

AMIRI BARAKA

ANIMALS ARE PASSING
FROM OUR LIVES

It's wonderful how I jog
on four honed-down ivory toes
my massive buttocks slipping
like oiled parts with each light step.

I'm to market. I can smell
the sour, grooved block. I can smell
the blade that opens the hole
and the pudgy white fingers

that shake out the intestines
like a hankie. In my dreams
the snouts drool on the marble,
suffering children, suffering flies,

suffering the consumers
who won't meet their steady eyes
for fear they could see. The boy
who drives me along believes

that any moment I'll fall
on my side and drum my toes
like a typewriter or squeal
and shit like a new housewife

discovering television,
or that I'll turn like a beast
cleverly to hook his teeth
with my teeth. No. Not this pig.

PHILIP LEVINE

IT IS THIS WAY WITH MEN

They are pounded into the earth
like nails; move an inch,
they are driven down again.
The earth is sore with them.
It is a spiny fruit
that has lost hope
of being raised and eaten.
It can only ripen and ripen.
And men, they too are wounded.
They too are sifted from their loss
and are without hope. The core
softens. The pure flesh softens
and melts. There are thorns, there
are the dark seeds, and they end.

C. K. WILLIAMS

THE WAR PRAYER

"O Lord our Father, our young patriots, idols of our hearts, go forth to battle—be Thou near them! With them—in spirit—we also go forth from the sweet peace of our beloved firesides to smite the foe. O Lord our God, help us to tear their soldiers to bloody shreds with our shells; help us to cover their smiling fields with the pale forms of their patriot dead; help us to drown the thunder of the guns with the shrieks of their wounded, writhing in pain; help us to lay waste their humble homes with a hurricane of fire; help us to wring the hearts of their unoffending widows with unavailing grief; help us to turn them out roofless with their little children to wander unfriended the wastes of their desolated land in rags and hunger and thirst, sports of the sun flames of summer and the icy winds of winter, broken in spirit, worn with travail, imploring Thee for the refuge of the grave and denied it—for our sakes who adore Thee, Lord, blast their hopes, blight their lives, protract their bitter pilgrimage, make heavy their steps, water their way with their tears, stain the white snow with the blood of their wounded feet! We ask it, in the spirit of love, of Him Who is the Source of Love, and Who is the ever-faithful refuge and friend of all that are sore beset and seek His aid with humble and contrite hearts.   Amen."

MARK TWAIN

Yeats says: "Why deny it? Christ's dark brother is on the way."

THE SECOND COMING

Turning and turning on the widening gyre,
The falcon cannot hear the falconer;
Things fall apart; the centre cannot hold;
Mere anarchy is loosed upon the world,
The blood-dimmed tide is loosed, and everywhere
The ceremony of innocence is drowned;
The best lack all conviction, while the worst
Are full of passionate intensity.

Surely some revelation is at hand;
Surely the Second Coming is at hand.
The Second Coming! Hardly are those words out
When a vast image out of *Spiritus Mundi*
Troubles my sight: Somewhere in the sands of the desert
A shape with a lion body and the head of a man,
A gaze blank and pitiless as the sun,
Is moving its slow thighs, while all about it
Reel shadows of the indignant desert birds.
The darkness drops again, but now I know
That twenty centuries of stony sleep
Were vexed to nightmare by a rocking cradle,
And what rough beast, its hour come round at last,
Slouches towards Bethlehem to be born?

WILLIAM BUTLER YEATS

The calmness of the TV anchorman, Ignatow says, teaches all citizens how not to feel the horror of what is happening.

A FIRST ON TV

For Walter Cronkite

This is the twentieth century,
you are there, preparing to skin
a human being alive. Your part
will be to remain calm
and to participate with the flayer
in his work as you follow his hand,
the slow, delicate way with the knife
between the skin and flesh,
and see the red meat emerge.
Tiny rivulets of blood will flow
from the naked flesh and over the hands
of the flayer. Your eyes will waver
and turn away but turn back to witness
the unprecedented, the incredible,
for you are there
and your part will be to remain calm.

You will smash at the screen
with your fist and try to reach
this program on the phone, like a madman
gripping it by the neck
as if it were the neck of the flayer
and you will scream into the receiver,
"Get me station ZXY at once, at once,
do you hear!" But your part
will be to remain calm.

DAVID IGNATOW

Making a Hole in Denial

In this poem a father is visiting his schizophrenic son at the asylum. To me, this is what poetry without denial would look like.

SUNDAY AT THE STATE HOSPITAL

I am sitting across the table
eating my visit sandwich.
The one I brought him stays suspended
near his mouth; his eyes focus
on the table and seem to think,
his shoulders hunched forward.
I chew methodically,
pretending to take him
as a matter of course.
The sandwich tastes mad
and I keep chewing.
My past is sitting in front of me
filled with itself
and trying with almost no success
to bring the present to its mouth.

DAVID IGNATOW

NO THEORY

No theory will stand up to a chicken's guts
being cleaned out, a hand rammed up
to pull out the wriggling entrails,
the green bile and the bloody liver;
no theory that does not grow sick
at the odor escaping.

DAVID IGNATOW

Why are we always so polite to our gods? Why not tell them what we think?

FUNERAL EVA

SOLO: Oh, Priest Pangeivi, you let go
my son, the canoe of his life
is dashed and sunk.

CHORUS: O Tane, you could have saved him,
made him return, a
sapling among our aging forest.
But he died, woman-like, wet
on his pillow, far from the
crash of spears and adzes. You could have
done better than god Turanga, a bag
of lies not worth our prayers.

Your belly full, you can't be bothered.
Let shitballs be thrown at you,
Let you be smeared all over,
Let piss and shit dribble down your
fat cheeks, you bum god. Any man
can do better.

SOLO: Fart, O Tiki, let your wind go.
Fart on this phoney god not worth
our curses.

CHORUS: Fart, fart, fart.
Swallow the wind, O Pangeivi.
Having eaten my son, you
shall eat our feces.

KORONEU
Mangaian, Polynesia

The ascensionist view that everything in our life should be fair and heavenly amounts to a massive denial. Crazy Jane says the body is not made that way.

CRAZY JANE
TALKS WITH THE BISHOP

I met the Bishop on the road
And much said he and I.
Those breasts are flat and fallen now,
Those veins must soon run dry;
Live in a heavenly mansion,
Not in some foul sty.

"Fair and foul and near of kin,
And fair needs foul," I cried.
"My friends are gone, but that's a truth
Nor grave nor bed denied,
Learned in bodily lowliness
And in the heart's pride.

"A woman can be proud and stiff
When on love intent;
But love has pitched his mansion in
The place of excrement;
For nothing can be sole or whole
that has not first been rent!"

WILLIAM BUTLER YEATS

Perhaps a horror is built right into this planet, and in every detail—that
is, the horror of life eating life.

DESIGN

I found a dimpled spider, fat and white,
On a white heal-all, holding up a moth
Like a white piece of rigid satin cloth—
Assorted characters of death and blight
Mixed ready to begin the morning right,
Like the ingredients of a witches' broth—
A snow-drop spider, a flower like a froth,
And dead wings carried like a paper kite.
What had that flower to do with being white,
The wayside blue and innocent heal-all?
What brought the kindred spider to that height,
Then steered the white moth thither in the night?
What but design of darkness to appall?—
If design govern in a thing so small.

ROBERT FROST

HAVE YOU ANYTHING TO SAY
IN YOUR DEFENSE?

Well, on the day I was born,
God was sick.

They all know that I'm alive,
that I'm vicious; and they don't know
the December that follows from that January.
Well, on the day I was born,
God was sick.

There is an empty place
in my metaphysical shape
that no one can reach:
a cloister of silence
that spoke with the fire of its voice muffled.

On the day I was born,
God was sick.

Brother, listen to me, listen . . .
Oh, all right. Don't worry, I won't leave
without taking my Decembers along,
without leaving my Januaries behind.
Well, on the day I was born,
God was sick.

They all know that I'm alive,
that I chew my food . . . and they don't know
why harsh winds whistle in my poems,
the narrow uneasiness of a coffin,

winds untangled from the Sphinx
who holds the desert for routine questioning.

Yes, they all know . . . Well, they don't know
that the light gets skinny
and the darkness gets bloated . . .
and they don't know that the Mystery joins things
    together . . .
that he is the hunchback
musical and sad who stands a little way off and foretells
the dazzling progression from the limits to the Limits.

On the day I was born,
God was sick,
gravely.

CÉSAR VALLEJO
translated by James Wright

THE SPIDER

It is a huge spider, which can no longer move;
a spider which is colorless, whose body,
a head and an abdomen, is bleeding.

Today I watched it with great care. With what tremendous
    energy
to every side
it was stretching out its many feet.
And I have been thinking of its invisible eyes,
the death-bringing pilots of the spider.

It is a spider which was shivering, fixed
on the sharp ridge of a stone;
the abdomen on one side,
and on the other, the head.

With so many feet the poor thing, and still it cannot
solve it! And seeing it
confused in such great danger,
what a strange pain that traveler has given me today!

It is a huge spider, whose abdomen
prevents him from following his head.
And I have been thinking of his eyes
and of his many, many feet . . .
And what a strange pain that traveler has given me!

CÉSAR VALLEJO
translated by R.B.

EIGHT

Loving
the Community
and Work

Dogs bark at people they don't know.
                              —HERACLITUS

The poems in this section speak in different ways about being in community. All the ways make a similar assumption: we don't so much build communities as we are already built into them. Just by being here in the world our life is with others. And it is in this communal context that work belongs. By throwing yourself into a task, you take part in the world, give it your gifts and bring it your love. Work may call for muscle, know-how, and a sweet hand, but, as soon as we are engaged with other people, something else more important is required, as William Stafford says in the first poem. All mutual relations depend on "awake people be[ing] awake. . . . the signals we give . . . should be clear," otherwise we don't know who the other person is or let the other know who we are. To love is to talk right. This clarity may be more essential to living and working with others than strong feelings and kind flowers.

So the first way of recognizing community is through work. Work is often coupled with love as its opponent or substitute, as if each were an escape from the other. But this coupling means that work and love are equivalent passions, that work is another mode of desire, a form of love itself, else work could not substitute for love. Freud thought the purpose of psychoanalysis was to resolve the twin problems of love and work, again suggesting they are of the same nature. Both give joy, put you in "the high seat," as Gary Snyder says, quickening your senses so that the truck's "Polished hubs gleam / And the shiny diesel stack / Warms." Work helps "shake off this sadness" (Unamuno).

When work is imagined different from love, work becomes a grueling job. We have to push ourselves to do it for money or to climb the ladder, and we have to look elsewhere for community. We forget that all work always implies other people. Jobs express communal needs. They say, "help wanted," you're needed. And a man's identity comes as much from what is wanted from him by others as from his own self-generated desires. Therefore, these writers say, don't sit around waiting for inspiration, that "winged energy of delight" (Rilke). ". . . [S]tart then, turn to the work" (Unamuno); "Whatever you can do, / or dream you can, begin it" (Goethe).

A second way of community derives from an alert sense of social justice. Lorca's furious, bitter, ideal Spanish passion is also compassion. Compassion is communal eros, being passionately moved by others, for others, toward others. Lorca, who was seized and shot by Franco's fascists, spoke his love as outrage. "The mountains exist. I know that." (Don't tell me about calm serenity and inspiring heights.) "I have not come to see the sky. I have come to see the stormy blood." He speaks for dead pigs and lambs and ducks, and all else that is murdered so that our civilization may go on as it is. This style of communal love attacks

> all those persons
> who know nothing of the other half. . . .
> I attack the conspiring
> of these empty offices
> that will not broadcast the sufferings.

All this was written long before the deceits of the Gulf War, the conspiracy of Irangate and the subversion of the Constitution, and the secretive statism of corporate America (which Lorca calls "New York"), which pays the hit men of species, soils, cultures, and children the world over (with the acquiescent complicity of taxpaying citizens). Of this terrorism, Lorca writes in terrifying lines with a terrible love. Men building community through recovery groups and personal support sharing may learn from Lorca another approach to community love.

That genius of enlightened rationalism Dr. Samuel Johnson, drinking dish after dish of tea in his candlelit chambers while inventing the dictionary of the English language, declares in a few terse words a conclusion similar to Lorca's: men are bound together by feelings of brotherhood. Within all community flows fellow feeling. Only when we are asleep are we alone, said Heraclitus.

Alfred Adler called fellow feeling *Gemeinschaftsgefühl,* which has been translated into "social feeling" and "community feeling." Adler, who originated psychoanalysis along with Freud and Jung, considered *Gemeinschaftsgefühl* ("the feeling of intimate belonging to the full spectrum, of humanity") to be the dominant motive of life, as basic as Freud's sexual drive and Jung's urge toward meaning. For him, "A man of genius is primarily a man of supreme usefulness."

So, third, the brotherhood of community arises when men can do useful things together. Jim Heynen conveys this fraternal feeling in his description of boys saving pheasants during an ice storm. Boys especially feel the bonds of brotherhood. Psychology calls this elemental association peer pressure; sociology, gang behavior; anthropology, the young male initiation group. These are ways that academic language can cover over the deepest emotion of "intimate belonging" that urges men to join together.

When this primary feeling is distorted by violence, by ideology, or by exploitation, that is, by leaders who cheapen and betray the emotions of brotherhood, it can turn nasty and fascist. But in the depths there remains a love *with* others that shows as love *for* others and that carries all teamwork from sports, group music, and construction to the gritty loyalty of a platoon under fire.

James Wright's account of his Scout troop evokes the perennial boy interior to every man. This boy still remembers the nicknames and odd peculiarities of his old companions, still thrills at recollections of their common adventures. For then were the first stirrings of deep friendship, group loyalty, and the mysterious free happiness that comes with doing things with other men. The two poems that follow, by Robert Francis and Kenneth Rexroth, move the sense of comradeship from young boys to old men, their reminiscences, delusions, sadness, and insane exhilaration in simply being together. "We were comrades together. / Life was good for us," says Rexroth, "[L]et us journey together," says Thomas McGrath.

J.H.

A RITUAL TO READ TO EACH OTHER

If you don't know the kind of person I am
and I don't know the kind of person you are
a pattern that others made may prevail in the world
and following the wrong god home we may miss our star.

For there is many a small betrayal in the mind,
a shrug that lets the fragile sequence break
sending with shouts the horrible errors of childhood
storming out to play through the broken dyke.

And as elephants parade holding each elephant's tail,
but if one wanders the circus won't find the park,
I call it cruel and maybe the root of all cruelty
to know what occurs but not recognize the fact.

And so I appeal to a voice, to something shadowy,
a remote important region in all who talk:
though we could fool each other, we should consider—
lest the parade of our mutual life get lost in the dark.

For it is important that awake people be awake,
or a breaking line may discourage them back to sleep;
the signals we give—yes or no, or maybe—
should be clear: the darkness around us is deep.

WILLIAM STAFFORD

THROW YOURSELF LIKE SEED

Shake off this sadness, and recover your spirit;
sluggish you will never see the wheel of fate
that brushes your heel as it turns going by,
the man who wants to live is the man in whom life is
  abundant.

Now you are only giving food to that final pain
which is slowly winding you in the nets of death,
but to live is to work, and the only thing which lasts
is the work; start then, turn to the work.

Throw yourself like seed as you walk, and into your own
  field,
don't turn your face for that would be to turn it to death,
and do not let the past weigh down your motion.

Leave what's alive in the furrow, what's dead in yourself,
for life does not move in the same way as a group of clouds;
from your work you will be able one day to gather yourself.

MIGUEL DE UNAMUNO
translated by R.B.

UNTIL ONE IS COMMITTED

Until one is committed, there is hesitancy, the chance to draw back, always ineffectiveness. Concerning all acts of initiative (and creation) there is one elementary truth, the ignorance of which kills countless ideas and splendid plans: that the moment one definitely commits oneself, then Providence moves too. All sorts of things occur to help one that would never otherwise have occurred. A whole stream of events issues from the decision, raising in one's favor all manner of unforeseen incidents and meetings and material assistance, which no man could have dreamed would have come his way.

> Whatever you can do,
> or dream you can, begin it.
> Boldness has genius,
> power and magic in it.

GOETHE

Being carried along by the wind is not enough. Build arches to reach across the chasms of hurt rather than rely on fragile puer wings. But a whining inner voice asks, Why bother? Work is so mundane and so hard. Rilke answers: not to build is hubris, that negative inflation of belief in a destiny superior to achievements. And Rilke adds a touch beyond moral exhortations. We work because the gods themselves learn from our doing.

JUST AS THE WINGED ENERGY
OF DELIGHT

Just as the winged energy of delight
carried you over many chasms early on,
now raise the daringly imagined arch
holding up the astounding bridges.

Miracle doesn't lie only in the amazing
living through and defeat of danger;
miracles become miracles in the clear
achievement that is earned.

To work with things is not hubris
when building the association beyond words;
denser and denser the pattern becomes—
being carried along is not enough.

Take your well-disciplined strengths
and stretch them between two
opposing poles. Because inside human beings
is where God learns.

Muzot, February 1924

RAINER MARIA RILKE
translated by R.B.

Unamuno says, Throw yourself like seed; Goethe says, Begin it now. But how? Where? Do what? The Hungarian poet Gyula Illyés answers: Be amazed, astonished. Be struck with admiration for someone, something, that reveals your desire. His is kindled by a moment in childhood watching a craftsman at work—the hand, the tool, the iron, the fire.

WORK

They stuck pigs in the throat. Might I not have done it myself? They tossed chickens with their heads cut off out into the courtyard. With a child's thirst for knowledge, I watched their final spasms with a heart hardly touched. My first really shattering experience came when I watched the hooping of a cartwheel.

From the huge coal fire, with pincers at least a yard long, the apprentices grabbed the iron loop, which by then was red hot up and down. They ran with it to the fresh-smelling oak wheel that had been fixed in place in the front of the blacksmith's shop. The flesh-colored wooden wheel was my grandfather's work; the iron hoop, which gave off a shower of sparks in its fiery agony, was my father's. One of the apprentices held the sledge hammer, the other the buckets. Places, everyone. As on shipboard. As at an execution. The hoop, which in its white-hot state had just expanded to the size of the wheel, was quickly placed on it; and they began to pry it out with their tongs. My father swung the hammer with lightning speed, giving orders all the while. The wood caught fire; they poured a bucket of water on it. The wheel sent up steam and smoke so thick you couldn't see it. But still the hammer pounded on, and still came the "Press hard!" uttered breathlessly from the corner of the mouth. The fire blazed up again. Water flung again as on a tortured man who has sunk into a coma. Then the last flourishing bush of steam evaporated while the apprentices poured a thin trickle from a can on the cooling iron which, in congealing, gripped lovingly its life-long companion to be. The men wiped the sweat from their brows, spat, shook their heads, satisfied. Nothing— not the slightest flicker of a movement—could have been executed differently.

GYULA ILLYÉS
translated by William Jay Smith

For some men what animals do and what we do with them kindles sympathy with all things, a response that says, In the animal kingdom we are all part of one another. Besides, animals teach us careful observation, a body-attentiveness such as they show each other. Here, the verb to see repeats twenty-eight times. Notice, too, how the poet's observation of the event becomes participation in the event, which includes everybody present, a communal circle. And there is no "I."

LAMB

Saw a lamb being born.
Saw the shepherd chase and grab a big ewe
and dump her on her side.
Saw him rub some stuff from a bottle on his hands.
Saw him bend and reach in.
Heard two cries from the ewe.
Two sharp quick cries. Like high grunts.
Saw him pull out a slack white package.
Saw him lay it out on the ground.
Saw him kneel and take his teeth to the cord.
Saw him slap the package around.
Saw it not move.
Saw him bend and put his mouth to it and blow.
Doing this calmly, half kneeling.
Saw him slap it around some more.
Saw my mother watching this. Saw Angela. Saw Peter.
Saw Mimi, with a baby in her belly.
Saw them standing in a row
by the dry stone wall, in the wind.
Saw the package move.
Saw it was stained with red and yellow.
Saw the shepherd wipe red hands on the ewe's wool.
Heard the other sheep in the meadow calling out.
Saw the package shaking its head.
Saw it try to stand. Saw it nearly succeed.
Saw it have to sit and think about it a bit.

Saw a new creature's first moments of thinking.
Felt the chill blowing through me.
Heard the shepherd say:
"Good day for lambing. Wind dries them out."
Saw the package start to stand. Get half-way. Kneeling.
Saw it push upward. Stagger, push. And make it.
Stand, standing.
Saw it surely was a lamb, a lamb, a lamb.
Saw a lamb being born!

MICHAEL DENNIS BROWNE

WHY LOG TRUCK DRIVERS RISE EARLIER THAN STUDENTS OF ZEN

In the high seat,
  before-dawn dark,

Polished hubs gleam
And the shiny diesel stack
Warms and flutters
Up the Tyler Road grade
To the logging on Poorman
                    Creek.
Thirty miles of dust.

There is no other life.

GARY SNYDER

Getting going doesn't mean the going is easy. The roads are bad, says Hölderlin. Besides, even as we begin, "a longing for disintegration constantly comes." Failure doesn't go away with achievement; failure sits on the shoulders and gives weight, gravitas. It adds lead to the keel even as we rock and sway and go off course.

ALL THE FRUIT

All the fruit is ripe, plunged in fire, cooked,
And they have passed their test on earth, and one law is this:
That everything curls inward, like snakes,
Prophetic, dreaming on
The hills of heaven. And many things
Have to stay on the shoulders like a load
Of failure. However the roads
Are bad. For the chained elements,
Like horses, are going off to the side,
And the old
Laws of the earth. And a longing
For disintegration constantly comes. Many things however
Have to stay on the shoulders. Steadiness is essential.
Forwards, however, or backwards we will
Not look. Let us learn to live swaying
As in a rocking boat on the sea.

FRIEDRICH HÖLDERLIN
translated by R.B.

NEW YORK
(Office and Attack)

For Fernando Vela

Beneath all the statistics
there is a drop of duck's blood.
Beneath all the columns
there is a drop of sailor's blood.
Beneath all the totals, a river of warm blood.
A river that goes singing
past the bedrooms of the suburbs,
and the river is silver, cement, or wind
in the lying daybreak of New York.
The mountains exist. I know that.
And the lenses ground for wisdom.
I know that. But I have not come to see the sky.
I have come to see the stormy blood,
the blood that sweeps the machines on to the waterfalls,
and the spirit on to the cobra's tongue.
Every day they kill in New York
ducks, four million,
pigs, five million,
pigeons, two thousand, for the enjoyment of dying men,
cows, one million,
lambs, one million,
roosters, two million
who turn the sky to small splinters.
You may as well sob filing a razor blade
or assassinate dogs
in the hallucinating foxhunts,
as try to stop in the dawnlight
the endless trains carrying milk,
the endless trains carrying blood,
and the trains carrying roses put in chains
by those in the field of perfume.

Loving the Community and Work

The ducks and the pigeons
and the hogs and the lambs
lay their drops of blood down
underneath all the statistics;
and the terrible bawling of the packed-in cattle
fills the valley with suffering
where the Hudson is getting drunk on its oil.
I attack all those persons
who know nothing of the other half,
the half who cannot be saved,
who raise their cement mountains
in which the hearts of the small
animals no one thinks of are beating,
and from which we will all fall
during the final holiday of the drills.
I spit in your face.
The other half hears me,
as they go on eating, urinating, flying in their purity
like the children of the janitors
who carry delicate sticks
to the holes where the antennas
of the insects are rusting.
This is not hell, it is a street.
This is not death, it is a fruit stand.
There is a whole world of crushed rivers
and unachievable distances
in the paw of the cat
crushed by a car,
and I hear the song of the worm
in the heart of so many girls.
Rust, rotting, trembling earth.
And you are earth, swimming
through the figures of the office.
What shall I do, set my landscapes in order?
Set in place the lovers who will afterwards be photographs,
who will be bits of wood

and mouthfuls of blood?
St. Ignatius of Loyola
murdered a small rabbit
and its lips moan still
high on the church steeples.
No, I won't; I attack,
I attack the conspiring
of these empty offices
that will not broadcast the sufferings,
that rub out the plans of the forest,
and I offer myself to be eaten
by the packed-in cattle
when their mooing fills the valley
where the Hudson is getting drunk on its oil.

FEDERICO GARCÍA LORCA
translated by R.B.

TO THE STATES
To Identify the 16th, 17th, or 18th Presidentiad

Why reclining, interrogating? why myself and all drowsing?
What deepening twilight—scum floating atop of the waters,
Who are they as bats and night-dogs askant in the capitol?
What a filthy Presidentiad! (O South, your torrid suns! O
    North, your arctic freezings!)
Are those really Congressmen; are those the great Judges? is
    that the President?
Then I will sleep awhile yet, for I see that these States
    sleep, for reasons;
(With gathering murk, with muttering thunder and lambent
    shoots we all duly awake,
South, North, East, West, inland and seaboard, we will
    surely awake).

WALT WHITMAN

THOUGHTS

A decent provision for the poor is the true test of a civilization.

It is our first duty to serve society, and after we have done that, we may attend wholly to the salvation of our own souls.

SAMUEL JOHNSON

THOUGHTS

Awake we share a common world; sleeping each turns to his private world.

People must fight for their law as for their city wall.

Thinking is common to all men.

It is necessary to be guided by what is common to all although many a man lives as if he followed his own private reason.

HERACLITUS

WHAT HAPPENED DURING THE ICE STORM

One winter there was a freezing rain. How beautiful! people said when things outside started to shine with ice. But the freezing rain kept coming. Tree branches glistened like glass. Then broke like glass. Ice thickened on the windows until everything outside blurred. Farmers moved their livestock into the barns, and most animals were safe. But not the pheasants. Their eyes froze shut.

Some farmers went ice-skating down the gravel roads with clubs to harvest pheasants that sat helplessly in the roadside ditches. The boys went out into the freezing rain to find pheasants too. They saw dark spots along a fence. Pheasants, all right. Five or six of them. The boys slid their feet along slowly, trying not to break the ice that covered the snow. They slid up close to the pheasants. The pheasants pulled their heads down between their wings. They couldn't tell how easy it was to see them huddled there.

The boys stood still in the icy rain. Their breath came out in slow puffs of steam. The pheasants' breath came out in quick little white puffs. Some of them lifted their heads and turned them from side to side, but they were blindfolded with ice and didn't flush. The boys had not brought clubs, or sacks, or anything but themselves. They stood over the pheasants, turning their own heads, looking at each other, each expecting the other to do something. To pounce on a pheasant, or to yell Bang! Things around them were shining and dripping with icy rain. The barbed wire fence. The fence posts. The broken stems of grass. Even the grass seeds. The grass seeds looked like little yolks inside gelatin whites. And the pheasants looked like unborn birds glazed in egg white. Ice was hardening on the boys' caps and coats. Soon they would be covered with ice too.

Then one of the boys said, Shh. He was taking off his coat, the thin layer of ice splintering in flakes as he pulled his arms from the sleeves. But the inside of the coat was dry and warm. He covered two of the crouching pheasants with his coat, rounding the back of it over them like a shell. The other boys did the same. They covered all the helpless pheasants. The small gray hens and the larger brown cocks. Now the boys felt the rain soaking through their shirts and freezing. They ran across the slippery fields, unsure of their footing, the ice clinging to their skin as they made their way toward the warm blurry lights of the house.

JIM HEYNEN

Ralph Neal was the Scoutmaster. He was still a young man. He liked us.

I have no doubt he knew perfectly well we were each of us masturbating unhappily in secret caves and shores.

The soul of patience, he waited while we smirked behind each other's backs, mocking and parodying the Scout Law, trying to imitate the oratorical rotundities of Winston Churchill in a Southern Ohio accent:

"Ay scout is trusswortha, loll, hailpful, frenly, curtchuss, kand, abaydent, chairful, thrifta, dapraved, clane, and letcherass."

Ralph Neal knew all about the pain of the aching stones in our twelve-year-old groins, the lava swollen halfway between our peckers and our nuts that were still green and sour as halfripe apples two full months before the football season began.

Socrates loved his friend the traitor Alcibiades for his beauty and for what he might become.

I think Ralph Neal loved us for our scrawniness, our acne, our fear; but mostly for his knowledge of what would probably become of us. He was not a fool. He knew he would never himself get out of that slime hole of a river valley, and maybe he didn't want to. The Vedantas illustrate the most sublime of ethical ideals of describing a saint who, having endured through a thousand lives every half-assed mistake and unendurable suffering possible to humanity from birth to death, refused at the last minute to enter Nirvana because he realized that his scruffy dog, suppurating at the nostrils and half mad with rabies, could not accompany him into perfect peace.

Some of us wanted to get out, and some of us wanted to and didn't.

The last I heard, Dickey Beck, a three-time loser at housebreaking, was doing life at the State Pen in Columbus.

The last I heard, Dale Headley was driving one of those

milk trucks where the driver has to stand up all day and rattle his spine over the jagged street-bricks.

The last I heard from my brother-in-law, Hub Snodgrass was still dragging himself home every evening down by the river to shine, shower, shave, and spend a good hour still trying to scrape the Laughlin steel dust out of his pale skin. He never tanned much, he just burned or stayed out of the river.

The last I heard, Mike Kottelos was making book in Wheeling.

I have never gone back there down home to see Ralph Neal. My portrait hangs on one of the walls of the Martins Ferry Public Library. Ralph Neal would think I've become something. And no doubt I have, though I don't know just what. Scribbling my name in books. Christ have mercy on me alive; and after I'm dead, as Pietro Aretino of Florence requested of the priest after he had received extreme unction on his deathbed, "Now that I've been oiled, keep me from the rats."

When I think of Ralph Neal's name, I feel some kind of ice breaking open in me. I feel a garfish escaping into a hill spring where the crawdads burrow down to the pure bottom in hot weather to get the cool. I feel a rush of long fondness for that good man Ralph Neal, that good man who knew us dreadful and utterly vulnerable little bastards better than we knew ourselves, who took care of us better than we took care of ourselves, and who loved us, I reckon, because he knew damned well what would become of most of us, and it sure did, and he knew it, and he loved us anyway. The very name of America often makes me sick, and yet Ralph Neal was an American. The country is enough to drive you crazy.

JAMES WRIGHT

WAXWINGS

Four tao philosophers as cedar waxwings
chat on a February berrybush
in sun, and I am one.

Such merriment and such sobriety—
the small wild fruit on the tall stalk—
was this not always my true style?

Above an elegance of snow, beneath
a silk-blue sky a brotherhood of four
birds. Can you mistake us?

To sun, to feast, and to converse
and all together—for this I have abandoned all my other
    lives.

ROBERT FRANCIS

FOR ELI JACOBSON
December, 1952

There are few of us now, soon
There will be none. We were comrades
Together, we believed we
Would see with our own eyes the new
World where man was no longer
Wolf to man, but men and women
Were all brothers and lovers
Together. We will not see it.
We will not see it, none of us.
It is farther off than we thought.
In our young days we believed
That as we grew old and fell
Out of rank, new recruits, young
And with the wisdom of youth,
Would take our places and they
Surely would grow old in the
Golden Age. They have not come.
They will not come. There are not
Many of us left. Once we
Marched in closed ranks, today each
Of us fights off the enemy,
A lonely isolated guerrilla.
All this has happened before,
Many times. It does not matter.
We were comrades together.
Life was good for us. It is
Good to be brave—nothing is
Better. Food tastes better. Wine
Is more brilliant. Girls are more
Beautiful. The sky is bluer
For the brave—for the brave and
Happy comrades and for the
Lonely brave retreating warriors.

You had a good life. Even all
Its sorrows and defeats and
Disillusionments were good,
Met with courage and a gay heart.
You are gone and we are that
Much more alone. We are one fewer,
Soon we shall be none. We know now
We have failed for a long time.
And we do not care. We few will
Remember as long as we can,
Our children may remember,
Some day the world will remember.
Then they will say, "They lived in
The days of the good comrades.
It must have been wonderful
To have been alive then, though it
Is very beautiful now."
We will be remembered, all
Of us, always, by all men,
In the good days now so far away.
If the good days never come,
We will not know. We will not care.
Our lives were the best. We were the
Happiest men alive in our day.

KENNETH REXROTH

EPITAPH

Again, traveller, you have come a long way led by that star.
But the kingdom of the wish is at the other end of the night.
May you fare well, compañero; let us journey together
   joyfully,
Living on catastrophe, eating the pure light.

THOMAS MCGRATH

DEATH

There is no needle without piercing point.
There is no razor without trenchant blade.
Death comes in many forms.

With our feet we walk the goat's earth.
With our hands we touch God's sky.
Some future day in the heat of noon,
I shall be carried shoulder high
through the village of the dead.
When I die, don't bury me under forest trees,
I fear their thorns.
When I die, don't bury me under forest trees,
I fear their dripping water.
Bury me under the great shade trees in the market,
I want to hear the drums beating,
I want to feel the dancers' feet.

Kuba, Zaire
translated by Ulli Beier

NINE

The Naïve Male

What has no shadow has no strength to live.

—CZESLAW MILOSZ

Each of us is a son of our mother (and of the Mother) and a son of our father (and of the Father). But each of us leans one way, usually. Naïveté is a quality we all know; and the Europeans feel it is a quality particularly characteristic of some American men.

For the mother's dependent son, all is infinite, endless, with no boundaries, like clouds or open water; all is possible, all mergings and identities. "I can become a saint, I can become a Hindu sannyasin, I can become the best friend of the feminine." Perhaps because his early merging with his mother in the kitchen was so intense, he believes that he can save women, hear them, take away their loneliness, make them happy and harmonious.

The naïve man often has difficulty in accepting the dark side of women, or the inelegant side of matter. Baudelaire says:

> I once knew a woman named Benedicta, who infused everything with the ideal. When one looked into her eyes one wanted nobility, glory, beauty, all those qualities that make us love immortality.

We can feel that this story is going to end badly.

Robert Hass tells a story that has a similar theme. A man about to make love to a woman is told by her that she has had a double mastectomy, and he says to her: "I'm sorry. I don't think I could."

> He walked back to his own cabin
> through the pines, and in the morning
> he found a small blue bowl on the
> porch outside his door. It looked to be
> full of rose petals, but he found when
> he picked it up that the rose petals were
> on top; the rest of the bowl—she must
> have swept them from the corners of
> her studio—was full of dead bees.

Czeslaw Milosz expresses the traditional European view that dead bees can be expected in the world. The shadow is a part of life.

> Look, see the long shadow cast by the tree;
> And flowers and people throw shadows on the earth:
> What has no shadow has no strength to live.

Sometimes naïve men are too trusting. The New Age saying expresses it: "All we need is love," or intuition, or bliss. Olav Hauge, out on a mountain lake in Norway, said:

> . . . you feel how the memory
> of that cold person
> who drowned himself here once
> helps hold up your frail boat.
> He, really crazy, trusted his life
> to water and eternity.

Some naïveté expresses itself in a boyish demand for protection, understanding, assurance, particularly from women. The naïve man is often the soaring man, the one who ascends into the high air of Hinduism, accomplishes amazing feats of devotion and elevation. He is the spiritual hero—whom Kabir calls "the spiritual athlete." But we often have the feeling that his heroic acts have been done for the eyes of his own mother. Ibsen created such a man, Peer Gynt, and the whole play begins with the mother saying to him, after he has told a story of his air-heroism, "You're lying, Peer!"

When I am possessed by my naïveté, I want to live a high and amazing life, in which I am a special person. This longing has come to be accepted as normal by the New Age. As such a man, I want to do what no one else has ever done.

So there is a great deal of poetry in the naïve man. He is his mother's favorite; he has been kissed by the moon. But sometimes that only makes it more difficult to know what masculinity is. Alden Nowlan says in his brilliant poem "The Rites of Manhood":

> he's finding out what it means
> to be a man and how different it is
> from the way that only hours ago he imagined it.

R.B.

The naïve man, from one point of view, cannot take in the harsh facts of life, or the earthly side of women.

WHICH ONE IS GENUINE?

I once knew a woman named Benedicta, who infused everything with the ideal. When one looked into her eyes one wanted nobility, glory, beauty, all those qualities that make us love immortality.

But this exquisite woman was too beautiful to live long; she died in fact shortly after I met her, and it was I who buried her one day when spring was waving his encensoir even through the cemetery gates. It was I who buried her, well enclosed in a coffin made of a wood scented and eternal as the treasure boxes of India.

And while my eyes remained fixed on that spot where my jewel lay entombed, I saw all at once a tiny human being much like the dead woman, doing a bizarre dance, violent and hysterical, on the loose earth. She howled with laughter as she spoke: "This is me! Benedicta, as she *is!* I'm trash, everyone knows it! And the punishment for your stupidity and your blind head is this: You'll have to love what I am!"

I went into a rage and said, "No! No! No! No!" And in order to give strength to my no, I stomped the earth so fiercely with my foot that my leg sank into the freshly turned earth up to my knee, and like a wolf caught in a trap, I am now tied, perhaps for the rest of my life, to the grave of the ideal.

CHARLES BAUDELAIRE
translated by R.B.

ONION

The smoothness of onions infuriates him
so like the skin of women or their expensive clothes
and the striptease of onions, which is also a disappearing act.
He says he is searching for the ultimate nakedness
but when he finds that thin green seed
that negligible sprout of a heart
we could have told him he'd only be disappointed.
Meanwhile the onion has been hacked to bits
and he's weeping in the kitchen most unromantic tears.

KATHA POLLITT

A STORY ABOUT THE BODY

The young composer, working that summer at an artist's colony, had watched her for a week. She was Japanese, a painter, almost sixty, and he thought he was in love with her. He loved her work, and her work was like the way she moved her body, used her hands, looked at him directly when she made amused and considered answers to his questions. One night, walking back from a concert, they came to her door and she turned to him and said, "I think you would like to have me. I would like that too, but I must tell you that I have had a double mastectomy," and when he didn't understand, "I've lost both my breasts." The radiance that he had carried around his belly and chest cavity—like music—withered, very quickly, and he made himself look at her when he said, "I'm sorry. I don't think I could." He walked back to his own cabin through the pines, and in the morning he found a small blue bowl on the porch outside his door. It looked to be full of rose petals, but he found when he picked it up that the rose petals were on top; the rest of the bowl—she must have swept them from the corners of her studio—was full of dead bees.

ROBERT HASS

THE RITES OF MANHOOD

It's snowing hard enough that the taxis aren't running.
I'm walking home, my night's work finished,
long after midnight, with the whole city to myself,
when across the street I see a very young American sailor
standing over a girl who's kneeling on the sidewalk
and refuses to get up although he's yelling at her
to tell him where she lives so he can take her there
before they both freeze. The pair of them are drunk
and my guess is he picked her up in a bar
and later they got separated from his buddies
and at first it was great fun to play at being
an old salt at liberty in a port full of women with
hinges on their heels, but by now he wants only to
find a solution to the infinitely complex
problem of what to do about her before he falls into
the hands of the police or the shore patrol
—and what keeps this from being squalid is
what's happening to him inside:
if there were other sailors here
it would be possible for him
to abandon her where she is and joke about it
later, but he's alone and the guilt can't be
divided into small forgettable pieces;
he's finding out what it means
to be a man and how different it is
from the way that only hours ago he imagined it.

ALDEN NOWLAN

HE LOVED THREE THINGS

He loved three things:
White fowls, evensong,
And antique maps of America.

He hated the crying of children,
Raspberry jam at tea,
And female hysteria.

And I was his wife.

ANNA AKHMATOVA
translated by Jerome Bullitt

A second view is that the naïve man loves dreams and oracles; he is a favorite not of the sun, but of the moon.

WHEN THE FATHER IS ABSENT

The missing father is not your or my personal father. He is the absent father of our culture, the viable senex who provides not daily bread but spirit through meaning and order. The missing father is the dead God who offered a focus for spiritual things. Without this focus, we turn to dreams and oracles, rather than to prayer, code, tradition, and ritual. When mother replaces father, magic substitutes for logos, and son-priests contaminate the puer spirit.

Unable to go backward to revive the dead father of tradition, we go downward into the mothers of the collective unconscious, seeking an all-embracing comprehension. We ask for help in getting through the narrow straits without harm; the son wants invulnerability. Grant us protection, foreknowledge; cherish us. Our prayer is to the night for a dream, to a love for understanding, to a little rite or exercise for a moment of wisdom. Above all we want assurance through a vision beforehand that it will all come out all right.

Without the father we lose also that capacity which the Church recognized as "discrimination of the spirits": the ability to know a call when we hear one and to discriminate between the voices. . . .

The mother encourages her son: go ahead, embrace it all. For her, all equals everything. The father's instruction, on the contrary, is: all equals nothing—unless the all be precisely discriminated.

JAMES HILLMAN

THE BLACK HAIRS

My darling, you know how much I like to see the light on a bird's wing, but I do not like the little hairs at the base of the beak.

The light on the bird's wing tells me that I am a Prince, that my body cells come from Brendan's Island. When I went on the Crusades, I did not feel the cold of the Muslim steel as I died, only that I, like Parsifal, was far from my mother. You were not there to protect me when I died.

I want to sail with the German moon through the eerie clouds, so that my body resembles rags thrown down in a sloppail. As I am moving with you, I am a part of what is noble, ethereal, spiritual, bodiless, gorgeous in its tinctures, in touch with the dying mother's word.

The light on the bird's wing tells me I am on a journey. I love being on a journey so that when people speak to me, I do not need to answer, so that I can overestimate others, so that I can say that conflict never does any good, that love is the only solution, and all will be well.

I know that women want revenge on men because women love the little black hairs at the base of the beak, but their rage cannot rouse me; I have been put to sleep by the light on the bird's wing.

HEINZ PASMAN
translated by R.B.

THE INDIAN SERENADE

I arise from dreams of Thee
In the first sweet sleep of night,
When the winds are breathing low
And the stars are shining bright:
I arise from dreams of thee,
And a spirit in my feet
Hath led me—who knows how?
To thy chamber-window, Sweet!

The wandering airs, they faint
On the dark, the silent stream—
The champak odors fail
Like sweet thoughts in a dream;
The nightingale's complaint,
It dies upon her heart,
As I must on thine,
Oh, beloved as thou art!

Oh, lift me from the grass!
I die, I faint, I fail!
Let thy love in kisses rain
On my lips and eyelids pale.
My cheek is cold and white, alas!
My heart beats loud and fast;
Oh! press it close to thine again,
Where it will break at last.

PERCY BYSSHE SHELLEY

THE GOOD DEEDS OF THE MOON

The moon, who is whimsicality itself, gazed into the window while you were sleeping in your cradle, and said to herself: "This child is my favorite."

And she descended with velvet steps down her staircase of cloud, and making no sound slipped through the window-panes. Then she threw herself over your body with the downy endearments of a mother, and she pressed her colors on your face. Ever after you've had green pupils, and remarkably pale cheeks. It was while brooding on your visitor that your eyes grew so astonishingly large; and she folded her arms so firmly and tenderly around your neck that you have kept ever since the desire to weep.

Meanwhile, as her delight grew, the Moon charged the whole room with a kind of phosphorescence or light-filled poison; and this fully alive light began to think and said, "You will be forever under the influence of my kiss. Your beauty will be my sort of beauty. You will love what I love, and love what loves me: the water and the clouds, also silence and the night; the endless and green ocean; waters chaotic and elegant, the place where you are not, the beloved whom you do not know; grotesque blossoms; perfumes that make you rave, and cats that drape themselves on pianos and who groan like a woman, with the voice husky and delicious.

"And you will be adored by those who adore me, and flattered by those who fawn on me. You will be queen of all green-eyed men whose neck I have firmly enfolded in my nighttime attentions; of those who love the ocean, the immense green troubled and tumbling ocean, the chaotic rivers and the elegant rivers, the place where you are not, the woman whom you have never met, the ominous flowers that resemble encensoirs from some unknown religion, the perfumes that disturb the will, and those savage and sensuous animals that are the symbols of such madness."

That is the reason, my dear spoiled and miserable boy,

that I stay here, watching at your feet, trying to glimpse anywhere in your being the reflected light from that terrible Goddess, from that godmother sans merci, the wetnurse who gives her poisoned breasts to the *moon-maddened men*.

CHARLES BAUDELAIRE
translated by R.B.

Here is the victim man, who always speaks in a flat voice, and is ready at any moment to be abandoned in the desert.

IN A TAVERN

"It's no use," he says, "she's left me." This is after several drinks. It's as if he had said "Van Gogh is my favorite painter." It's a dimestore print he has added to his collection. He's been waiting all evening to show it to me. He doesn't see it. To him it's an incredible landscape, empty, a desert. "My life is empty." He likes the simplicity. "My life is empty. She won't come back." It is a landmark, like the blue mountains in the distance that never change. The crust of sand gives way with each step, tiny lizards skitter out of the way. . . . Even after walking all day there is no change in the horizon. "We're lost," he says. "No," I say, "let's go on." He says, "You go on. Take my canteen. You've got a reason to live." "No," I say, "we're in this together and we'll both make it out of here."

LOUIS JENKINS

FAITH

The word Faith means when someone sees
A dew-drop or a floating leaf, and knows
That they are, because they have to be.
And even if you dreamed, or closed your eyes
And wished, the world would still be what it was,
And the leaf would still be carried down the river.

It means that when someone's foot is hurt
By a sharp rock, he also knows that rocks
Are here so they can hurt our feet.
Look, see the long shadow cast by the tree;
And flowers and people throw shadows on the earth:
What has no shadow has no strength to live.

CZESLAW MILOSZ
translated by Robert Hass
and Robert Pinsky with Renata Gorczynski

A third view of the naïve man is that he lives almost entirely without boundaries; he sympathizes too much, disbelieves in limits, wants to be unchecked nature.

from
SONG OF MYSELF

I celebrate myself, and sing myself,
And what I assume you shall assume,
For every atom belonging to me as good belongs to you.

I loaf and invite my soul,
I lean and loaf at my ease observing a spear of summer grass.

My tongue, every atom of my blood, formed from this soil,
    this air,
Born here of parents born here from parents the same, and
    their parents the same,
I, now thirty-seven years old in perfect health begin,
Hoping to cease not till death.

Creeds and schools in abeyance,
Retiring back a while suffered at what they are, but never
    forgotten,
I harbor for good or bad, I permit to speak at every hazard,
Nature without check with original energy.

WALT WHITMAN

ACROSS THE SWAMP

It is the roots from all the trees that have died
out here, that's how you can walk
safely over the soft places.
Roots like these keep their firmness, it's possible
they've lain here centuries.
And there is still some dark remains
of them under the moss.
They are still in the world and hold
you up so you can make it over.
And when you push out into the mountain lake, high
up, you feel how the memory
of that cold person
who drowned himself here once
helps hold up your frail boat.
He, really crazy, trusted his life
to water and eternity.

OLAV H. HAUGE
translated by R.B.

Ibsen here expresses beautifully the vertical quality of a naïve mother's son. He is the one who is always ascending and falling, and the falls are as spectacular as the ascensions.

PEER GYNT TELLS HIS MOTHER
ABOUT HIS NEWEST ADVENTURE

OHSA: You're lying, Peer!

PEER: No way!

OHSA: Is it true or not?

PEER: It's true as truth and truer than true. . . .

OHSA: Lies and lies; Just lies and more lies.
By the way where was that buck?

PEER: On the big ridge . . .
                    I hear a sound—
He's digging in the snow—hidden by a clump
of bushes, and digging—for moss under snow . . .
             Within a second
I'm astride him, my knife out.
I grab his left ear, I'm about
to drive the knife in— Holy Gods! . . .
                 You remember
how that ridge runs? It thins out,
it goes along three whole miles
skinny edged like a machete!
You see mountain peaks and glaciers
around; if you look down it's
straight down into a lake
lying heavy and black, sleeping
three thousand feet below!

Along that knife edge he and I
cut our way through wicked wind.
What a ride! Suns glittered
ahead of us, shining; below
dizzying nothingness, and in it
eagles swimming— Have you seen
their brown backs from above? . . .
      The buck turned
in midair, and kicking off, threw
himself out in the naked air,
with me on his back!
(Ohsa sways a little and reaches for the tree trunk.)
Black mountain wall behind us,
and ahead, nothing, nothing, nothing!
First a zone of mist—we cut through it,
then dove into a flock of seagulls.
How they screeched, wheeling
and crying at the terror of it.
Downwards nothing to stay the fall . . .
But something gleamed in the lake below—
something creamy, like a reindeer belly.
Mother, that was us! It was our image
hurtling from the mountain floor
up through stillness to the surface,
matching second by second
our insane speed in hurtling down!

OHSA: Holy Jesus! Hurry, say it! . . .

PEER: We thrashed around, we splashed a lot,
    Then slowly—oh so slow—we swam
    off toward shore, the northern shore.
    The buck swam, actually, I just held on. . . .

OHSA: I can't believe you've been so lucky!
    Ribs all right? All your legs all right?

No twists to the back? Your neck all right? . . .
(She suddenly stops, looks at him with big eyes, mouth
fallen open. Silent a moment, she finally breaks out:)
Oh my God how you can lie! Lie!
You give me this stuff—it's all garbage,
and give it to me, and I remember now
I heard it as a girl! It was Gudbrand
that happened to . . . a man named Gudbrand,
not you!

PEER: Why not me too?
        Things happen more than once, you know.

HENRIK IBSEN
translated by R.B.

THE HOPEFUL SPIRITUAL ATHLETE

The spiritual athlete often changes the color of his clothes,
and his mind remains gray and loveless.

Or he sits inside a shrine room all day,
so that God has to go out and praise the rocks.

He drills holes in his ears, his beard grows enormous and
    matted,
people mistake him for a goat. . . .
He goes out into wilderness areas, strangles his impulses,
makes himself neither male nor female. . . .

He shaves his skull, puts his robe in an orange vat,
reads the Bhagavad-Gita, and becomes a terrific talker.

Kabir says: Actually you are going in a hearse to the country
    of death,
bound hand and foot!

KABIR
version by R.B.

HOW MUCH IS NOT TRUE

There is nothing but water in the holy pools.
I know, I have been swimming in them.
All the gods sculpted of wood or ivory can't say a word.
I know, I have been crying out to them.
The Sacred Books of the East are nothing but words.
I looked through their covers one day sideways.
What Kabir talks of is only what he has lived through.
If you have not lived through something, it is not true.

KABIR
version by R.B.

TEN

The Second Layer: Anger, Hatred, Outrage

If you are never angry, then you are unborn.

—*African proverb, Bassa tribe*

If the First Layer of human interaction is the common ground of manners, kind speech, polite greeting, and working agreements; if the Third Layer is the area of deeply shared humanity, the universal brotherhood and sisterhood of all people, of the underlying, fundamental oneness of human love, justice, and peaceful coexistence; then the Second Layer is the territory of anger, hatred, wrath, rage, outrage, jealousy, envy, contempt, disgust, and acrimony. It is the Via Negativa, the field of Conflict, the plain of Discord, the hills of Turmoil. And, the Second Layer always exists between the First Layer and the Third.

All three layers are necessary for a society to continue, for a relationship to endure, for an individual to persist. The First Layer is the immediate area of surface courtesies that make life in passing possible. Without this overlay, the simplest tasks of survival could not be accomplished. We reinforce the daily social world by the common greeting, "How are you?" followed by the appropriate First Layer answer, "Fine," and the concluding blessing, "Well, have a nice day." What is being stated is not TRUTH, but the attempt to reinforce the basic agreements of society and the relationships within it. This layer is dedicated to the simple harmony of status quo. "How are you?" is not a penetrating request for soul-searching. "Fine" is not a well-reflected self-evaluation. "Have a nice day" is not a deeply emotional prayer intended to alter an individual's fate. The clue to the ritual of courtesy is the word *nice*. The First Layer is constantly converting things to "right on," "thumbs up," "OK," "nice." I may wish that I didn't have to see you at all, but I say, "How are you?" You may be feeling that if one more thing goes wrong, you'll begin pouring hot coffee over the feet of anyone who approaches you at all, but you answer, "Fine." We may each wish all the bad karma, all the pigeon droppings, and all the wrong turns of a lifetime on the other, but we each say, "Have a nice day." We know that the decency of the First Layer must be kept intact most of the time, for the sake of social survival. The First Layer doesn't have to carry true emotions, hard-learned insights, or personal authenticity. But if an individual or a society stays only in the surface layer of life, a huge shadow starts to grow in the Second Layer.

The Third Layer is the province of deep unity with all things and with the great themes and images of life. Without some experience of the Third Layer, we die. Societies, alliances, relationships, and individual souls must occasionally fall into these pools of unity or else they dry out or blow up. When we "fall in love," it's the ground of the Third Layer we fall upon. In this country, "all you need is love" and "love is all there is." Or, finally, "justice is served" and the wrongs are righted. And for a moment all is "right with the world." The Third Layer is where the unifying images of god exist, where prayers are answered, where healing mends the wounds of life, where peace becomes real and contagious. "Visualize World Peace" is a Third Layer bumper sticker; so are "Jesus Loves You" and "This Car Stops for Ducks." We all want to be in the warmth and peace of the Third Layer. All utopias reside in the Third Layer. We mount great efforts to get there through meditation and prayer, through working at relationships, through great social movements. We can sit there rent-free and see how it was all worth it. In the clear skies and fresh air of the Third Layer we can truly forgive the insults, punishments, and injustices heaped upon us. Here at the depths a rare stream of humor cleanses the old wounds and makes our eyes bright for life.

Here's the bad news: the Third Layer is constantly moving

its location; its not to be found today where it was yesterday. We can go through the motions, exactly repeating everything that previously got us to that state of peace, love, bliss; and we get nowhere. We return to places where we fell deep into love and find the view obscured by a new factory; the romantic restaurant has been replaced by a fast-food joint. We bow in all directions, say the prayers just as before, but there's no sense or sight of god; we come up empty. The Third Layer is mysterious, unpredictable, leaves no forwarding address.

The First Layer is always in the same place: it's predictable, it's certain—superficially certain, like a sidewalk or a sign. But the signs in the Second Layer say "Beware of the Dog," "Shit Happens," "Get a Life," "Up Your Day." The Second Layer says: "I can't take it anymore, I won't stand for it, I've had enough." The Second Layer sends postcards from Hell, greetings from the underworld: "How about a nice, special-delivery order of rage pie, a fillet of hatred, a salad of jealousy, a side of envy, a plate of wrath?" It is a stove that seethes with an adverse, acidic, acrid, avaricious, acrimonious, angry stew. It bubbles with feelings, emotions, and indelible attitudes we'd rather not have, wouldn't choose, and shouldn't express. Movements beneath the surface can be minor tremors that rattle a few dishes and then subside or can be earthquakings that shatter, rend, and collapse whatever has been built up above. If a major fault is involved, a volcanic eruption can spew deep-core hot magma to the surface, melting, burning, swallowing whole areas of the First Layer. Is it better that the volcano vent steam, or should it be corked?

The population of the Second Layer includes a high percentage of giants, hags, trolls, boxers, bears, street criminals, cops, vultures, gargoyles, streetwalkers, and outraged motorists. The sidewalks are cracked, the stores are closed, the lights don't work, and there is no one who'll listen to you. When people avoid entering this territory, they begin attracting shadowy figures who will one day explode into their life. Or, like a TV evangelist, they are compulsively drawn to the figures of the night. Cultures that try to shut out the Second Layer wind up with overcrowded prisons, high crime rates, huge black markets, and, finally, riots in the streets.

There's more bad news. The only way out of the First Layer, the only way to break the spell of niceness when it has shifted from ensuring life's continuance to insulting life's purpose is to enter the turmoil of the Second Layer. Furthermore —and don't blame this on me—the only way to find the next location of the Third Layer is by traversing the battle-scarred, dog-infested terrain of the Second Layer.

The following poems are letters from the Second Layer. Some of the messages may shock or burn in the hand, but, as Claude McKay says:

> My being would be a skeleton, a shell,
> If this dark passion . . .
> Did not forever feed me vital blood.

Strange as it may seem, without the irrational fires in the Second Layer, activity on the First Level would freeze up and everything on the Third Level would be shrouded in a mist so rare and white that not one thing could be discerned from another. Unpleasant ideas and words inhabit each of these poems. They don't seek agreement or approval. They permeate the history of poetry the way that dark and fierce emotions permeate our lives. All emotions have a purpose, as Yeats finds in anger and hate a light that shows "How soul may walk when all such things are past." Emily Dickinson in not turning away from the rough terrain finds:

> The palate of the hate departs; . . .
> Anger as soon as fed is dead;
> 'Tis starving makes it fat.

M.J.M.

THE BLACK RIDERS

There are blows in life so violent—Don't ask me!
Blows as if from the hatred of God; as if before them,
the deep waters of everything lived through
were backed up in the soul . . . Don't ask me!

Not many; but they exist . . . They open dark ravines
in the most ferocious face and in the most bull-like back.
Perhaps they are the horses of that heathen Attila,
or the black riders sent to us by Death.

They are the slips backward made by the Christs of the soul,
away from some holy faith that is sneered at by Events.
These blows that are bloody are the crackling sounds
from some bread that burns at the oven door.

And man . . . poor man! . . . poor man! He swings his eyes, as
when a man behind us calls us by clapping his hands;
swings his crazy eyes, and everything alive
is backed up, like a pool of guilt, in that glance.

There are blows in life so violent . . . Don't ask me!

CÉSAR VALLEJO
translated by R.B.

THE TWINS

Good and bad are in my heart,
But I cannot tell to you—
—For they never are apart—
Which is better of the two.

I am this! I am the other!
And the devil is my brother!
But my father He is God!
And my mother is the Sod!
I am safe enough, you see,
Owing to my pedigree.

So I shelter love and hate
Like twin brothers in a nest;
Lest I find when it's too late,
That the other was the best.

JAMES STEPHENS

INDEED INDEED, I CANNOT TELL

Indeed indeed, I cannot tell,
Though I ponder on it well,
Which were easier to state,
All my love or all my hate.
Surely, surely, thou wilt trust me
When I say thou dost disgust me.
O, I hate thee with a hate
That would fain annihilate;
Yet sometimes against my will,
My dear friend, I love thee still.
It were treason to our love,
And a sin to God above,
One iota to abate
Of a pure impartial hate.

HENRY DAVID THOREAU

Olav H. Hauge spent several months in a mental institution in Norway, and this poem was written during that time.

I STAND HERE, DO YOU UNDERSTAND

I stand here, do you understand.
I stood here last year too, do you understand.
I am going to stand here too, do you understand.
I take it too, do you understand.
There's something you don't know, do you understand.
You just got here, do you understand.
How long are we to stand here?
We have to eat too, do you understand.
I stand when I eat too, I do that, do you understand,
and throw the plates at the wall.
We have to rest too, do you understand.
We have to piss and shit too, do you understand.
How long are we to stand here?
I stand all right, do you understand.
I take it too, do you understand.
I'm going to stand here, do you understand.

OLAV H. HAUGE
translated by R.B.

HATRED

I shall hate you
Like a dart of singing steel
Shot through still air
At even-tide.
Or solemnly
As pines are sober
When they stand etched
Against the sky.
Hating you shall be a game
Played with cool hands
And slim fingers.
Your heart will yearn
For the lonely splendor
Of the pine tree;
While rekindled fires
In my eyes
Shall wound you like swift arrows.
Memory will lay its hands
Upon your breast
And you will understand
My hatred.

GWENDOLYN BENNETT

RIBH CONSIDERS CHRISTIAN LOVE
INSUFFICIENT

Why should I seek for love or study it?
It is of God and passes human wit;
I study hatred with great diligence,
For that's a passion in my own control,
A sort of besom that can clear the soul
Of everything that is not mind or sense.

Why do I hate man, woman or event?
That is a light my jealous soul has sent.
From terror and deception freed it can
Discover impurities, can show at last
How soul may walk when all such things are past,
How soul could walk before such things began.

Then my delivered soul herself shall learn
A darker knowledge and in hatred turn
From every thought of God mankind has had.
Thought is a garment and the soul's a bride
That cannot in that trash and tinsel hide:
Hatred of God may bring the soul to God.

At stroke of midnight soul cannot endure
A bodily or mental furniture.
What can she take until her Master give!
Where can she look until He make the show!
What can she know until He bid her know!
How can she live till in her blood He live!

WILLIAM BUTLER YEATS

LINES FOR AN OLD MAN

The tiger in the tiger-pit
Is not more irritable than I.
The whipping tail is not more still
Than when I smell the enemy
Writhing in the essential blood
Or dangling from the friendly tree.
When I lay bare the tooth of wit
The hissing over the archèd tongue
Is more affectionate than hate,
More bitter than the love of youth,
And inaccessible by the young.
Reflected from my golden eye
The dullard knows that he is mad.
Tell me if I am not glad!

T. S. ELIOT

THE HILL

It is sometime since I have been
to what it was had once turned me backwards,
and made my head into
a cruel instrument.

It is simple
to confess. Then done,
to walk away, walk away,
to come again.

But that form, I must answer,
is dead in me, completely,
and I will not allow it
to reappear—

Saith perversity, the willful,
the magnanimous cruelty,
which is in me
like a hill.

ROBERT CREELEY

THE ANGER THAT BREAKS THE MAN
INTO CHILDREN

The anger that breaks the man into children,
that breaks the child into equal birds,
and the bird, afterward, into little eggs;
the anger of the poor
has one oil against two vinegars.

The anger that breaks the tree into leaves,
the leaf into unequal buds
and the bud, into telescopic grooves;
the anger of the poor
has two rivers against many seas.

The anger that breaks the good into doubts,
the doubt, into three similar arcs
and the arc, later on, into unforeseeable tombs;
the anger of the poor
has one steel against two daggers.

The anger that breaks the soul into bodies;
the body into dissimilar organs
and the organ, into octave thoughts;
the anger of the poor
has one central fire against two craters.

CÉSAR VALLEJO
*translated by Clayton Eshleman
and José Rubia Barcia*

THE MAN WATCHING

I can tell by the way the trees beat, after
so many dull days, on my worried windowpanes
that a storm is coming,
and I hear the far-off fields say things
I can't bear without a friend,
I can't love without a sister.

The storm, the shifter of shapes, drives on
across the woods and across time,
and the world looks as if it had no age:
the landscape, like a line in the psalm book,
is seriousness and weight and eternity.

What we choose to fight is so tiny!
What fights with us is so great!
If only we would let ourselves be dominated
as things do by some immense storm,
we would become strong too, and not need names.

When we win it's with small things,
and the triumph itself makes us small.
What is extraordinary and eternal
does not *want* to be bent by us.
I mean the Angel who appeared
to the wrestlers of the Old Testament:
when the wrestlers' sinews
grew long like metal strings,
he felt them under his fingers
like chords of deep music.

Whoever was beaten by this Angel
(who often simply declined the fight)
went away proud and strengthened

and great from that harsh hand,
that kneaded him as if to change his shape.
Winning does not tempt that man.
This is how he grows: by being defeated, decisively,
by constantly greater beings.

RAINER MARIA RILKE
translated by R.B.

FIRE ON THE HILLS

The deer were bounding like blown leaves
Under the smoke in front of the roaring wave of the
    brushfire;
I thought of the smaller lives that were caught.
Beauty is not always lovely; the fire was beautiful, the terror
Of the deer was beautiful; and when I returned
Down the black slopes after the fire had gone by, an eagle
Was perched on the jag of a burnt pine,
Insolent and gorged, cloaked in the folded storms of his
    shoulders.
He had come from far off for the good hunting
With fire for his beater to drive the game; the sky was
    merciless
Blue, and the hills merciless black,
The sombre-feathered great bird sleepily merciless between
    them.
I thought, painfully, but the whole mind,
The destruction that brings an eagle from heaven is better
    than mercy.

ROBINSON JEFFERS

THE SONG OF THE BLACK BEAR

My moccasins are black obsidian,
My leggings are black obsidian,
My shirt is black obsidian.
I am girded with a black arrowsnake.
Black snakes go up from my head.
With zigzag lightning darting from the ends of my feet I
    step,
With zigzag lightning streaming out from my knees I step,
With zigzag lightning streaming from the tip of my tongue
    I speak.
Now a disk of pollen rests on the crown of my head.
Gray arrowsnakes and rattlesnakes eat it.
Black obsidian and zigzag lightning streams out from me in
    four ways,
Where they strike the earth, bad things, bad talk does not
    like it.
It causes the missiles to spread out.
Long Life, something frightful I am.
Now I am.

There is danger where I move my feet.
I am whirlwind.
There is danger when I move my feet.
I am a gray bear.
When I walk, where I step, lightning flies from me,
Where I walk, one to be feared [I am].

Where I walk, Long Life.
One to be feared I am.
There is danger where I walk.

Navajo

The Second Layer: Anger, Hatred, Outrage

301

A POISON TREE

I was angry with my friend:
I told my wrath, my wrath did end.
I was angry with my foe:
I told it not, my wrath did grow.

And I water'd it in fears,
Night & morning with my tears;
And I sunned it with smiles,
And with soft deceitful wiles.

And it grew both day and night,
Till it bore an apple bright;
And my foe beheld it shine,
And he knew that it was mine,

And into my garden stole
When the night had veil'd the pole:
In the morning glad I see
My foe outstretch'd beneath the tree.

WILLIAM BLAKE

THE ENGLISH ARE SO NICE!

The English are so nice
so awfully nice
they're the nicest people in the world.
And what's more, they're very nice about being nice
about your being nice as well!
If you're not nice, they soon make you feel it.

Americans and French and Germans and so on
they're all very well
but they're not *really* nice, you know.
They're not as nice in *our* sense of the word, are they now?

That's why one doesn't have to take them seriously.
We must be nice to them, of course,
of course, naturally—
But it doesn't really matter what you say to them,
they don't really understand—
you can just say anything to them:
be nice, you know, just be nice—
but you must never take them seriously, they wouldn't
    understand
just be nice, you know! oh, fairly nice,
not too nice of course, they take advantage—
but nice enough, just nice enough
to let them feel they're not quite as nice as they might be.

D. H. LAWRENCE

MINE ENEMY IS GROWING OLD

Mine enemy is growing old,—
I have at last revenge.
The palate of the hate departs;
If any would avenge,—

Let him be quick, the viand flits,
It is a faded meat.
Anger as soon as fed is dead;
'Tis starving makes it fat.

EMILY DICKINSON

THE ASCENSIONS

You, Marc Chagall, should be able to tell us
what was cremated in Thor's ovens,
you who were always painting ascensions.

The ascensions of priestly violinists,
the ascension of white-gowned brides,
the ascension of purple donkeys,
of lovers, of bouquets, of golden cockerels,
ascensions into the clair-de-lune.

O this soaring
out of shanties and cellars!
the folk spirit ascending
through enchanted alphabets,
through magical numbers,
to a wandering in bluest realms.

The ascension
(from sewers, dives, back-alleys)
of folk-songs to the new moon,
to the feast of lights,
to the silences of Friday evening . . .

. . . and suddenly
in the quietude of steppes
a thin column of smoke ascending
and after that
no more ascensions.

* * *

No more ascensions!

Only stone chimneys
heavily clinging
to the earth of Poland.
Not even a marker saying:
Here the Zhids
en-masse ascended.

WILLIAM PILLIN

THE UNITED FRUIT CO.

When the trumpet sounded, it was
all prepared on the earth,
and Jehovah parceled out the earth
to Coca-Cola, Inc., Anaconda,
Ford Motors, and other entities:
The Fruit Company, Inc.
reserved for itself the most succulent,
the central coast of my own land,
the delicate waist of America.
It rechristened its territories
as the "Banana Republics"
and over the sleeping dead,
over the restless heroes
who brought about the greatness,
the liberty and the flags,
it established the comic opera:
abolished the independencies,
presented crowns of Caesar,
unsheathed envy, attracted
the dictatorship of the flies,
Trujillo flies, Tacho flies,
Carías flies, Martínez flies,
Ubico flies, damp flies
of modest blood and marmalade,
drunken flies who zoom
over the ordinary graves,
circus flies, wise flies
well trained in tyranny.
Among the bloodthirsty flies
the Fruit Company lands its ships,
taking off the coffee and the fruit;
the treasure of our submerged
territories flows as though
on plates into the ships.

The Second Layer: Anger, Hatred, Outrage

Meanwhile Indians are falling
into the sugared chasms
of the harbors, wrapped
for burial in the mist of the dawn:
a body rolls, a thing
that has no name, a fallen cipher,
a cluster of dead fruit
thrown down on the dump.

PABLO NERUDA
translated by R.B.

THE WHITE CITY

I will not toy with it nor bend an inch.
Deep in the secret chambers of my heart
I muse my life-long hate, and without flinch
I bear it nobly as I live my part.
My being would be a skeleton, a shell,
If this dark Passion that fills my every mood,
And makes my heaven in the white world's hell,
Did not forever feed me vital blood.
I see the mighty city through a mist—
The strident trains that speed the goaded mass,
The poles and spires and towers vapor-kissed,
The fortressed port through which the great ships pass,
The tides, the wharves, the dens I contemplate,
Are sweet like wanton loves because I hate.

CLAUDE MCKAY

HARLEM

What happens to a dream deferred?

Does it dry up
like a raisin in the sun?

Or fester like a sore—
And then run?
Does it stink like rotten meat?
Or crust and sugar over—
like a syrupy sweet?

Maybe it just sags
like a heavy load.

Or does it explode?

LANGSTON HUGHES

FIRE AND ICE

Some say the world will end in fire,
Some say in ice.
From what I've tasted of desire
I hold with those who favor fire.
But if it had to perish twice,
I think I know enough of hate,
To say that for destruction ice
Is also great
And would suffice.

ROBERT FROST

ELEVEN

Earthly Love

A night full of talking that hurts,
my worst held-back secrets: Everything
has to do with loving and not loving.

—RUMI

When we tell these poems at gatherings of men, the room stretches out, seems to open into various landscapes of loving that the men carry inside themselves. All the great ways of organizing the world are abandoned as each finds the places of "loving and not loving" inside. Neruda says: "when you surrender you stretch out like the world." Through surrendering one world we enter another. We become earth's creatures, earthladen, and a particular place stretches within us, as Rilke says of a young man:

... The wind that rises
of their rising rustles in the leaves of his body. His brooks run sparkling into the distance.

He is stirred by love and basks in the warm light, learning of rivers inside himself. While another, whom love has forsaken and left clumsy:

> ... The man who
> has wandered pathless at night
> in the mountain-range of his feelings:
> is silent.

Once we surrender, earth surrounds and claims our bodies. We find ourselves standing in "a river of swirling eddies" or "a resurrected field in bloom," in "total desert" or else "anklebones in leaf-mush . . ." We become part of the sensual intimacy of the surprising earth. The "mole on Ahmad's cheek" becomes an entire rose garden complete with gardener.

Unawares, we have entered the precincts of the earth gods, of Aphrodite who inhabits all landscapes and moves from one to another on the crest of sea-waves or the rippling surface of a brook. This is not a distant Venus, nor the all-containing bosom of Mother Earth. We have entered the domains of green-eyed Aphrodite, whose every step pulls three fresh flowers from the forest floor, whose mantle is the ground cover of the earth. She is the Mistress of Animals and of the "body immediate." She brightens the physical world, stretches senses, and expands feelings. Always a part of loving is an offering to Aphrodite and thereby to the earth. A man loves a woman, or loves a man, and part of that loving is not human. The loved one is connected to but not the same as the goddess. The universal gift of lovers—flowers, foods, gems, and oils—are the charms of Aphrodite grown in the fertile carpet of the earth. The exchange of gifts brings the grace of Aphrodite present whenever a loving body approaches another.

Of course any earthly loving is subject to seasons, sudden storms, and droughts. And whoever can tie together can tear asunder. Aphrodite can rend any bond and strip the grace of nature from any relationship. The poems reveal Aphrodite of the "holy confusion," whose grinding teeth and growling song Carolyn Kizer hears:

> I'm going to murder you with love;
> I'm going to suffocate you with embraces;
> I'm going to hug you, bone by bone,
> Till you're dead all over.
> Then I will dine on your delectable marrow.

The intimacies we risk with each other are the sweet moments that sustain our mutual lives. And the intimate ones know where exactly to hurt each other. As Samuel Butler said, "Eating is touch carried to the bitter end."

But it is not only Aphrodite whose touch we feel in earthly love. Wherever Aphrodite is present, Eros the boy-man god is there as well. It was said that Eros was present when the egg of the earth cracked open and Life began to flourish in rivers, swell the trees with sap, saturate the wind with pollen. Eros is love in its masculine tone, permeating in cellular glue but also thrown across the world in great longing. Neruda names him: "My thirst, my desire without end, my wavering road!" Eros is in the seductions of the road, the loneliness of empty highways, and the surprise encounters, the side roads that lead us astray. For earthly love seduces, and everyone is seduced and led aside by the erotics of the senses. Eros is in the eye of Roethke that must follow:

> . . . a woman, lovely in her bones, . . .
> My eyes, they dazzled at her flowing knees;
> Her several parts could keep a pure repose,
> Or one hip quiver with a mobile nose
> (She moved in circles, and those circles moved).

Eros darts out in the eye of Walt Whitman in "A Glimpse" that pierces through ". . . a crowd of workmen and drivers" to find ". . . a youth who loves me, and whom I love." And Eros sticks moments in the memory as Whitman says later: "All else has long been forgotten by me" except the one who "long and long held me by the hand." Eros is in the memories that pull us back and the circle that moves far out into the world on the old roads of longing.

No one alive can avoid the pull or the spark of Eros. Eros is the tie that binds the teacher with the watchful pupil. Eros hides inside things and pulls us toward them as mementos and keepsakes of love. It is the sudden spark of longing for a loved one that seems to come from nowhere. It is a simple human touch that opens "Dark riverbeds down which the eternal thirst is flowing." Eros keeps us in a marriage or relationship long enough to arrive at "the silent drifting hours . . . yet no pathway worn between." And Eros sits inexhaustible within times of loss, within bitter times as Thomas McGrath has it in "A Coal Fire in Winter":

> Something old and tyrannical burning there.
> . . . heat
> From the time before there was fire.
> . . . a captive prince
> From the sunken kingdom of the father coal.

M.J.M.

I have seen the victor Dioxippos subdue all contenders at Olympia and be thrown on his back by the glance of a girl.

DIOGENES

THE MOLE

There is a mole on Ahmad's cheek that draws all those who
    are not now in love;
it is like a rose-garden, whose gardener is an Abyssinian.

AL-MUNTAFIL
translated by R.B.

THE GUEST

Everything's just as it was: fine hard snow
beats against the dining room windows,
and I myself have not changed:
even so, a man came to call.

I asked him: "What do you want?"
He said, "To be with you in hell."
I laughed: "It seems you see
plenty of trouble ahead for us both."

But lifting his dry hand
he lightly touched the flowers.
"Tell me how they kiss you,
tell me how you kiss."

And his half-closed eyes
remained on my ring.
Not even the smallest muscle moved
in his serenely angry face.

Oh, I know it fills him with joy—
this hard and passionate certainty
that there is nothing he needs,
and nothing I can keep from him.

1 January 1914

ANNA AKHMATOVA
translated by Jane Kenyan and Vera Dunham

THREE QUATRAINS

I

Never too many fish in a swift creek,
never too much water for fish to live in.

No place is too small for lovers,
nor can lovers see too much of the world.

2

Let the lover be disgraceful, crazy,
absentminded. Someone sober
will worry about events going badly.
Let the lover be.

3

A night full of talking that hurts,
my worst held-back secrets: Everything
has to do with loving and not loving.
This night will pass.
Then we have work to do.

RUMI
translated by John Moyne and Coleman Barks

A GLIMPSE

A glimpse, through an interstice caught,
Of a crowd of workmen and drivers in a bar-room, around
the stove, late of a winter night—and I unremarked,
seated in a corner,
Of a youth who loves me, and whom I love, silently
approaching, and seating himself near, that he may hold
me by the hand,
A long while, amid the noises of coming and going—of
drinking and oath and smutty jest,
There we two, content, happy in being together, speaking
little, perhaps not a word.

WALT WHITMAN

BODY OF A WOMAN

Body of a woman, white hills, white thighs,
when you surrender, you stretch out like the world.
My body, savage and peasant, undermines you
and makes a son leap in the bottom of the earth.

I was lonely as a tunnel. Birds flew from me.
And night invaded me with her powerful army.
To survive I forged you like a weapon,
like an arrow for my bow, or a stone for my sling.

But now the hour of revenge falls, and I love you.
Body of skin, of moss, of firm and thirsty milk!
And the cups of your breasts! And your eyes full of absence!
And the roses of your mound! And your voice slow and sad!

Body of my woman, I will live on through your
  marvelousness.
My thirst, my desire without end, my wavering road!
Dark river beds down which the eternal thirst is flowing,
and the fatigue is flowing, and the grief without shore.

PABLO NERUDA
translated by R.B.

& BALLS

Actually: it's the balls I look for, always.
Men in the street, offices, cars, restaurants.
it's the nuts I imagine—
firm, soft, in hairy sacks
the way they are
down there rigged between the thighs,
the funny way they are.
One in front, a little in front of the other,
slightly higher. The way they slip
between your fingers, the way they
slip around in their soft sack.
The way they swing when he walks,
hang down when he bends
over. You see them sometimes bright pink
out of a pair of shorts
when he sits wide and unaware,
the hair sparse and wiry
like that on a poland china pig.
You can see the skin right through—speckled,
with wrinkles like a prune, but loose,
slipping over those kernels
rocking the smooth, small huevos.
So delicate, the cock becomes a diversion,
a masthead overlarge, its flag distracting
from beautiful pebbles beneath.

ANNE MCNAUGHTON

O WHA'S THE BRIDE?

O wha's the bride that carries the bunch
O' thistles blinterin' white?
Her cuckold bridegroom little dreids
What he sall ken this nicht.

For closer than gudeman can come
And closer to'r than hersel',
Wha didna need her maidenheid
Has wrocht his purpose fell.

O wha's been here afore me, lass,
And hoo did he get in?
—*A man that deed or was I born*
This evil thing has din.

And left, as it were on a corpse,
Your maidenheid to me?
—*Nae lass, gudeman, sin' Time began*
'S hed ony mair to gi'e.

But I can gi'e ye kindness, lad,
And a pair o' willin' hands,
And you sall ha'e my breists like stars,
My limbs like willow wands.

And on my lips ye'll heed nae mair,
And in my hair forget,
The seed o' a' the men that in
My virgin womb ha'e met. . . .

1. wha's: who is. *2. blinterin':* gleaming. *3. dreids:* dreads. *4. sall ken:* shall know.
5. gudeman: husband. *8. wrocht:* worked. *10. hoo:* how. *11. deed:* died.
12. din: done. *15. sin':* since. *16. 'S:* Has. *ony . . . gi'e:* any more to give.
19. sall: shall. *breists:* breasts.

HUGH MACDIARMID

GREED AND AGGRESSION

Someone in Quaker meeting talks about greed and aggression
and I think of the way I lay the massive
weight of my body down on you
like a tiger lying down in gluttony and pleasure on the
elegant heavy body of the eland it eats,
the spiral horn pointing to the sky like heaven.
Ecstasy has been given to the tiger,
forced into its nature the way the
forcemeat is cranked down the throat of the held goose,
it cannot help it, hunger and the glory of
eating packed at the center of each
tiger cell, for the life of the tiger and the
making of new tigers, so there will
always be tigers on the earth, their stripes like
stripes of night and stripes of fire-light—
so if they had a God it would be striped,
burnt-gold and black, the way if
I had a God it would renew itself the
way you live and live while I take you as if
consuming you while you take me as if
consuming me, it would be a God of
love as complete satiety,
greed and fullness, aggression and fullness, the
way we once drank at the body of an animal
until we were so happy we could only
faint, our mouths running, into sleep.

SHARON OLDS

GENTLEMAN WITHOUT COMPANY

The homosexual young men and the love-mad girls,
and the long widows who suffer from a delirious inability to
   sleep,
and the young wives who have been pregnant for thirty
   hours,
and the hoarse cats that cross my garden in the dark,
these, like a necklace of throbbing sexual oysters,
surround my solitary house,
like enemies set up against my soul,
like members of a conspiracy dressed in sleeping costumes,
who give each other as passwords long and profound kisses.

The shining summer leads out the lovers
in low-spirited regiments that are all alike,
made up of fat and thin and cheerful and sullen pairs;
under the elegant coconut palms, near the sea and the moon,
there is a steady movement of trousers and petticoats,
and a hum from the stroking of silk stockings,
and women's breasts sparkling like eyes.

The small-time employee, after many things,
after the boredom of the week, and the novels read in bed at
   night,
has once and for all seduced the woman next door,
and now he escorts her to the miserable movies,
where the heroes are either colts or passionate princes,
and he strokes her legs sheathed in their sweet down
with his warm and damp hands that smell of cigarettes.

The evenings of the woman-chaser and the nights of the
   husbands
come together like two bed-sheets and bury me,
and the hours after lunch, when the young male students

and the young female students, and the priests are
   masturbating,
and the animals are riding each other frankly,
and the bees have an odor of blood, and the flies buzz in
   anger,
and cousins play strange games with their girl-cousins,
and doctors look with rage at the husband of the young
   patient,
and the morning hours, when the professor, as if
   absentminded,
performs his marital duty, and his breakfast,
and still more, the adulterers, who love each other with a real
   love
on beds high and huge as ocean liners,
this immense forest, entangled and breathing,
hedges me around firmly on all sides forever
with huge flowers like mouths and rows of teeth
and black roots that look like fingernails and shoes.

PABLO NERUDA
translated by R.B.

LAST GODS

She sits naked on a rock
a few yards out in the water.
He stands on the shore,
also naked, picking blueberries.
She calls. He turns. She opens
her legs showing him her great beauty,
and smiles, a bow of lips
seeming to tie together
the ends of the earth.
Splashing her image
to pieces, he wades out
and stands before her, sunk
to the anklebones in leaf-mush
and bottom-slime—the intimacy
of the visible world. He puts
a berry in its shirt
of mist into her mouth.
She swallows it. He puts in another.
She swallows it. Over the lake
two swallows whim, juke, jink,
and when one snatches
an insect they both whirl up
and exult. He is swollen
not with ichor but with blood.
She takes him and sucks him
more swollen. He kneels, opens
the dark, vertical smile
linking heaven with the underearth
and licks her smoothest flesh more smooth.
On top of the rock they join.
Somewhere a frog moans, a crow screams.
The hair of their bodies
startles up. They cry
in the tongue of the last gods,

who refused to go,
chose death, and shuddered
in joy and shattered in pieces,
bequeathing their cries
into the human mouth. Now in the lake
two faces float, looking up
at a great maternal pine whose branches
open out in all directions
explaining everything.

GALWAY KINNELL

COCKS AND MARES

Every man wants to be a stud.
His nature drives him.
Hanging between his legs
The heavy weight of scrotum.
He wants to bring forth God.
He wants God to come
Out of those common eggs.
But he can't tell his cock
From a rooster's. However,
I'm a horse, he says,
Prancing up and down.
What am I doing here
In the hen house?
Diddle you. Doodle doo.
In this fashion he goes on
Pretending that women are fowl
And that he is a stallion.
You can hear him crowing
When the wild mares
Come up out of the night fields
Whistling through their nostrils
In their rhythmic pounding,
In the sound of their deep breathing.

RUTH STONE

I KNEW A WOMAN

I knew a woman, lovely in her bones,
When small birds sighed, she would sigh back at them;
Ah, when she moved, she moved more ways than one:
The shapes a bright container can contain!
Of her choice virtues only gods should speak,
Or English poets who grew up on Greek
(I'd have them sing in chorus, cheek to cheek).

How well her wishes went! She stroked my chin,
She taught me Turn, and Counter-turn, and Stand;
She taught me Touch, and undulant white skin;
I nibbled meekly from her proffered hand;
She was the sickle; I, poor I, the rake,
Coming behind her for her pretty sake
(But what prodigious mowing we did make).

Love likes a gander, and adores a goose:
Her full lips pursed, the errant note to seize;
She played it quick, she played it light and loose,
My eyes, they dazzled at her flowing knees;
Her several parts could keep a pure repose,
Or one hip quiver with a mobile nose
(She moved in circles, and those circles moved).

Let seed be grass, and grass turn into hay:
I'm martyr to a motion not my own;
What's freedom for? To know eternity.
I swear she cast a shadow white as stone.
But who would count eternity in days?
These old bones live to learn her wanton ways:
(I measure time by how a body sways).

THEODORE ROETHKE

FOOD OF LOVE

Eating is touch carried to the bitter end.
—SAMUEL BUTLER II

I'm going to murder you with love;
I'm going to suffocate you with embraces;
I'm going to hug you, bone by bone,
Till you're dead all over.
Then I will dine on your delectable marrow.

You will become my personal Sahara;
I'll sun myself in you, then with one swallow
Drain your remaining brackish well.
With my female blade I'll carve my name
In your most aspiring palm
Before I chop it down
Then I'll inhale your last oasis whole.

But in the total desert you become
You'll see me stretch, horizon to horizon,
Opulent mirage!
Wisteria balconies dripping cyclamen.
Vistas ablaze with crystal, laced in gold.

So you will summon each dry grain of sand
And move towards me in undulating dunes
Till you arrive at sudden ultramarine:
A Mediterranean to stroke your dusty shores;
Obstinate verdure, creeping inland, fast renudes
Your barrens; succulents spring up everywhere,
Surprising life! And I will be that green.

When you are fed and watered, flourishing
With shoots entwining trellis, dome and spire,
Till you are resurrected field in bloom,
I will devour you, my natural food,
My host, my final supper on the earth,
And you'll begin to die again.

CAROLYN KIZER

FEEDING THE DOG

An old woman likes to melt her husband. She puts him in a melting device, and he pours out the other end in a hot bloody syrup, which she catches in a series of little husband molds.

What splatters on the floor the dog licks up.

When they have set she has seventeen little husbands. One she throws to the dog because the genitals didn't set right, too much like a vulva because of an air bubble.

Then there are sixteen naked little husbands standing in a row across the kitchen table.

She diddles them and they produce sixteen little erections.

She thinks she might melt her husband again. She likes melting him.

She might pour him into an even smaller series of husband molds . . .

RUSSELL EDSON

I WRUNG MY HANDS
UNDER MY DARK VEIL

I wrung my hands under my dark veil . . .
"Why are you pale, what makes you reckless?"
—Because I have made my loved one drunk
with an astringent sadness.

I'll never forget. He went out, reeling;
his mouth was twisted, desolate . . .
I ran downstairs, not touching the banisters,
and followed him as far as the gate.

And shouted, choking: "I meant it all
in fun. Don't leave me, or I'll die of pain."
He smiled at me—oh so calmly, terribly—
and said: "Why don't you get out of the rain?"

ANNA AKHMATOVA
translated by Max Hayward and Stanley Kunitz

TO WOMEN, AS FAR AS I'M CONCERNED

The feelings I don't have, I don't have.
The feelings I don't have, I won't say I have.
The feelings you say you have, you don't have.
The feelings you would like us both to have, we neither of
   us have.

The feelings people ought to have, they never have.
If people say they've got feelings, you may be pretty sure
   they haven't got them.

So if you want either of us to feel anything at all
you'd better abandon all idea of feelings altogether.

D. H. LAWRENCE

INTIMATES

Don't you care for my love? she said bitterly.

I handed her the mirror, and said:
Please address these questions to the proper person!
Please make all requests to head-quarters!
In all matters of emotional importance
please approach the supreme authority direct!—
So I handed her the mirror.

D. H. LAWRENCE

BALLAD OF THE DESPAIRING HUSBAND

My wife and I lived all alone,
contention was our only bone.
I fought with her, she fought with me,
and things went on right merrily.

But now I live here by myself
with hardly a damn thing on the shelf,
and pass my days with little cheer
since I have parted from my dear.

Oh come home soon, I write to her.
Go screw yourself, is her answer.
Now what is that, for Christian word?
I hope she feeds on dried goose turd.

But still I love her, yes I do.
I love her and the children too.
I only think it fit that she
should quickly come right back to me.

Ah no, she says, and she is tough,
and smacks me down with her rebuff.
Ah no, she says, I will not come
after the bloody things you've done.

Oh wife, oh wife—I tell you true,
I never loved no one but you.
I never will, it cannot be
another woman is for me.

That may be right, she will say then,
but as for me, there's other men.
And I will tell you I propose
to catch them firmly by the nose.

And I will wear what dresses I choose!
And I will dance, and what's to lose!
I'm free of you, you little prick,
and I'm the one can make it stick.

Was this the darling I did love?
Was this that mercy from above
did open violets in the spring—
and made my own worn self to sing?

She was. I know. And she is still,
and if I love her? then so I will.
And I will tell her, and tell her right . . .

Oh lovely lady, morning or evening or afternoon.
Oh lovely lady, eating with or without a spoon.
Oh most lovely lady, whether dressed or undressed or
    partly.
Oh most lovely lady, getting up or going to bed or sitting
    only.

Oh loveliest of ladies, than whom none is more fair, more
    gracious, more beautiful.
Oh loveliest of ladies, whether you are just or unjust,
    merciful, indifferent, or cruel.
Oh most loveliest of ladies, doing whatever, seeing
    whatever, being whatever.
Oh most loveliest of ladies, in rain, in shine, in any
    weather.

Oh lady, grant me time,
please, to finish my rhyme.

ROBERT CREELEY

ALL THAT IS LOVELY IN MEN

Nothing for a dirty man
but soap in his bathtub, a

greasy hand, lover's
nuts

perhaps. Or else

something like sand
with which to scour him

for all
that is lovely in women.

ROBERT CREELEY

SEPARATION BY DEATH

She was pure and white, resembling the sun as it rises.
All other women were merely stars!
Love for her has made my heart fly off its permanent branch,
And after stopping a while, it is still hovering in the air!

IBN HAZM
version by Robert Bly
adapted from the translation by A. R. Nykl

FEELING FUCKED UP

Lord she's gone done left me done packed / up and split
and I with no way to make her
come back and everywhere the world is bare
bright bone white crystal sand glistens
dope death dead dying and jiving drove
her away made her take her laughter and her smiles
and her softness and her midnight sighs—

Fuck Coltrane and music and clouds drifting in the sky
fuck the sea and trees and the sky and birds
and alligators and all the animals that roam the earth
fuck marx and mao fuck fidel and nkrumah and
democracy and communism fuck smack and pot
and red ripe tomatoes fuck joseph fuck mary fuck
god jesus and all the disciples fuck fanon nixon
and malcolm fuck the revolution fuck freedom fuck
the whole muthafucking thing
all i want now is my woman back
so my soul can sing

ETHERIDGE KNIGHT

THE IMPULSE

It was too lonely for her there,
　And too wild,
And since there were but two of them,
　And no child,

And work was little in the house,
　She was free,
And followed where he furrowed field,
　Or felled tree.

She rested on a log and tossed
　The fresh chips,
With a song only to herself
　On her lips.

And once she went to break a bough
　Of black alder.
She strayed so far she scarcely heard
　When he called her—

And didn't answer—didn't speak—
　Or return.
She stood, and then she ran and hid
　In the fern.

He never found her, though he looked
　Everywhere,
And he asked at her mother's house
　Was she there.

Sudden and swift and light as that
　The ties gave,
And he learned of finalities
　Besides the grave.

ROBERT FROST

GRIEF

Grief reached across the world to get me,
sadness carries me across seas and countries
to your grave, my brother,

to offer the only gift I still can give you—
words you will not hear.

Fortune has taken you from me. You.
No reason, nothing fair.
I didn't deserve losing you.

Now, in the silence since,
as is the ancient custom of our people,
I say the mourner's prayer,
do the final kindness.

Accept and understand it, brother.
My head aches from crying.
Forever, goodbye.

GAIUS VALERIUS CATULLUS
translated by Jacob Rabinowitz

THE
RIVER-MERCHANT'S WIFE:
A LETTER

While my hair was still cut straight across my forehead
I played about the front gate, pulling flowers.
You came by on bamboo stilts, playing horse,
You walked about my seat, playing with blue plums.
And we went on living in the village of Chokan:
Two small people, without dislike or suspicion.

At fourteen I married My Lord you.
I never laughed, being bashful.
Lowering my head, I looked at the wall.
Called to, a thousand times, I never looked back.

At fifteen I stopped scowling,
I desired my dust to be mingled with yours
Forever and forever and forever.
Why should I climb the look out?

At sixteen you departed,
You went into far Ku-to-yen, by the river of swirling eddies,
And you have been gone five months.
The monkeys make sorrowful noise overhead.

You dragged your feet when you went out.
By the gate now, the moss is grown, the different mosses,
Too deep to clear them away!
The leaves fall early this autumn, in wind.
The paired butterflies are already yellow with August
Over the grass in the West garden;
They hurt me. I grow older.

If you are coming down through the narrows of the river
   Kiang,
Please let me know beforehand,
And I will come out to meet you
               As far as Cho-fu-Sa.

By Rihaku

EZRA POUND

"WE MUST DIE
BECAUSE WE HAVE KNOWN THEM"

(Papyrus Prisse. From the sayings of Ptah-hotep, manuscript from 2000 B.C.)

"We must die because we have known them." Die
of their smile's unsayable flower. Die
of their delicate hands. Die
of women.

Let the young man sing of them, praise
these death-bringers, when they move through his heart-
    space,
high overhead. From his blossoming breast
let him sing to them:
unattainable! Ah, how distant they are.
Over the peaks
of his feeling, they float and pour down
sweetly transfigured night into the abandoned
valley of his arms. The wind
of their rising rustles in the leaves of his body. His brooks
    run
sparkling into the distance.

But the grown man
shudders and is silent. The man who
has wandered pathless at night
in the mountain-range of his feelings:
is silent.

As the old sailor is silent,
and the terrors that he has endured
play inside him as though in quivering cages.

Paris, July 1914

RAINER MARIA RILKE
translated by Stephen Mitchell

Earthly Love
349

A MARRIAGE

The first retainer
he gave to her
was a golden
wedding ring.

The second—late at night
he woke up,
leaned over on an elbow,
and kissed her.

The third and the last—
he died with
and gave up loving
and lived with her.

ROBERT CREELEY

AND IF HE HAD BEEN WRONG FOR ME

yet he was there, and all my thirst
gatherd in the thought of him that year,
a tall liquid presence of the man,
a river running in the sound of him,

sun dazzle in the shallows, shadows
in the pool beneath the rocks.

It is a place of early lonely thought,
impatient revery of a cool green.

It is a glass of water
ever just pourd for me, a memory
kept silent come to speak.

ROBERT DUNCAN

LISTENING TO THE KÖLN CONCERT

After we had loved each other intently,
we heard notes tumbling together,
in late winter, and we heard ice
falling from the ends of twigs.

The notes abandon so much as they move.
They are the food not eaten, the comfort
not taken, the lies not spoken.
The music is my attention to you.

And when the music came again,
later in the day, I saw tears in your eyes.
I saw you turn your face away
so that the others would not see.

When men and women come together,
how much they have to abandon! Wrens
make their nests of fancy threads
and string ends, animals

abandon all their money each year.
What is that men and women leave?
Harder than wrens' doing, they have
to abandon their longing for the perfect.

The inner nest not made by instinct
will never be quite round,
and each has to enter the nest
made by the other imperfect bird.

ROBERT BLY

ONCE I PASSED THROUGH
A POPULOUS CITY

Once I passed through a populous city, imprinting on my
   brain, for future use, its shows, architecture, customs and
   traditions
But now of all that city I remember only the man who
   wandered with me there, for love of me,
Day by day, and night by night, we were together.
All else has long been forgotten by me—I remember, I say,
   only one rude and ignorant man who, when I departed,
   long and long held me by the hand, with silent lips, sad
   and tremulous.

WALT WHITMAN

HISTORY

The listless beauty of the hour
When snow fell on the apple-trees
And the wood-ash gathered in the fire
And we faced our first miseries.

Then the sweeping sunshine of noon
When the mountains like chariot cars
Were ranked to blue battle—and you and I
Counted our scars.

And then in a strange, grey hour
We lay mouth to mouth, with your face
Under mine like a star on the lake,
And I covered the earth, and all space.

The silent, drifting hours
Or morn after morn
And night drifting up to the night
Yet no pathway worn.

Your life, and mine, my love
Passing on and on, the hate
Fusing closer and closer with love
Till at length they mate.

The Cearne

D. H. LAWRENCE

A COAL FIRE IN WINTER

Something old and tyrannical burning there.
(Not like a wood fire which is only
The end of a summer, or a life)
But something of darkness: heat
From the time before there was fire.
And I have come here
To warm that blackness into forms of light,
To set free a captive prince
From the sunken kingdom of the father coal.

A warming company of the cold-blooded—
These carbon serpents of bituminous gardens,
These inflammable tunnels of dead song from the black pit,
This sparkling end of the great beasts, these blazing
Stone flowers diamond fire incandescent fruit.
And out of all that death, now,
At midnight, my love and I are riding
Down the old high roads of inexhaustible light.

THOMAS MCGRATH

TWELVE

The Cultivated Heart

How blessed is the man who like Hafez
Has tasted in his heart the wine made before Adam.

—version by R.B.

What is the cultivated heart? We know that we are not talking about the educated mind, though the subtle mind is not ruled out, or the disciplined body, though a vigorous body is not ruled out. We aren't talking of the intense will either, that intensified clarity of purpose, which, in a warrior, carries him past childish distractions and adolescent comfort-longings to his goal. The heart is a place of tenderness. The cultivated heart receives intensification toward tenderness.

In Europe love and the cultivated heart become noticeable in the twelfth century. Men were working on the cultivation of the heart when they accepted vows to be courteous. To be courteous meant to honor elders, to offer praise and support to other men, whose fragility was kept in mind, and, above all, to do honor in the most difficult situations to women. When we read the literature of the time, we realize what an enormous step that was for Western or European man.

To judge by stories, reports, poems, and memoirs, a typical male act before the time of courtesy would have been this: a man on a horse—enjoying some wealth and privilege—riding through a farm valley sees a young woman gathering hay: he gets off and makes love to her and that's that. Then he gets on his horse and rides on. This situation turns up in poems over several hundred years. Once the southern European man took vows of courtesy, the details of the narrative changed. First, the man may talk, and even try to speak to the young woman personally. He may make promises—"Come live with me and be my love"—which he may or may not intend to keep. Eventually, he may listen for her reply. Perhaps she says she wants some proof of the sincerity of his promises, or perhaps she tells him not to bother getting off his horse, just to ride on. If he obeys, it amounts to some evidence that he has a tender heart.

People in the Provence region eventually adopted the word *amor* to describe this new emotion associated in their minds with passionate delicacy and courteous affection. This emotion may have been well known in earlier Celtic culture, but it felt new in much of continental Europe. It involved rejection of many Catholic doctrines, including the self-disgust taught by the Church. Lovers of language felt a great thrill when they realized that if you spelled Roma backward it turned into "*amor.*" The Church did feel that admirers of Amor were enemies, and allegiance to Amor was one of the reasons the Church launched the Albigensian Crusade, which effectively destroyed the entire Provençal culture. We would say today that the man who felt Amor had made himself transparent to the "Great Feminine," without denying his masculinity or becoming an imitation woman.

It was a lady
    accompanied
by goat men
    leading her.

Her hair held earth.
    Her eyes were dark.
A double flute
    made her move.

"O love,
    where are you
leading
    me now?

(Robert Creeley)

The Rag and Bone Shop of the Heart

I don't mean to imply that "New Love" suggests atheism or hatred of God; on the contrary, the cultivated heart is religious, courteous toward God and His Mother. People noticed, however, that Augustinian self-disgust and hatred of sexuality did not mingle well with Amor.

Dante, inheriting two centuries of this embodied speculation, wrote a famous poem that clarified the images for many people.

Amor e cor gentil sono una cosa,
Siccom 'il Saggio in suo dittato pone;
E così senza l'un l'altro esser osa,
Com' alma razional senza ragione.

New Love and the gentle heart are the same thing,
Just as the wise man has set down in his poems,
And one without the other could no more exist
Than the thoughtful soul exist if thought did not.

He goes on to say that the gentle or cultivated heart resembles a large house, and far inside that house Amor is sleeping. The problem is how the New Love—so well insulated from noise—can be awakened. He says that beauty glimpsed by the eyes begins the process, and not the beauty of a teenager or a model, but the beauty of a savvy woman, who we assume would be a woman with a serious and educated heart.

The cultivated heart, imagined then as a house with many rooms, or an alchemical vase able to sustain high temperatures to assist creation of new substances, or imagined as a walled garden with rare flowers, order, solitude, place for intimacy with another, disdain of ordinary chaotic life, represented immense effort. It still does. Male initiation does not move toward machoism; on the contrary, it moves toward achieving a cultivated heart before we die.

I am not I.
　　　　I am this one
Walking beside me whom I do not see,
Whom at times I manage to visit,
And at other times I forget.

(Juan Ramón Jiménez)

For us in the West, it is humbling to realize that this move-
ment was pursued more enthusiastically, more massively, more
subtly, more widely in the Middle Ages and early Renaissance
than it is today. Much of the impulse for this movement came
directly from Persian and Arabic piety and Muslim ideas of chiv-
alry, which Spain and France absorbed.

For many years, French scholars insisted that the first Pro-
vençal love poems came directly out of French folk life and owed
nothing to the Arabs. Now we know that the early poems of
Guillaume X were in fact virtual translations from the Arabic;
the original Arabic poems, with the rhyme structure intact, have
been found. Islamic civilization at its highest point encouraged
and achieved marvelous cultivation of the lover's heart. Rumi
says: "No one knows our name until our last breath goes out."

American readers have adopted Rumi and Kabir and Mira-
bai poems with great joy recently, as if they were long-lost chil-
dren. And they are.

If the heart is a garden, then, it's clear we don't mean an
open garden, a garden set on the prairie through which horses
or pigs could run if they wished. The open heart paradoxically
needs walls, firm ones, so that it is a *hortus inclusus,* a closed
garden, a garden with limits. Only there, in a space withdrawn
from the public, can we grow the vines that require sun and
quiet, those vines trained by our ancestors. Hafez says:

How blessed is the man who like Hafez
Has tasted in his heart the wine made before Adam.

　　　　　　　　　　　　　　　　　　　　　　　R.B.

The next three poems speak of a man who learns to love "the guiding woman." He cultivates the heart that way.

THE SONG OF WANDERING AENGUS

I went out to the hazel wood,
Because a fire was in my head,
And cut and peeled a hazel wand,
And hooked a berry to a thread;
And when white moths were on the wing,
And moth-like stars were flickering out,
I dropped the berry in a stream
And caught a little silver trout.

When I had laid it on the floor
I went to blow the fire aflame,
But something rustled on the floor,
And someone called me by my name;
It had become a glimmering girl
With apple blossom in her hair
Who called me by my name and ran
And faded through the brightening air.

Though I am old from wandering
Through hollow lands and hilly lands,
I will find out where she has gone,
And kiss her lips and take her hands;
And walk among long dappled grass,
And pluck till time and times are done
The silver apples of the moon,
The golden apples of the sun.

WILLIAM BUTLER YEATS

NEW LOVE AND THE GENTLE HEART

New Love and the gentle heart are the same thing,
Just as the wise man has set down in his poems,
And one without the other could no more exist
Than the thoughtful soul exist if thought did not.

Nature made them both one day when amorous,
New Love as Lord, and the heart as his great seat;
Inside that house New Love lies there sleeping,
Perhaps a month or two, perhaps for years—

Then it is beauty in a savvy woman that appears,
And beauty pleases his eyes so much that deep inside
A desire is born toward this desirable thing,

And sometimes the desire remains alive in him
So long that it makes the spirit of New Love wake up.
A generous man has the same effect upon a woman.

DANTE
translated by R.B.

AS I WAS WALKING

As I was walking
   I came upon
chance walking
   the same road upon.

As I sat down
   by chance to move
later
   if and as I might,

light the wood was,
   light and green,
and what I saw
   before I had not seen.

It was a lady
   accompanied
by goat men
   leading her.

Her hair held earth.
   Her eyes were dark.
A double flute
   made her move.

"O love,
   where are you
leading
   me now?"

ROBERT CREELEY

The Cultivated Heart

The next three poems speak of a man who takes a different route: he works to welcome back into himself his "male twin," whom he sent away early in his life.

from
MORAL PROVERBS AND FOLK SONGS

I

Don't trace out your profile—
forget your side view—
all that is outer stuff.

II

Look for your other half
who walks always next to you
and tends to be who you aren't.

III

Narcissism
is an ugly fault,
and now it's a boring fault too.

IV

But look in your mirror for the other one,
the other one who walks by your side.

ANTONIO MACHADO
translated by R.B.

I AM NOT I

I am not I.
       I am this one
Walking beside me whom I do not see,
Whom at times I manage to visit,
And at other times I forget.
The one who remains silent when I talk,
The one who forgives, sweet, when I hate,
The one who takes a walk when I am indoors,
The one who will remain standing when I die.

JUAN RAMÓN JIMÉNEZ
translated by R.B.

THE ONE WHO IS AT HOME

Each day I long so much to see
The true teacher. And each time
At dusk when I open the cabin
Door and empty the teapot,
I think I know where he is:
West of us, in the forest.

Or perhaps I am the one
Who is out in the night,
The forest sand wet under
My feet, moonlight shining
On the sides of the birch trees,
The sea far off gleaming.

And he is the one who is
At home. He sits in my chair
Calmly; he reads and prays
All night. He loves to feel
His own body around him;
He does not leave his house.

FRANCISCO ALBÁNEZ
translated by R.B.

Some poets say that what you hope for in the afterlife is to be experienced here—through intensity of longing. This is a cultivation of the heart through longing.

TO BE A SLAVE OF INTENSITY

Friend, hope for the Guest while you are alive.
Jump into experience while you are alive!
Think . . . and think . . . while you are alive.
What you call "salvation" belongs to the time before death.

If you don't break your ropes while you're alive,
do you think
ghosts will do it after?

The idea that the soul will join with the ecstatic
just because the body is rotten—
that is all fantasy.
What is found now is found then.
If you find nothing now,
you will simply end up with an apartment in the City of
    Death.
If you make love with the divine now, in the next life you
    will have the face of satisfied desire.

So plunge into the truth, find out who the Teacher is,
    Believe in the Great Sound!

Kabir says this: When the Guest is being searched for, it is
    the intensity of the longing for the Guest that does all the
    work.
Look at me, and you will see a slave of that intensity.

KABIR
version by R.B.

ARCHAIC TORSO OF APOLLO

We cannot know his legendary head
with eyes like ripening fruit. And yet his torso
is still suffused with brilliance from inside,
like a lamp, in which his gaze, now turned to low,

gleams in all its power. Otherwise
the curved breast could not dazzle you so, nor could
a smile run through the placid hips and thighs
to that dark center where procreation flared.

Otherwise this stone would seem defaced
beneath the translucent cascade of the shoulders
and would not glisten like a wild beast's fur:

would not, from all the borders of itself,
burst like a star: for here there is no place
that does not see you. You must change your life.

RAINER MARIA RILKE
translated by Stephen Mitchell

SOMEONE DIGGING IN THE GROUND

An eye is meant to see things.
The soul is here for its own joy.
A head has one use: For loving a true love.
Legs: To run after.

Love is for vanishing into the sky. The mind,
for learning what men have done and tried to do.
Mysteries are not to be solved. The eye goes blind
when it only wants to see *why*.

A lover is always accused of something.
But when he finds his love, whatever was lost
in the looking comes back completely changed.
On the way to Mecca, many dangers: Thieves,
the blowing sand, only camel's milk to drink.
Still, each pilgrim kisses the black stone there
with pure longing, feeling in the surface
the taste of the lips he wants.

This talk is like stamping new coins. They pile up,
while the real work is done outside
by someone digging in the ground.

RUMI
translated by Coleman Barks

A fourth way of cultivation Antonio Machado refers to in this fine poem.
He calls it working with "your old failures."

LAST NIGHT

Last night, as I was sleeping,
I dreamt—marvellous error!—
that a spring was breaking
out in my heart.
I said: Along which secret aqueduct,
Oh water, are you coming to me,
water of a new life
that I have never drunk?

Last night, as I was sleeping,
I dreamt—marvellous error!—
that I had a beehive
here inside my heart.
And the golden bees
were making white combs
and sweet honey
from my old failures.

Last night, as I was sleeping,
I dreamt—marvelous error!—
that a fiery sun was giving
light inside my heart.
It was fiery because I felt
warmth as from a hearth,
and sun because it gave light
and brought tears to my eyes.

Last night, as I slept,
I dreamt—marvellous error!—
that it was God I had
here inside my heart.

ANTONIO MACHADO
translated by R.B.

PORTRAIT

My childhood is memories of a patio in Seville,
and a garden where sunlit lemons are growing yellow;
my youth twenty years on the earth of Castile;
what I lived a few things you'll forgive me for omitting.

A great seducer I was not, nor the lover of Juliet;
—the oafish way I dress is enough to say that—
but the arrow Cupid planned for me I got,
and I loved whenever women found a home in me.

A flow of leftist blood moves through my body,
but my poems rise from a calm and deep spring.
There is a man of rule who behaves as he should, but more
than him, I am, in the good sense of the word, good.

I adore beauty, and following contemporary thought
have cut some old roses from the garden of Ronsard;
but the new lotions and feathers are not for me;
I am not one of the blue jays who sing so well.

I dislike hollow tenors who warble of love,
and the chorus of crickets singing to the moon.
I fall silent so as to separate voices from echoes,
and I listen among the voices to one voice and only one.

Am I classic or Romantic? Who knows. I want to leave
my poetry as a fighter leaves his sword, known
for the masculine hand that closed around it,
not for the coded mark of the proud forger.

I talk always to the man who walks along with me;
—men who talk to themselves hope to talk to God
   someday—

My soliloquies amount to discussions with this friend,
who taught me the secret of loving human beings.

   In the end, I owe you nothing; you owe me what I've
      written.
I turn to my work; with what I've earned I pay
for my clothes and hat, the house in which I live,
the food that feeds my body, the bed on which I sleep.

   And when the day arrives for the last leaving of all,
and the ship that never returns to port is ready to go,
you'll find me on board, light, with few belongings,
almost naked like the children of the sea.

ANTONIO MACHADO
translated by R.B.

NAMES

You should try to hear the name the Holy One has for
   things.
There is something in the phrase: "The Holy One taught him
   names."
We name everything according to the number of legs it has;
The holy one names it according to what is inside.
Moses waved his stick; he thought it was a "rod."
But inside its name was "dragonish snake."
We thought the name of Umar meant: "agitator against
   priests";
But in eternity his name is "the one who believes."
No one knows our name until our last breath goes out.

RUMI
version by R.B.

THAT JOURNEYS ARE GOOD

If a fir tree had a foot or two like a turtle, or a wing,
Do you think it would just wait for the saw to enter?

You know the sun journeys all night under the earth;
If it didn't, how could it throw up its flood of light in the
    east?

And salt water climbs with such marvellous swiftness to the
    sky.
If it didn't, how would the cabbages be fed with the rain?

Have you thought of Joseph lately? Didn't he leave his father
    in tears, going?
Didn't he then learn how to understand dreams, and give
    away grain?

Didn't Mohammed set out on a journey to Medina,
And found dominion there and became Shah of a hundred
    lands?

And you, if you have no feet to leave your country, go
Into yourself, become a ruby mine, open to the gifts of the
    sun.

You could travel from your outer man into your inner man.
By a journey of that sort earth became a place where you find
    gold.

So give up your bitterness, and your acidity, and your heavy-
    heartedness.
Don't you realize how many fruits have already escaped out
    of sourness into sweetness?

A good source of sweetness is a teacher, mine is named
  Shams.
You know every fruit grows more handsome in the light of
  the sun.

RUMI
version by R.B.

ADVICE FROM HERACLITUS

Men who love wisdom should acquaint themselves with many particulars.

Eyes and ears are bad witnesses for men with barbarous souls.

Nature loves to hide.

ADVICE FROM PYTHAGORAS

Do not eat the black-tailed fish.

Avoid the flesh of animals that die on their own.

Do not polish a seat with oil.

Never speak when facing the sun.

THE WAKING

I wake to sleep, and take my waking slow.
I feel my fate in what I cannot fear.
I learn by going where I have to go.

We think by feeling. What is there to know?
I hear my being dance from ear to ear.
I wake to sleep, and take my waking slow.

Of those so close beside me, which are you?
God bless the Ground! I shall walk softly there,
And learn by going where I have to go.

Light takes the Tree; but who can tell us how?
The lowly worm climbs up a winding stair;
I wake to sleep, and take my waking slow.

Great Nature has another thing to do
To you and me; so take the lively air,
And, lovely, learn by going where to go.

This shaking keeps me steady. I should know.
What falls away is always. And is near.
I wake to sleep, and take my waking slow.
I learn by going where I have to go.

THEODORE ROETHKE

THE HOLY LONGING

Tell a wise person, or else keep silent,
Because the massman will mock it right away.
I praise what is truly alive,
what longs to be burned to death.

In the calm water of the love-nights,
where you were begotten, where you have begotten,
a strange feeling comes over you
when you see the silent candle burning.

Now you are no longer caught
in the obsession with darkness,
and a desire for higher love-making
sweeps you upward.

Distance does not make you falter,
now, arriving in magic, flying,
and finally, insane for the light,
you are the butterfly and you are gone.

And so long as you haven't experienced
this: to die and so to grow,
you are only a troubled guest
on the dark earth.

GOETHE
translated by R.B.

THIRTEEN

Mother and Great Mother

The Mother of Songs, the mother of our whole seed, bore us in the beginning. She is the mother of all races of men and the mother of all tribes. She is the mother of the thunder, the mother of the rivers, the mother of trees . . . the mother of songs and dances. She is the mother of the older brother stones . . . and of the strangers . . . and the only mother we have.

—*Song of the Kagaba Indians, Colombia*

Our memories are permeated with Mother. Not only do our bodies begin in her body but our psyches begin in hers and remain attached to hers by means of the scenes, feelings, and habits that compose our life. Memory, and therefore Mother, affects us continually. We are and always will be "stuck" in Mother because she is the ground of the experiencing soul. That umbilical cord is never bitten through, even if I put Mom right out of my mind, or pack off my actual mother to a nursing home in a pine forest. *I Remember Mama,* the title of an old Broadway play, tells it like it is because I can't forget Mama. She lives on in the memorial rooms of the soul as the happiness and fear of childhood, family, home, and the earliest desires and pain. She is like a permanent stain, a dominant chord, the warp of the carpet structuring us as we are.

C. G. Jung lists these qualities associated with the mother archetype:

> Maternal solicitude and sympathy; the magic authority of the female principle; the wisdom and spiritual exaltation that transcend reason; also, all that is benign, all that cherishes and sustains, furthers growth and fertility. . . . On the negative side, the mother archetype may connote what devours, seduces, and poisons; it is terrifying and inescapable like fate. I have expressed the ambivalence of these attributes in the phrase "the loving and terrible mother."

Essentially, Jung continues, she brings cherishing and nourishing kindness, orgiastic emotionality, and the Stygian depths of death and the underworld.

In another passage he says of her: "Intimately known and yet strange like Nature, lovingly tender and yet cruel like fate, joyous and the untiring giver of life. . . . Mother is mother-love, is *my* experience, *my* secret." She is the "carrier . . . of that great experience which includes herself and myself and all mankind, and indeed the whole of created nature, the experience of life whose children we are."

As original ground of soul she is also final ground, burial ground in symbolisms worldwide, whether as Maria holding the dead Jesus or Kali dancing among the bones. She goes on triumphant; her sons, her heroes and warriors fall. And so we bring fear to her, and mourning. The great size of these emotions finds its equivalence in the figure of the Great Mother, such as the goddesses in myths and grandmothers, stepmothers, wise women, and witches in fairy tales, those power-ladies who mother a man with care and advice all the while smothering his free spirit. Jung says, "Crudely or delicately, consciously or unconsciously, she cannot help touching in some way upon the son's masculinity." In five of the following poems, the mother's "touch" is presented quite literally as her hand.

By admitting the deep love and equally deep terror Mother inspires, the poems in this section display the range of every mother's greatness. They allow Mother to enter consciousness in the guise of remembrances and mournings, and they muse the memories and sorrows into art.

According to the Greeks, memory (Mnemosyne) is the mother of all the arts, so that art—such as these poems for, to, and about Mother—is the best way "out" of the mother complex, a way of working it so that we please Mother with our art rather than sacrifice to her with our lives. That term, *mother complex,* at its deepest refers to the emotional memories distilled into our most intimate habits of feeling to which we cling as if for survival. We don't want to give up what we require in love, how we style our bodies, what we feel to be homecoming, the fears to which we have become accustomed. This is all mother memory ruling a man's life. She is the continuity of patterns we have lived with for so long that we have become them, thereby living in the ground of her body, still. She persists in these patterns until we can admit to our fascination with—now called addiction to—likes and dislikes that seem so secretly and intimately mine yet attest to my origins in her.

J.H.

Citations from C. G. Jung from "The Psychological Aspects of the Mother Archetype," translated by Cary F. Baynes and Ximena de Angulo, original version (1938), as published in *Spring 1943* and again in *Fathers and Mothers*, Patricia Berry, ed. (Dallas: Spring Publications, 1990), 237, 240, 246.

Here, the man is a boy in his dream perched like a bird, escaping from the protective mothers by soaring to a taller tree. But memory can move, as age moves from thirty to thirty-five, and, instead of warnings and flight, there are the sweet cherries.

CHERRIES

When I was five, we lived in Tesuque,
in a mud house with walls two feet
thick. I dreamt I was perched in
the top of our cherry tree. Mom and
aunt Owane paced in small circles far
below. Cupping their hands, they yelled,
"Come down. You'll fall!" I watched
the wind billow their long dresses,
and soared to a taller tree.

When I was thirty, I remembered this
dream.

When I was thirty-five, I remembered
the cherries were thick, sweet, and
yellow.

JOE LAMB

He is held to his mother's hand by an enchantment that disrupts the wonderful aloneness and enormous riches of the boy's imagination. What grips us like this—the mother? or the entrancing power of memory?

FROM CHILDHOOD

The darkness in the room was like enormous riches;
there the child was sitting, wonderfully alone.
And when the mother entered, as if in a dream,
a glass quaked in the silent china closet.
She felt it, how the room was betraying her,
and kissed the child, saying, "Are you here?"
Then both looked toward the piano in fear,
for often at evening they would have a song
in which the child found himself strangely caught.

He sat stone still. His great gaze hung
upon her hand, which, totally bowed down by the ring,
walked over the white keys
as if plowing through deep drifts of snow.

RAINER MARIA RILKE
translated by R.B.

Seduction is subtle, and "abuse" is sometimes hardly different from a touch on the earlobe, a casual caress.

MOTHER AND SON

She goes on with her story,
this woman whose twelve-year-old son
has drifted into the party;
her mind is still with the guests.
But her flesh has claimed possession of his.

She pushes his hair back from his eyes,
curls a lock of it around her finger,
while continuing to entertain us
with her wit. The touch of her hand
embarrasses him, but only a little;
he shrugs slightly, that is all.
Now she smiles at him
as if conscious of his presence
for the first time.
It's a loving smile, of course,
but not altogether a friendly one:
there's a pride in that smile
and a sense of power,
even a hint of cruelty. She's a normal parent.

She pinches his earlobe now, plays with the buttons
on his shirt, talking with us all the while.
He wriggles for an instant, and then
surrenders, half-gratefully,
half-resentfully, to her caresses.

They both know she's the stronger,
that she'll be the stronger for a while yet,
that he couldn't break away from her
even if he could make up his mind
that it's what he wants.

ALDEN NOWLAN

The mother's puer-son, that high-flying, sharp-eyed falcon, returns to her hand no matter how far he flies. One psychological trait after another unfolds from the poem's rhythm: the urge to be perfect; the vicious attack on the hand that feeds you; the hooded, dreamy isolation; the flowery, airy language; and the desire to be carried by her arm forever.

from
MY MOTHER WOULD BE
A FALCONRESS

My mother would be a falconress,
And I her gay falcon treading her wrist,
would fly to bring back
from the blue of the sky to her, bleeding, a prize,
where I dream in my little hood with many bells
jangling when I'd turn my head.

My mother would be a falconress,
and she sends me as far as her will goes.
She lets me ride to the end of her curb
where I fall back in anguish.

I dread that she will cast me away,
for I fall, I mis-take, I fail in her mission.

She would bring down the little birds.
And I would bring down the little birds.
When will she let me bring down the little birds,
pierced from their flight with their necks broken,
their heads like flowers limp from the stem?

I tread my mother's wrist and would draw blood.
Behind the little hood my eyes are hooded.
I have gone back into my hooded silence,
talking to myself and dropping off to sleep.

For she has muffled my dreams in the hood she has made
   me,
sewn round with bells, jangling when I move.
She rides with her little falcon upon her wrist.
She uses a barb that brings me to cower.
She sends me abroad to try my wings
and I come back to her. I would bring down
the little birds to her
I may not tear into, I must bring back perfectly.
I tear at her wrist with my beak to draw blood,
and her eye holds me, anguisht, terrifying.
She draws a limit to my flight.
Never beyond my sight, she says.

She trains me to fetch and to limit myself in fetching.
She rewards me with meat for my dinner.
But I must never eat what she sends me to bring her.

Yet it would have been beautiful, if she would have carried
   me,
always, in a little hood with the bells ringing,
at her wrist, and her riding
to the great falcon hunt, and me
flying up to the curb of my heart from her heart
to bring down the skylark from the blue to her feet,
straining, and then released for the flight. . . .

ROBERT DUNCAN

Mother and Great Mother

THE RIGHT MEANING

"Mother, you know there is a place somewhere called Paris. It's a huge place and a long way off and it really is huge."

My mother turns up my coat collar, not because it's starting to snow, but in order that it may start.

My father's wife is in love with me, walking up, always keeping her back to my birth, and her face toward my death. Because I am hers twice: by my good-bye and by my coming home. When I return home, I close her. That is why her eyes gave me so much, pronounced innocent of me, caught in the act of me, everything occurs through finished arrangements, through convenants carried out.

Has my mother confessed me, has she been named publicly? Why doesn't she give so much to my other brothers? To Victor, for example, the oldest, who is so old now that people say, "He looks like his father's youngest brother!" It must be because I have traveled so much! It must be because I have lived more!

My mother gives me illuminated permissions to explore my coming-home tales. Face to face with my returning-home life, remembering that I journeyed for two whole hearts through her womb, she blushes and goes deathly pale when I say in the discourse of the soul: "That night I was happy!" But she grows more sad, she grew more sad.

"How old you're getting, son!"

And she walks firmly through the color yellow to cry, because I seem to her to be getting old, on the blade of the sword, in the delta of my face. Weeps with me, grows sad with me. Why should my youth be necessary, if I will always be her son? Why do mothers feel pain when their sons get old, if their age will never equal anyway the age of the mothers? And why, if the sons, the more they get on, merely come nearer to the age of the fathers? My mother cries because I am old in my time and because I will never get old enough to be old in hers!

My good-byes left from a point in her being more toward the outside than the point in her being to which I come back. I am, because I am so overdue coming back, more the man to my mother than the son to my mother. The purity that lights us both now with three flames lies precisely in that. I say then until I finally fall silent:

"Mother, you know there is a place somewhere called Paris. It's a huge place and a long way off and it really is huge."

The wife of my father, hearing my voice, goes on eating her lunch, and her eyes that will die descend gently along my arms.

CÉSAR VALLEJO
translated by R.B.

KADDISH

Mother of my birth, for how long were we together
in your love and my adoration of your self?
For the shadow of a moment as I breathed your pain
and you breathed my suffering, as we knew
of shadows in lit rooms that would swallow the light.

Your face beneath the oxygen tent was alive
but your eyes were closed. Your breathing was hoarse
but your sleep was with death. I was alone with you
as it was when I was young but only alone now
and now with you. I was to be alone forever
as I was learning, watching you become alone.

Earth is your mother as you were mine, my earth,
my sustenance, my comfort and my strength
and now without you I turn to your mother
and seek from her that I may meet you again
in rock and stone: whisper to the stone,
I love you; whisper to the rock, I found you;
whisper to earth, Mother, I have found my mother
and I am safe and always have been.

DAVID IGNATOW

SONNET TO MY MOTHER

Most near, most dear, most loved and most far,
Under the window where I often found her
Sitting as huge as Asia, seismic with laughter,
Gin and chicken helpless in her Irish hand,
Irresistible as Rabelais but most tender for
The lame dogs and hurt birds that surround her,—
She is a procession no one can follow after
But be like a little dog following a brass band.
She will not glance up at the bomber or condescend
To drop her gin and scuttle to a cellar,
But lean on the mahogany table like a mountain
Whom only faith can move, and so I send
O all her faith and all my love to tell her
That she will move from mourning into morning.

GEORGE BARKER

IN MEMORY OF MY MOTHER

I do not think of you lying in the wet clay
Of a Monaghan graveyard; I see
You walking down a lane among the poplars
On your way to the station, or happily

Going to second Mass on a summer Sunday—
You meet me and you say:
"Don't forget to see about the cattle—"
Among your earthiest words the angels stray.

And I think of you walking along a headland
Of green oats in June,
So full of repose, so rich with life—
And I see us meeting at the end of a town

On a fair day by accident, after
The bargains are all made and we can walk
Together through the shops and stalls and markets
Free in the oriental streets of thought.

O you are not lying in the wet clay,
For it is a harvest evening now and we
Are piling up the ricks against the moonlight
And you smile up at us—eternally.

PATRICK KAVANAGH

THE LAST WORDS
OF MY ENGLISH GRANDMOTHER

There were some dirty plates
and a glass of milk
beside her on a small table
near the rank, disheveled bed—

Wrinkled and nearly blind
she lay and snored
rousing with anger in her tones
to cry for food,

Gimme something to eat—
They're starving me—
I'm all right I won't go
to the hospital. No, no, no

Give me something to eat
Let me take you
to the hospital, I said
and after you are well

you can do as you please.
She smiled, Yes
you do what you please first
then I can do what I please—

Oh, oh, oh! she cried
as the ambulance men lifted
her to the stretcher—
Is this what you call

making me comfortable?
By now her mind was clear—
Oh you think you're smart
you young people,

she said, but I'll tell you
you don't know anything.
Then we started.
On the way

we passed a long row
of elms. She looked at them
awhile out of
the ambulance window and said,

What are all those
fuzzy-looking things out there?
Trees? Well, I'm tired
of them and rolled her head away.

WILLIAM CARLOS WILLIAMS

I AM ASKING YOU
TO COME BACK HOME

I am asking you to come back home
before you lose the chance of seein' me alive.
You already missed your daddy.
You missed your uncle Howard.
You missed Luciel.
I kept them and I buried them.
You showed up for the funerals.
Funerals are the easy part.

You even missed that dog you left.
I dug him a hole and put him in it.
It was a Sunday morning, but dead animals
don't wait no better than dead people.

My mamma used to say she could feel herself
runnin' short of the breath of life. So can I.
And I am blessed tired of buryin' things I love.
Somebody else can do that job to me.
You'll be back here then; you come for funerals.

I'd rather you come back now and got my stories.
I've got whole lives of stories that belong to you.
I could fill you up with stories,
stories I ain't told nobody yet,
stories with your name, your blood in them.
Ain't nobody gonna hear them if you don't
and you ain't gonna hear them unless you get back home.

When I am dead, it will not matter
how hard you press your ear to the ground.

JO CARSON

Mother and Great Mother

A man's idealized love, as well as his panic and hatred, in regard to his mother may all be because he can never really know her. Most simply, she is a woman, the eternal other, separated by the laws of gender. An Ethiopian woman reportedly made this speech to a European anthropologist to make clear what a man cannot ever know about the phenomenon Mother.

KORE

"How can a man know what a woman's life is? A woman's life is quite different from a man's. God has ordered it so. A man is the same from the time of his withering. He is the same before he has sought out a woman for the first time, and afterwards. But the day when a woman enjoys her first love cuts her in two. She becomes another woman on that day. The man is the same after his first love as he was before. The woman is from the day of her first love another that continues all through life. The man spends a night by a woman and goes away. His life and body are always the same. The woman conceives. As a mother she is another person than the woman without child. She carries the fruit of the night for nine months in her body. Something grows. Something grows into her life that never again departs from it. She is a mother. She is and remains a mother even though her child dies. For at one time she carried the child under her heart. And it does not go out of her heart ever again. Not even when it is dead. All this, the man does not know, he knows nothing. He does not know the difference before love and after love, before motherhood and after motherhood. He can know nothing. Only a woman can know that and speak of that. That is why we won't be told what to do by our husbands. A woman can only do one thing. She can respect herself. She can keep herself decent. She must always be as her nature is. She must always be maiden and always be mother. Before every love she is a maiden, after every love she is a mother. In this you can see if she is a good woman or not.

AN ETHIOPIAN WOMAN
as reported by Carl Kerényi

Behind each mother is a greatness, the Great Mother, whom Barker de-
scribed as seismic with laughter, and Kavanagh as smiling eternally. This
greatness brings an ample joy to life, as if we are all bouncing in her lap;
it also gives her hand such a hold. Here Robert Graves brings in the
symbolisms that extend her range to the ordered stars above and coiled
snake below. In view of this sublime power, as large as the cosmos, it is
best, Graves says, to "dwell on her graciousness, dwell on her smiling."

TO JUAN
AT THE WINTER SOLSTICE

There is one story and one story only
That will prove worth your telling,
Whether as learned bard or gifted child;
To it all lines or lesser gauds belong
That startle with their shining
Such common stories as they stray into.

Is it of trees you tell, their months and virtues,
Of strange beasts that beset you,
Of birds that croak at you the Triple will?
Or of the Zodiac and how slow it turns
Below the Boreal Crown,
Prison of all true kings that ever reigned?

Water to water, ark again to ark,
From woman back to woman:
So each new victim treads unfalteringly
The never altered circuit of his fate,
Bringing twelve peers as witness
Both to his starry rise and starry fall.

Or is it of the Virgin's silver beauty,
All fish below the thighs?
She in her left hand bears a leafy quince;
When with her right hand she crooks a finger, smiling,

How may the King hold back?
Royally then he barters life for love.

Or of the undying snake from chaos hatched,
Whose coils contain the ocean,
Into whose chops with naked sword he springs,
Then in black water, tangled by the reeds,
Battles three days and nights,
To be spewed up beside her scalloped shore?

Much snow is falling, winds roar hollowly,
The owl hoots from the elder,
Fear in your heart cries to the loving-cup:
Sorrow to sorrow as the sparks fly upward.
The log groans and confesses
There is one story and one story only.

Dwell on her graciousness, dwell on her smiling,
Do not forget what flowers
The great boar trampled down in ivy time.
Her brow was creamy as the long ninth wave,
Her sea-blue eyes were wild.
But nothing promised that is not performed.

ROBERT GRAVES

THE THIEF

Having myself been scared silly when I was young
of any girl made of flesh and, God help us, blood,
I am in sympathy with the boy, said to be slow but not
    retarded,
who has been taken into custody for stealing panties
from the laundry rooms in our apartment building.
They say he had a trunkful of them. It reminds me
of those other thieves, treated as praiseworthy,
in the old folk tales; Jack of Jack and the Beanstalk
climbing in through a window of a castle to snitch a harp;
it was no crime to rob a giant in those days.
If the King heard about it, he gave the thief his daughter
in marriage; and, as everybody knows that carried with it a
    guarantee
of living happily ever after. Mind you, that was well before
the invention of panties; for that matter, drawers of any kind
are believed to have been unknown before the 16th century
and, naturally, are first mentioned in a sermon
by the Cardinal-Archbishop of Milan in which he said that
    God Almighty
intended women to keep her bottom bare, in remembrance
of Mother Eve's weakness. All that was long, long ago,
and once upon a time; but I can tell you this from
    experience:
that to a boy like that—who would even today trade his
    cow, if he had one,
for a handful of beans, not so much because he was a fool
as because he was too bashful to argue, and afterwards
hate himself with an almost murderous hatred for being such
    a bumpkin—
to a boy like that, every female, without exception,
is a giantess, ready and able to grind his bones to bake her
    bread.

ALDEN NOWLAN

The giantess may also appear in the shopping mall.

WHAT I HEARD
AT THE DISCOUNT DEPARTMENT STORE

Don't touch that. And stop your whining too.
Stop it. I mean it. You know I do.
If you don't stop, I'll give you fucking something
to cry about right here
and don't you think I won't either.

So she did. She slapped him across the face.
And you could hear the snap of flesh against the flesh
halfway across the store. Then he wasn't whining anymore.
Instead, he wept. His little body heaved and shivered and
    wept.
He was seven or eight. She was maybe thirty.
Above her left breast, the pin said: Nurse's Aide.

Now they walk hand in hand down the aisle
between the tables piled with tennis shoes
and underpants and plastic bags of socks.

I told you I would. You knew I would.
You can't get away with shit like that with me,
you know you can't.
You're not in school anymore
You're with your mother now.
You can get away with fucking murder there,
but you can't get away with shit like that with me.

Stop that crying now I say
or I'll give you another little something
like I did before.

Stop that now. You'd better stop.

That's better. That's a whole lot better.
You know you can't do that with me.
You're with your mother now.

DAVID BUDBILL

THE WITCH

1

I have cut the plaintain grove
I have taken off my clothes
I have learnt from my mother-in-law
How to eat my husband
On the hills the wind blows
I have cut the thatching grass
I have grown weary
Weary of eating rice

2

The weapons are ready
The axe glitters
Over the smooth verandah
The wasps are swarming
O Bagru leave us
Kill the young servants
Kill the girls, kill the boys

SANTAL
India

She had opened an immense hole in the soft ground, which she quickly digs up with her skeleton fingers, and bending her ribs and inclining her white smooth skull, she heaps together in the abyss old men and youths, women and children, cold, pale, and stiff, whose lids she silently closes.

"Ah," sighs the dreamer, who sadly and with heavy heart sees her accomplish her work, "accursed, accursed be thou, destroyer of beings, detestable and cruel Death, and mayest thou be dominated and desolated by the ever-renewed floods of mortal life!"

The grave-digger has arisen. She turns her face; she is now made of pink and charming flesh; her friendly brow is crowned with rosy corals. She bears in her arms fair naked children, who laugh to the sky, and she says softly to the dreamer, while gazing at him with eyes full of joy:

"I am she who accomplishes without cease and without end the transformation of all. Beneath my fingers the flowers that have become cinders bloom once more, and I am both She whom thou namest Death, and She whom thou namest Life!"

THÉODORE DE BANVILLE
translated by Stuart Merrill

Nikki Giovanni calls this chant "Ego Tripping." Some ego! But not the one we learn about in psychology. This is a poem in the "I am" tradition. It raises the spirit by exaggeration, extending the imagination to the four corners of the earth and the farthest reaches of history. It says, Your mother isn't just a me; she's a myth. Of course, she's too much! The poem tells what really lies within a man's complaint that his mother is egocentric.

EGO TRIPPING
(there may be a reason why)

I was born in the congo
I walked to the fertile crescent and built
     the sphinx
I designed a pyramid so tough that a star
     that only glows every one hundred years falls
     into the center giving divine perfect light
I am bad

I sat on the throne
     drinking nectar with allah
I got hot and sent an ice age to europe
     to control my thirst
My oldest daughter is nefertiti
     the tears from my birth pains
     created the nile
I am a beautiful woman

I gazed on the forest and burned
     out the sahara desert
     with a packet of goat's meat
     and a change of clothes
I crossed it in two hours
I am a gazelle so swift
     so swift you can't catch me

For a birthday present when he was three
I gave my son hannibal an elephant
        he gave me rome for mother's day
My strength flows ever on

My son noah built new/ark and
I stood proudly at the helm
        as we sailed on a soft summer day
I turned myself into myself and was
        jesus
        men intone my loving name
        All praises All praises
I am the one who would save

I sowed diamonds in my back yard
My bowels deliver uranium
        the filings from my fingernails are
        semi-precious jewels
        On a trip north
I caught a cold and blew
My nose giving oil to the arab world
I am so hip even my errors are correct
I sailed west to reach east and had to round off
        the earth as I went
        The hair from my head thinned and gold was laid
        across three continents

I am so perfect so divine so ethereal so surreal
I cannot be comprehended
        except by my permission

I mean . . . I . . . can fly
        like a bird in the sky . . .

NIKKI GIOVANNI

BIRDS NEST

Birds nest in my arms,
on my shoulders, behind my knees,
between my breasts there are quails,
they must think I'm a tree.
The swans think I'm a fountain,
they all come down and drink when I talk.
When sheep pass, they pass over me,
and perched on my fingers, the sparrows eat,
the ants think I'm earth,
and men think I'm nothing.

GLORIA FUERTES
translated by Philip Levine

OLD WOMAN NATURE

Old Woman Nature
naturally has a bag of bones
tucked away somewhere.
a whole room full of bones!

A scattering of hair and cartilage
bits in the woods.

A fox scat with hair and a tooth in it.
a shellmound
a bone flake in a streambank.

A purring cat, crunching
the mouse head first,
eating on down toward the tail—

The sweet old woman
calmly gathering firewood in the
moon . . .

Don't be shocked,
She's heating you some soup.

VII, '81, Seeing Ichikawa Ennosuke
in "Kurozuka"—"Demoness"—
at the Kabuki-za in Tokyo

GARY SNYDER

FOURTEEN

The
Spindrift Gaze
Toward Paradise

A man deprived of the function of unreality is just
as neurotic as the man deprived of the function of
reality.

—GASTON BACHELARD
translated by Colette Gaudin

Moments come when we feel outside time, seized by a long-ing, moved by an image, in touch with invisible voices. We realize that we do not live in one world only. As Rilke says, "[W]e are grasped by what we cannot grasp." And James Wright says, "The air fills with delicate creatures / From the other world." Something beyond life lives within life and calls the soul. Several of the following poems warn about forgetting this fact. I don't hear these voices if I am, as Wright says, "lost in myself." The gaze beyond narrows to tunnel vision inward, and we miss what else there might be. Repair of the soul ("the damage I have done to myself," as Kabir says) and focus on the job at hand are only half; a man has metaphysical tasks, too. Unless his spirit ventures toward the invisible, a man will be unable to perform the daily round with purpose. He will have little joy, only duty —and rebelliousness. The deepest cause of our discontent and of our confused yearnings is the loss of Paradise. The human soul needs anchoring in something beyond itself, in that vision which is the ground of all initiations, a vision which hints that life on earth reflects ideals of perfection.

The first initiation of youth detaches a man from the inno-cence of Paradise, releasing his strength into the world. Later initiations open the eyes and ears to further realities. Religions describe these realities literally as "above" and "beyond," and locate them in "heaven." The longing for the "heavenly" affects much of what we do. We idealize our loves, our children, our projects and intentions, because an image of Paradise lies at the root of wanting to do the right thing and to make things better. An urge to perfection calls every one of us. And although utopias may never be fully realized, the urge toward ideal love and beauty never lets go of human nature. The mind wants to break out of the skull and think its way to the stars just as the heart's beat cannot be held in a rib cage. Desire yearns for "more" and calls this more, Paradise. The gaze above and beyond seems an archetypal requisite of the soul to live a life on earth with passionate purpose.

An otherwordly longing becomes particularly necessary for older age, according to Yeats's majestic poem "Sailing to Byzantium." "An aged man is but a paltry thing, / A tattered coat upon a stick" unless he transcends the mortal fall by envisioning eternal images.

The ecstatic traditions of Rumi and Kabir insist that transcendent joy and love are immediately close. "Byzantium" is right at hand, if you "[s]ay *yes* quickly" (Rumi). "Those who hope to be reasonable about it fail," says Kabir. These schools teach the work of loss and surrender, a sinking that is also a lifting. Emily Dickinson, too, speaks of "surrender."

Surrender to what? First of all, surrender to the yearning itself (which the Greeks called *pothos* and the German Romantics, *Sehnsucht*)—and this disciplines desire by *not* fulfilling it. We learn that this longing cannot be satisfied, is not meant to be satisfied, because the soul gazes beyond toward Paradise. So yearning keeps the soul "in growing orbits, / which move out over the things of the world" (Rilke), searching, asking, risking "even if we do not reach it" (Rilke).

At some point, however, we furl the sails and let the questing come to rest. It becomes less a matter of seeking Paradise than of receiving its gifts. Perhaps, this too is a surrender. Instead of your knocking on the door, it swings on its own hinges. Or maybe you and the door, both unhinged. No longer on a journey, you are simply at home waiting for guests. So the great mystical philosopher Plotinus, speaking of his relation with the figures of "paradise," said: "It is for them to come to me, not for me to go to them." I think he is saying, You don't will yourself upward and out of this world with ascetic struggle. Rather, keep alert for visitations. Even "this concrete world" is "full of souls," sings Bob Dylan.

We would like otherworldly visitations to come as distinct voices with clear instructions, but they may only give small signs in dreams, or as sudden hunches and insights that cannot be denied. They feel more as if they emerge from inside and steer you from within like an inner guardian angel, who, as Rolf Jacobsen says, puts its "mouth against your heart / though you're not aware of it." And, most amazing, it has never forgotten you, although you may have spent most of your life ignoring it. Sometimes when you sink into yourself and listen or when you talk with a particularly moving or beautiful figure of your dream an utterly surprising window opens.

But that open window is also "dangerous," according to Felix Pollak, even unbalancing. Several of the poems speak of falling. These moments outside time can feel like death, and philosophers like Socrates and Spinoza consider the aim of life to be the study of "dying." I understand them to be agreeing with Rumi and Kabir—open your heart, your gaze, to the visitations of angels, even if the gifts they bring may not be centeredness and balance but eccentricity and a wholly unfamiliar sense of pleasure called joy.

J.H.

CONVERSATION IN THE MOUNTAINS

If you were to ask me why I dwell among green mountains,
I should laugh silently; my soul is serene.
The peach blossom follows the moving water;
There is another heaven and earth beyond the world of men.

LI PO
translated by Robert Payne

I THINK CONTINUALLY OF THOSE

I think continually of those who were truly great.
Who, from the womb, remembered the soul's history
Through corridors of light where the hours are suns,
Endless and singing. Whose lovely ambition
Was that their lips, still touched with fire,
Should tell of the spirit clothed from head to foot in song.
And who hoarded from the spring branches
The desires falling across their bodies like blossoms.

What is precious is never to forget
The delight of the blood drawn from ageless springs
Breaking through rocks in worlds before our earth;
Never to deny its pleasure in the simple morning light,
Nor its grave evening demand for love;
Never to allow gradually the traffic to smother
With noise and fog the flowering of the spirit.

Near the snow, near the sun, in the highest fields
See how these names are fêted by the waving grass,
And by the streamers of white cloud,
And whispers of wind in the listening sky;
The names of those who in their lives fought for life,
Who wore at their hearts the fire's center.
Born of the sun they traveled a short while towards the sun,
And left the vivid air signed with their honor.

STEPHEN SPENDER

As Spender tells of an "ambition . . . clothed from head to foot in song,"
Rilke imagines the very being of man as a great song. And both say that
for this song to sing through you, to be you, you must live life ever more
widely. And that is just what ambition means: walking the ambit, going
the limits of the perimeter in ever-growing orbits.

I LIVE MY LIFE

I live my life in growing orbits,
which move out over the things of the world.
Perhaps I can never achieve the last,
but that will be my attempt.

I am circling around God, around the ancient tower,
and I have been circling for a thousand years,
and I still don't know if I am a falcon, or a storm,
or a great song.

RAINER MARIA RILKE
translated by R.B.

A WALK

My eyes already touch the sunny hill,
going far ahead of the road I have begun.
So we are grasped by what we cannot grasp;
it has its inner light, even from a distance—

and changes us, even if we do not reach it,
into something else, which, hardly sensing it, we already are;
a gesture waves us on, answering our own wave . . .
but what we feel is the wind in our faces.

Muzot, March 1924

RAINER MARIA RILKE
translated by R.B.

MILKWEED

While I stood here, in the open, lost in myself,
I must have looked a long time
Down the corn rows, beyond grass,
The small house,
White walls, animals lumbering toward the barn.
I look down now. It is all changed.
Whatever it was I lost, whatever I wept for
Was a wild, gentle thing, the small dark eyes
Loving me in secret.
It is here. At a touch of my hand,
The air fills with delicate creatures
From the other world.

JAMES WRIGHT

THE INVISIBLE MEN

There is a tribe of invisible men
who move around us like shadows—have you felt them?
They have bodies like ours and live just like us,
using the same kind of weapons and tools.
You can see their tracks in the snow sometimes
and even their igloos
but never the invisible men themselves.
They cannot be seen except when they die
for then they become visible.

It once happened that a human woman
married one of the invisible men.
He was a good husband in every way:
He went out hunting and brought her food,
and they could talk together like any other couple.
But the wife could not bear the thought
that she did not know what the man she married looked like.
One day when they were both at home
she was so overcome with curiosity to see him
that she stabbed with a knife where she knew he was sitting.
And her desire was fulfilled:
Before her eyes a handsome young man fell to the floor.
but he was cold and dead, and too late
she realized what she had done,
and sobbed her heart out.

When the invisible men heard about this murder
they came out of their igloos to take revenge.
Their bows were seen moving through the air
and the bow strings stretching as they aimed their arrows.
The humans stood there helplessly
for they had no idea what to do or how to fight
because they could not see their assailants.
But the invisible men had a code of honor

that forbade them to attack opponents
who could not defend themselves,
so they did not let their arrows fly,
and nothing happened; there was no battle after all
and everyone went back to their ordinary lives.

NAKASAK
Eskimo
translated by Edward Field

THREE ANGELS

Three angels up above the street,
Each one playing a horn,
Dressed in green robes with wings that stick out,
They've been there since Christmas morn.
The wildest cat from Montana passes by in a flash,
Then a lady in a bright orange dress,
One U-Haul trailer, a truck with no wheels,
The Tenth Avenue bus going west.
The dogs and pigeons fly up and they flutter around,
A man with a badge skips by,
Three fellas crawlin' on their way back to work,
Nobody stops to ask why.
The bakery truck stops outside of that fence
Where the angels stand high on their poles,
The driver peeks out, trying to find one face
In this concrete world full of souls.
The angels play on their horns all day,
The whole earth in progression seems to pass by.
But does anyone hear the music they play,
Does anyone even try?

BOB DYLAN

GUARDIAN ANGEL

I am the bird that flutters against your window in the
   morning,
and your closest friend, whom you can never know,
blossoms that light up for the blind.

I am the glacier shining over the woods, so pale,
and heavy voices from the cathedral tower.
The thought that suddenly hits you in the middle of the day
and makes you feel so fantastically happy.

I am the one you have loved for many years.
I walk beside you all day and look intently at you
and put my mouth against your heart
though you're not aware of it.

I am your third arm, and your second
shadow, the white one,
whom you cannot accept,
and who can never forget you.

ROLF JACOBSEN
translated by R.B.

A MAN LOST BY A RIVER

There is a voice inside the body.

There is a voice and a music,
a throbbing, four-chambered pear
that wants to be heard, that sits
alone by the river with its mandolin
and its torn coat, and sings
for whomever will listen
a song that no one wants to hear.

But sometimes, lost,
on his way to somewhere significant,
a man in a long coat, carrying
a briefcase, wanders into the forest.

He hears the voice and the mandolin,
he sees the thrush and the dandelion,
and he feels the mist rise over the river.

And his life is never the same,
for this having been lost—
for having strayed from the path of his routine,
for no good reason.

MICHAEL BLUMENTHAL

Tranströmer notices how strange churches seem in a totally secular welfare state. The Swedes are like Nicodemus the Forgetful in the Gospel of John. Still, the bells ring even if buried, he says, and you are on the way even if you don't know where you are going.

THE SCATTERED CONGREGATION

I

We got ready and showed our home.
The visitor thought: you live well.
The slum must be inside you.

2

Inside the church, pillars and vaulting
white as plaster, like the cast
around the broken arm of faith.

3

Inside the church there's a begging bowl
that slowly lifts from the floor
and floats along the pews.

4

But the church bells have gone underground.
They're hanging in the drainage pipes.
Whenever we take a step, they ring.

5

Nicodemus the sleepwalker is on his way
to the Address. Who's got the Address?
Don't know. But that's where we're going.

TOMAS TRANSTRÖMER
translated by R.B.

Other invisible voices—cynical, conventional, clever—try to dissuade us.
They laugh at our heart's longing. They would kill the spirit, as the voice
in Bukowski's lines that follow. You have to know who shares your house
and whispers through the walls. Pollak's poem slyly discriminates among
the voices, while Rumi warns against smart Freudian-style reductions and
biological explanations that serve only to keep us in the dark. So, too, he
says, does hanging on to your anger.

THE SECRET

don't worry, nobody has the
beautiful lady, not really, and
nobody has the strange and
hidden power, nobody is
exceptional or wonderful or
magic, they only seem to be.
it's all a trick, an in, a con,
don't buy it, don't believe it.
the world is packed with
billions of people whose lives
and deaths are useless and
when one of these jumps up
and the light of history shines
upon them, forget it, it's not
what it seems, it's just
another act to fool the fools
again.

there are no strong men, there
are no beautiful women.
at least, you can die knowing
this
and you will have
the only possible
victory.

CHARLES BUKOWSKI

The Spindrift Gaze Toward Paradise

THE DREAM

He dreamed of
an open window.
A vagina, said
his psychiatrist.
Your divorce, said
his mistress.
Suicide, said
an ominous voice within him.
It means you should close the window
or you'll catch cold, said
his mother.
His wife said
nothing.
He dared not tell her
such a
dangerous dream.

FELIX POLLAK

THE LIGHT YOU GIVE OFF

The light you give off
did not come from a pelvis.
Your features did not begin in semen.
Don't try to hide inside anger
radiance that cannot be hidden.

RUMI
translated by Coleman Barks and John Moyne

LEDA

When the god, needing something, decided to become a
   swan,
he was astounded how lovely the bird was;
he was dizzy as he disappeared into the swan.
But his deceiving act soon pulled him into the doing,

before he had a chance to test all the new feelings
inside the being. And the woman, open to him,
recognized the One Soon To Be Born
and she knew: what he asked for

was something which, confused in her defending, she
could no longer keep from him. He pressed closer
and pushing his neck through her less and less firm hand

let the god loose into the darling woman.
Then for the first time he found his feathers marvelous
and lying in her soft place he became a swan.

RAINER MARIA RILKE
translated by R.B.

A BLESSING

Just off the highway to Rochester, Minnesota,
Twilight bounds softly forth on the grass.
And the eyes of those two Indian ponies
Darken with kindness.
They have come gladly out of the willows
To welcome my friend and me.
We step over the barbed wire into the pasture
Where they have been grazing all day, alone.
They ripple tensely, they can hardly contain their happiness
That we have come.
They bow shyly as wet swans. They love each other.
There is no loneliness like theirs.
At home once more,
They begin munching the young tufts of spring in the
    darkness.
I would like to hold the slenderer one in my arms,
For she has walked over to me
And nuzzled my left hand.
She is black and white,
Her mane falls wild on her forehead,
And the light breeze moves me to caress her long ear
That is delicate as the skin over a girl's wrist.
Suddenly I realize
That if I stepped out of my body I would break
Into blossom.

JAMES WRIGHT

TWO YEARS LATER

The hollow eyes of shock remain
Electric sockets burnt out in the
      skull.

The beauty of men never disappears
But drives a blue car through the
           stars.

JOHN WIENERS

THE GUEST IS INSIDE

The Guest is inside you, and also inside me;
you know the sprout is hidden inside the seed.
We are all struggling; none of us has gone far.
Let your arrogance go, and look around inside.

The blue sky opens out farther and farther,
the daily sense of failure goes away,
the damage I have done to myself fades,
a million suns come forward with light,
when I sit firmly in that world.

I hear bells ringing that no one has shaken,
inside "love" there is more joy than we know of,
rain pours down, although the sky is clear of clouds,
there are whole rivers of light.
The universe is shot through in all parts by a single sort of
   love.
How hard it is to feel that joy in all our four bodies!

Those who hope to be reasonable about it fail.
The arrogance of reason has separated us from that love.
With the word "reason" you already feel miles away.

How lucky Kabir is, that surrounded by all this joy
he sings inside his own little boat.
His poems amount to one soul meeting another.
These songs are about forgetting dying and loss.
They rise above both coming in and going out.

KABIR
version by R.B.

SAY YES QUICKLY

Forget your life. Say *God is Great*. Get up.
You think you know what time it is. It's time to pray.
You've carved so many little figurines, too many.
Don't knock on any random door like a beggar.
Reach your long hand out to another door, beyond where
you go on the street, the street
where everyone says, "How are you?"
and no one says *How aren't you?*

Tomorrow you'll see what you've broken and torn tonight,
thrashing in the dark. Inside you
there's an artist you don't know about.
He's not interested in how things look different in
   moonlight.

If you are here unfaithfully with us,
you're causing terrible damage.
If you've opened your loving to God's love,
you're helping people you don't know
and have never seen.

Is what I say true? Say *yes* quickly,
if you know, if you've known it
from before the beginning of the universe.

RUMI

translated by Coleman Barks and John Moyne

THE NEW RULE

It's the old rule that drunks have to argue
and get into fights.
The lover is just as bad: He falls into a hole.
But down in that hole he finds something shining,
worth more than any amount of money or power.

Last night the moon came dropping its clothes in the street.
I took it as a sign to start singing,
falling *up* into the bowl of sky.
The bowl breaks. Everywhere is falling everywhere.
Nothing else to do.

Here's the new rule: Break the wineglass,
and fall toward the glassblower's breath.

RUMI

translated by Coleman Barks

Images by Emily Dickinson offer two very different entrances to another world, the one wild, the other safe. In both, reason and will are surrendered.

WILD NIGHTS—WILD NIGHTS!

Wild Nights—Wild Nights!
Were I with thee
Wild Nights should be
Our luxury!

Futile—the Winds—
To a Heart in port—
Done with the Compass—
Done with the Chart!

Rowing in Eden—
Ah, the Sea!
Might I but moor—Tonight—
In Thee!

EMILY DICKINSON

SAFE IN THEIR ALABASTER CHAMBERS

Safe in their Alabaster Chambers—
Untouched by Morning—
And untouched by Noon—
Lie the meek members of the Resurrection—
Rafter of Satin—and Roof of Stone!
Grand go the Years—in the Crescent—above them—
Worlds scoop their Arcs—
And Firmaments—row—
Diadems—drop—and Doges—surrender—
Soundless as dots—on a Disc of Snow—

EMILY DICKINSON
version of 1861

Yeats agreed at the end of his life with Blake that man's highest conscious-ness is not "detachment" or "noninvolvement" but a passionate love of art, and love for the magnificent works of art. By reminding us of eternity, great art teaches the soul to sing louder than human mortality. So Yeats's image for rebirth is a stylized bird that a goldsmith might make.

SAILING TO BYZANTIUM

I

That is no country for old men. The young
In one another's arms, birds in the trees
—Those dying generations—at their song,
The salmon-falls, the mackerel-crowded seas,
Fish, flesh, or fowl, commend all summer long
Whatever is begotten, born, and dies.
Caught in that sensual music all neglect
Monuments of unageing intellect.

II

An aged man is but a paltry thing,
A tattered coat upon a stick, unless
Soul clap its hands and sing, and louder sing
For every tatter in its mortal dress,
Nor is there singing school but studying
Monuments of its own magnificence;
And therefore I have sailed the seas and come
To the holy city of Byzantium.

III

O sages standing in God's holy fire
As in the gold mosaic of a wall,
Come from the holy fire, perne in a gyre,
And be the singing-masters of my soul.

Consume my heart away; sick with desire
And fastened to a dying animal
It knows not what it is; and gather me
Into the artifice of eternity.

IV

Once out of nature I shall never take
My bodily form from any natural thing,
But such a form as Grecian goldsmiths make
Of hammered gold and gold enamelling
To keep a drowsy Emperor awake;
Or set upon a golden bough to sing
To lords and ladies of Byzantium
Of what is past, or passing, or to come.

WILLIAM BUTLER YEATS

This poem is a companion to Moby-Dick. In this excerpt the man loving the sea asks that we not die until we have experienced the intensity of that gaze toward Paradise that the sea animals have already achieved. Crane's extraordinary images, the rhythms and sounds in the lines, all together lift you beyond the ordinary sense of things.

from
VOYAGES II

And yet this great wink of eternity,
Of rimless floods, unfettered leewardings,
Samite sheeted and processioned where
Her undinal vast belly moonward bends,
Laughing the wrapt inflections of our love;

Take this Sea, whose diapason knells
On scrolls of silver snowy sentences,
The sceptred terror of whose sessions rends
As her demeanors motion well or ill,
All but the pieties of lovers' hands.

And onward, as bells off San Salvador
Salute the crocus lustres of the stars,
In these poinsettia meadows of her tides,—
Adagios of islands, O my Prodigal,
Complete the dark confessions her veins spell.

Mark how her turning shoulders wind the hours,
And hasten while her penniless rich palms
Pass superscription of bent foam and wave,—
Hasten, while they are true,—sleep, death, desire,
Close round one instant in one floating flower.

Bind us in time, O Seasons clear, and awe.
O minstrel galleons of Carib fire,
Bequeath us to no earthly shore until
Is answered in the vortex of our grave
The seal's wide spindrift gaze toward paradise.

HART CRANE

FIFTEEN

Zaniness

FATHER WILLIAM
(After Southey)

"You are old, Father William," the young man said,
  "And your hair has become very white;
And yet you incessantly stand on your head—
  Do you think, at your age, it is right?"

"In my youth," Father William replied to his son,
  "I feared it might injure the brain;
But, now that I'm perfectly sure I have none,
  Why, I do it again and again."

—LEWIS CARROLL

The gift of zaniness is one of the great gifts that human beings have. Men love zaniness, love to be in zaniness, love to watch zaniness. The Sioux man rushing up to touch an enemy with a wand and then rushing away is zany. So is the Navajo Trickster, *be'gotcidi*, who played pranks on hunters. Just as a hunter was ready to shoot, he would sneak up, grab the man's testicles, and shout.

The stilts walker is zany. Yeats, defending zaniness, said: "Processions that lack high stilts have nothing that catches the eye." When Yeats goes on about that, we realize that certain rhetorical forms—usually considered literary—are really zany. The old Norse poets loved a zany rhetoric of the image. They refused to call the sea "sea"; it is "the whale's road." The wind is not "wind"—that's too boring—it is "the wolf of the air." A mast is not a mast, but "a thorn," etc. A sail, then, is "a friend of the thorn of the water-cradle that the wolf of the air bites on the whale's road." In a single eight-line poem they pile metaphor on metaphor, so one can hardly tell what the subject matter of the poem is. The joy of their poems is the zany multiplication of images.

Bob Dylan says:

> I like to do just like the rest, I like my
> sugar sweet,
> But guarding fumes and making haste,

It ain't my cup of meat. . . .
But when Quinn the Eskimo gets here,
All the pigeons gonna run to him.
Come all without, come all within,
You'll not see nothing like the mighty
   Quinn.

Or, instead of a multiplication of images, a poet can take just one image and encourage it until it goes beyond all conventional limits.

Suppose you have an elaborate tattoo of an old Western town on your chest, but can't remember where you got it. Or suppose you're playing football. When you take the snap from center, it's not a football but a brown leather oxford. Is it right to throw it downfield? It's a moral question. Louis Jenkins takes up both of those questions.

Russell Edson likes to take a social situation. A man sits down to dinner perhaps expecting roast beef, but his wife serves him a roast ape with a little ribbon around the privates. If you are the poet writing, every detail you add will reveal more of yourself. To preserve the zaniness without collapsing into banality or meaninglessness—that is the discipline.

How stale and flat the day when nothing zany happens. How badly we need jokes: the old Sunday funnies; the comic strips and cartoons; Krazy Kat; Buster Keaton; Stan Laurel; Harpo Marx under his curls and hat squeezing his bulb-horn honker; the Dadaists; and the contorted Yogins swallowing their tongues, eyes popping; the stand-up comedians making silly faces and imitating sounds like vacuum cleaners and espresso machines. The spirit wants to leap with the joy of young kids—both goat and human—to change direction in midair. It is as if the spirit at its freshest and freest is zany, offering no explanation of itself; its justification solely the delight of risk, a flip into nonsense at the same time inventing ideas, words, images, and postures—insane or zany?

The zany poem in general has no message for professors, no moral for moralists to draw, it does not urge you to admire goodness or beauty. The zany poem is a testimony to the beauty of zaniness itself.

R.B., J.H., M.J.M.

NECESSITY

Work?
I don't have to work.
I don't have to do nothing
but eat, drink, stay black, and die.
This little old furnished room's
so small I can't whip a cat
without getting fur in my mouth
and my landlady's so old
her features is all run together
and God knows she sure can overcharge—
Which is why I reckon I *does*
have to work after all.

LANGSTON HUGHES

WALKING THROUGH A WALL

Unlike flying or astral projection, walking through walls is a totally earth-related craft, but a lot more interesting than pot making or driftwood lamps. I got started at a picnic up in Bowstring in the northern part of the state. A fellow walked through a brick wall right there in the park. I said "Say, I want to try that." Stone walls are best, then brick and wood. Wooden walls with fiberglass insulation and steel doors aren't so good. They won't hurt you. If your wall walking is done properly, both you and the wall are left intact. It is just that they aren't pleasant somehow. The worst things are wire fences, maybe it's the molecular structure of the alloy or just the amount of give in a fence, I don't know, but I've torn my jacket and lost my hat in a lot of fences. The best approach to a wall is, first, two hands placed flat against the surface; it's a matter of concentration and just the right pressure. You will feel the dry, cool inner wall with your fingers, then there is a moment of total darkness before you step through on the other side.

LOUIS JENKINS

FOOTBALL

I take the snap from center, fake to the right, fade back . . . I've got protection. I've got a receiver open downfield. . . . What the hell is this? This isn't a football it's a shoe. A man's brown leather oxford. A cousin to a football, maybe, the same skin, but not the same, a thing made for the earth, not the air. I realize that this is a world where anything is possible and I understand, also, that one often has to make do with what one has. I have eaten pancakes, for instance, with that clear corn syrup on them because there was no maple syrup and they weren't very good. Well, anyway, this is different. (My man downfield is waving his arms.) One has certain responsibilities, one has to make choices. This isn't right and I'm not going to throw it.

LOUIS JENKINS

THE LEAVES OF HEAVEN

The leaves of heaven
are ever greene,
& the leaves of the
soul are Sere
& cold

I have failed
my mother
& she has
failed me

Everything about
a human
is doomed
his life, his
things, his
hope, his
work—

The pallbearer
barfs on the
diaper

The phantoms,
The phantoms,
what to do
about the
phantoms?

kiss a hot
wet lightbulb

ED SANDERS

CONFESSIONAL POEM

I have this large tattoo on my chest. It is like a dream I have while I am awake. I see it in the mirror as I shave and brush my teeth, or when I change my shirt or make love. What can I do? I can't remember where I got the tattoo. When in the past did I live such a life? And the price of having such a large tattoo removed must be completely beyond reason. Still, the workmanship of the drawing is excellent, a landscape 8x10 inches in full color, showing cattle going downhill into a small western town. A young man, who might have been my great-grandfather, dressed as a cowboy and holding a rifle, stands at the top of the hill and points down toward the town. The caption beneath the picture reads: "Gosh, I didn't know we were this far west."

LOUIS JENKINS

APPOINTED ROUNDS

At first he refused to deliver junk mail because it was stupid, all those deodorant ads, money-making ideas and contests. Then he began to doubt the importance of the other mail he carried. He began to select first class mail randomly for non-delivery. After he had finished his mail route each day he would return home with his handful of letters and put them in the attic. He didn't open them and never even looked at them again. It was as if he were an agent of Fate, capricious and blind. In the several years before he was caught, friends vanished, marriages failed, business deals fell through. Toward the end he became more and more bold, deleting houses, then whole blocks, from his route. He began to feel he'd been born in the wrong era. If only he could have been a Pony Express rider galloping into some prairie town with an empty bag, or the runner from Marathon collapsing in the streets of Athens, gasping, "No news."

LOUIS JENKINS

QUINN THE ESKIMO
(The Mighty Quinn)

Ev'rybody's building the big ships and the boats,
Some are building monuments,
Others, jotting down notes,
Ev'rybody's in despair,
Ev'ry girl and boy
But when Quinn the Eskimo gets here,
Ev'rybody's gonna jump for joy.
Come all without, come all within,
You'll not see nothing like the mighty Quinn.

I like to do just like the rest, I like my sugar sweet,
But guarding fumes and making haste,
It ain't my cup of meat.
Ev'rybody's 'neath the trees,
Feeding pigeons on a limb
But when Quinn the Eskimo get here,
All the pigeons gonna run to him.
Come all without, come all within,
You'll not see nothing like the mighty Quinn.

A cat's meow and a cow's moo, I can recite 'em all,
Just tell me where it hurts yuh, honey,
And I'll tell you who to call.
Nobody can get no sleep,
There's someone on ev'ryone's toes
But when Quinn the Eskimo gets here,
Ev'rybody's gonna wanna doze.
Come all without, come all within,
You'll not see nothing like the mighty Quinn.

BOB DYLAN

RED LIP

Seventeen years later I sat down on a rock. It was under a tree next to an old abandoned shack that had a sheriff's notice nailed like a funeral wreath to the front door.

NO TRESPASSING
4/17 OF A HAIKU

Many rivers had flowed past those seventeen years, and thousands of trout, and now beside the highway and the sheriff's notice flowed yet another river, the Klamath, and I was trying to get thirty-five miles downstream to Steelhead, the place where I was staying.

It was all very simple. No one would stop and pick me up even though I was carrying fishing tackle. People usually stop and pick up a fisherman. I had to wait three hours for a ride.

The sun was like a huge fifty-cent piece that someone had poured kerosene on and then had lit with a match and said, "Here, hold this while I go get a newspaper," and put the coin in my hand, but never came back.

I had walked for miles and miles until I came to the rock under the tree and sat down. Every time a car would come by, about once every ten minutes, I would get up and stick out my thumb as if it were a bunch of bananas and then sit back down on the rock again.

The old shack had a tin roof colored reddish by years of wear, like a hat worn under the guillotine. A corner of the roof was loose and a hot wind blew down the river and the loose corner clanged in the wind.

A car went by. An old couple. The car almost swerved off the road and into the river. I guess they didn't see many hitch-hikers up there. The car went around the corner with both of them looking back at me.

I had nothing else to do, so I caught salmon flies in my landing net. I made up my own game. It went like this: I

Zaniness
459

couldn't chase after them. I had to let them fly to me. It was something to do with my mind. I caught six.

A little ways up from the shack was an outhouse with its door flung violently open. The inside of the outhouse was exposed like a human face and the outhouse seemed to say, "The old guy who built me crapped in here 9,745 times and he's dead now and I don't want anyone else to touch me. He was a good guy. He built me with loving care. Leave me alone. I'm a monument now to a good ass gone under. There's no mystery here. That's why the door's open. If you have to crap, go in the bushes like the deer."

"Fuck you," I said to the outhouse. "All I want is a ride down the river."

RICHARD BRAUTIGAN

from
A THOUSAND CHINESE DINNERS

From a thousand Chinese dinners, one cookie:
Good fortune in love, also a better position.

So much for both. Too many humorless people
Who can't believe that God could have made the cunt.

Maybe he didn't make it. Maybe hydrogen
Made nitrogen and one thing led to another.

Some hold that early man stumbled upon it
While dreaming of the perfect end to a long day's hunt.

But I say only Italians, with their flavor for drama,
Could have invented this fragrant envelope.

Let's drink to the Italians, especially Catullus,
Who knew it was no joke but couldn't help laughing.

ROBERT MEZEY

WELCOME BACK, MR. KNIGHT:
LOVE OF MY LIFE

Welcome back, Mr. K: Love of My Life—
How's your drinking problem?—your thinking
Problem? you / are / pickling
Your liver—
Gotta / watch / out for the
"Ol Liver": Love of My Life.
How's your dope
Problem?—your marijuana, methadone, and cocaine
Problem / too?—your lustful problem—
How's your weight problem—your eating problem?
How's your lying and cheating and
Staying out all / night long problem?
Welcome back, Mr. K: Love of My Life
How's your pocket / book problem?—your / being
broke problem? you still owe and borrowing mo'
25 dollar problems from other / po / poets?
Welcome back, Mr. K: Love of My Life.
How's your ex-convict problem?—your John Birch
Problem?—your preacher problem?—your fat
Priests sitting in your / chair, saying
How racist and sexist they / will / forever / be
Problem?—How's your Daniel Moynihan
Problem?—your crime in the streets, runaway
Daddy, Black men with dark shades
And bulging crotches problem?
How's your nixon-agnew—j. edgar hoover
Problem?—you still paranoid? still schizoid?—
Still scared shitless?
How's your bullet-thru-the-brain problem?—or
A needle-in-your-arm problem?
Welcome back, Mr. K:—Love of My Life.
You gotta watch / out for the "Ol Liver."
How's your pussy

Problem?—lady-on-top—
smiling like God, titty-in-your-mouth
Problem? Welcome back, Mr. K:
Love of My Life. How's your peace
Problem?—your no / mo' war
Problem—your heart problem—your belly / problem?—
You gotta watch / out for the "Ol Liver."

ETHERIDGE KNIGHT

FREUD TALKS OF THE PRIMAL MEAL

It is the privilege of age to correct the follies of youth—even one's own. Years ago I discovered that children's fantasies interpreting their parents' intercourse as a sadistic act determined the course of their future neuroses. These primal fantasies, as I termed them, circling about the disappearance of parents and the subsequent whispers and strangulated moans from behind closed doors, could so delay dinner, burn the roast, or let the soup get cold, that a child's instinctual gratifications could suffer nearly irreversible damage.

The correction I am now able to bring after decades of silent attention to the fantasies of my patients is not directed at the primal fantasies themselves. The core of the theory has been confirmed in case after case: neurotics suffering from reminiscences. But the focus of this suffering is not, as I thought then, the bed. It is the table! It is not the imagined sadism of the primal scene that harms the child, but the actual sadism of the primal meal.

These reminiscences are usually covered by screen memories of the family romance: the little loving clan gathered around the table, smiling mother spooning warm *Knödels,* bearded father bowed in grace, the children giggling, little kicks and pinches between the chairs, perhaps some *Schmarotzer* of a dear impoverished uncle making jokes.

Then, as the analysis proceeds, the truth is laid bare. The repressed reminiscence returns: one sits again, three years old face-to-face with strained spinach and mashed meat congealing on the plate under the brutal command: "Stop playing around and eat!" The crucial factor here is that of distancing. The small child has no distance between his face and the food: his head is barely six inches from his plate. The sadistic torture of this position is made all the worse by parents with long necks and long arms who ignore the injustice of the child's inferior size. All the while the child is told that only if one eats can one grow.

We thus see how the imagined sadism of the bedroom—

that the parents may be murdering each other—is actually a wish to escape from the terror of the primal meal, and the desire to watch big people in the bedroom actually a conversion of the memory of being watched by big people at the table.

Of the various neurotic symptoms that can be traced back to the primal meal, none is more devastating than carrot envy. The child staring into his soup fixes his or her gaze on a piece of carrot submerged there. "Must I eat that, all of that? It is so big!"

He or she then looks into the soups of siblings, rivalrously discovering that they have what seems a smaller carrot, or better yet, none at all. Intense carrot envy ensues, which emerges in adolescence as a curiosity about all carrot-shaped objects, their size and length—and absence.

But let us return to the primal meal itself and the command: "Stop playing around and eat!"

Here are sown the seeds for that long-lasting opposition between playing around and eating. *Essen ohne Freud,* we call it, a joylessness in food; for playing around has become the alternative to a good dinner. Don Juanism, coupled with the fast-food habit *(consummatio rapida),* can be expected as a consequence.

(This condition, I am told by Minna, is witnessed in modern cinema, where it is the fashion for the flirtatious heroine in restaurant scenes to toy with her food, and for the conquering hero never to pause to see what is in the icebox or make himself a little sandwich. I do not favor the cinema myself; not only because there is never enough time to get there with all that we have to do for dinner, but because when one has seen as many screen memories as I have, who needs celluloid?)

JAMES HILLMAN and CHARLES BOER

THE AUTOMOBILE

A man had just married an automobile.

But I mean to say, said his father, that the automobile is not a person because it is something different.

For instance, compare it to your mother. Do you see how it is different from your mother? Somehow it seems wider, doesn't it? And besides, your mother wears her hair differently.

You ought to try to find something in the world that looks like mother.

I have mother, isn't that enough of a thing that looks like mother? Do I have to gather more mothers?

They are all old ladies who do not in the least excite any wish to procreate, said the son.

But you cannot procreate with an automobile, said father.

The son shows father an ignition key. See, here is a special penis which does with the automobile as the man with the woman; and the automobile gives birth to a place far from this place, dropping its puppy miles as it goes.

Does that make me a grandfather? said father.

That makes you where you are when I am far away, said the son.

Father and mother watch an automobile with a *just married* sign on it growing smaller in a road.

RUSSELL EDSON

APE

You haven't finished your ape, said mother to father, who had monkey hair and blood on his whiskers.

I've had enough monkey, cried father.

You didn't eat the hands, and I went to all the trouble to make onion rings for its fingers, said mother.

I'll just nibble on its forehead, and then I've had enough, said father.

I stuffed its nose with garlic, just like you like it, said mother.

Why don't you have the butcher cut these apes up? You lay the whole thing on the table every night; the same fractured skull, the same singed fur; like someone who died horribly. These aren't dinners, these are post-mortem dissections.

Try a piece of its gum, I've stuffed its mouth with bread, said mother.

Ugh, it looks like a mouth full of vomit. How can I bite into its cheek with bread spilling out of its mouth? cried father.

Break one of the ears off, they're so crispy, said mother.

I wish to hell you'd put underpants on these apes; even a jockstrap, screamed father.

Father, how dare you insinuate that I see the ape as anything more than simple meat, screamed mother.

Well, what's with this ribbon tied in a bow on its privates? screamed father.

Are you saying that I am in love with this vicious creature? That I would submit my female opening to this brute? That after we had love on the kitchen floor I would put him in the oven, after breaking his head with a frying pan; and then serve him to my husband, that my husband might eat the evidence of my infidelity . . . ?

I'm just saying that I'm damn sick of ape every night, cried father.

RUSSELL EDSON

THE OX

There was once a woman whose father over the years had become an ox.

She would hear him alone at night lowing in his room.

It was one day that she looked up into his face that she suddenly noticed the ox.

She cried, you're an ox!

And he began to moo with his great pink tongue hanging out of his mouth.

He would stand over his newspaper, turning the pages with his tongue, while he evacuated on the rug.

When this was brought to his attention he would low with sorrow, and slowly climb the stairs to his room, and there spend the night in mournful lowing.

RUSSELL EDSON

HIGH TALK

Processions that lack high stilts have nothing that catches
the eye.
What if my great-granddad had a pair that were twenty
foot high,
And mine were but fifteen foot, no modern stalks upon
higher,
Some rogue of the world stole them to patch up a fence
or a fire.
Because piebald ponies, led bears, caged lions, make but
poor shows,
Because children demand Daddy-long-legs upon his timber
toes,
Because women in the upper storeys demand a face at the
pane,
That patching old heels they may shriek, I take to chisel
and plane.

Malachi Stilt-Jack am I, whatever I learned has run wild,
From collar to collar, from stilt to stilt, from father to
child.
All metaphor, Malachi, stilts and all. A barnacle goose
Far up in the stretches of night; night splits and the dawn
breaks loose;
I, through the terrible novelty of light, stalk on, stalk on;
Those great sea-horses bare their teeth and laugh at the
dawn.

WILLIAM BUTLER YEATS

SIXTEEN

Loving the World Anyway

I should be content
to look at a mountain
for what it is
and not as a comment
on my life.

—DAVID IGNATOW

We spend so much of our modern urban time shutting out the world. We are busy "getting and spending," in Wordsworth's phrase. And we are depressed, focusing narrowly on our "problems." The world becomes a disturbance. It gets in the way of what has to be done today, or it breaks into our mood with its noisy demands. Rain is a bother; winter nights come too early; things break down and require attention. How can I possibly love a world that consists so largely in Muzak, traffic, and bad coffee? "All is seared with trade; bleared, smeared with toil," Hopkins writes. Besides, I am so preoccupied with my life that I can't follow David Ignatow. Everything I see becomes "a comment on my life." What do I feel about it? What does it mean? How can it do me some good? These reactions built into our psychological wiring show that "my" subjective self is bigger than Ignatow's mountain. I love myself, even meditate upon it to help its growth, to the exclusion of the world.

So how do we love the world anyway? Is there any way to bless it and be blest by it, to use the language of Yeats in the last poems of this section? Despite all my revulsions over its ugliness and injustice, and my bitterness over defeat at its hands, the world remains lovable anyway. But *anyway* also means any which way, any way at all, implying that there are many different openings out of self-enclosure and toward love of the world.

One way I've found is through memory images. When I

feel cut off and so preoccupied that the world around me seems dead, I sometimes turn to recollections of years ago: the empty winter beach in south Jersey where I grew up, the gray sand, sea gulls cawing, and the wet wind coming off the breakers. I believe anybody can find a way into the world: some landscape, a particular room, neighborhood street, a building such as a barn with its smells, or a thing privately treasured, for instance, a baseball glove or a pair of shoes.

"All things are full of Gods" is an ancient Greek saying; "In my Father's house are many mansions," a Christian one. These suggest that there is something divine even in the baseball glove and the neighborhood street. Pavese's poem "Grappa in September" reveals, even blesses, this divine quality of ordinary life, which comes to us through our senses. We see, hear, smell the world, and this, the poets are saying, is the true ground of our love for it. Our enlivened senses rejoice in it and bring us to praise it.

Praise is an old-fashioned virtue. It goes much further than honor and respect, which feel like moral duties: you "should" love the world and show it respect. Praise, however, delights in the world and brings delight to it, as biblical psalms and old hymns praise the beauties and pleasures of creation. Hopkins in his adorations doesn't simply accept the world's strange deformities. He loves them, and sings their praises.

On the following pages, Neruda praises a pair of wool socks, Ponge a door, McGrath bread, Simic the breasts of a woman, Merwin apricots, and Carl Sandburg the great bestial menagerie that inhabits each man's own chest.

How excessive some of these poems seem! It's as if once we begin to notice the world and enjoy it, we fall in love with its marvels. "The world is too much with us," Wordsworth says. But the "too muchness" of Hopkins's ecstatic celebrations, or of Simic's and Sandburg's exuberances, corresponds with the "too muchness," the extraordinary richness, of the world itself. Anything you attend to carefully can bring blessing, like Neruda's socks and Yeats's empty cup.

The world's excess of riches tempts human ambition and also keeps it within bounds. "Old Song" from West Africa says, "Excel when you must," take the heroic course, "but do not excel the world." The world is always more than anything you do in it, to it, with it. No invention can surpass the creation, and no story can encompass the planet's history. The world sets limits to the heroic urge. Not only because the world is larger and older, but because of its supreme indifference. We would not need psychologists to warn about inflation and preachers to exhort modesty if we bore in mind the world's dispassionate habits as it goes its way, the days and nights, tides and seasons, which keep human actions in humbler proportion.

Auden's remarkable poem, commenting on Brueghel's painting of the fall of Icarus, makes this humbling indifference very clear. The puer-boy Icarus may perform "something amazing," flying and falling through the sky, but the horizontal world of earth and sea and daily work continue "calmly on."

Excess, exuberance, ecstatic adoration, yes, and also Creeley's rain falling, Auden's plowman, Martinson's earthworm, Frost's rough earth, Eberhart's groundhog, and Yeats's ditch. Loving the world's many ways.

J.H.

THE WORLD IS TOO MUCH WITH US

The world is too much with us; late and soon,
Getting and spending, we lay waste our powers;
Little we see in Nature that is ours;
We have given our hearts away, a sordid boon!
This Sea that bares her bosom to the moon,
The winds that will be howling at all hours,
And are up-gathered now like sleeping flowers,
For this, for everything, we are out of tune;
It moves us not.—Great God! I'd rather be
A Pagan suckled in a creed outworn;
So might I, standing on this pleasant lea,
Have glimpses that would make me less forlorn;
Have sight of Proteus rising from the sea;
Or hear old Triton blow his wreathéd horn.

WILLIAM WORDSWORTH

GOD'S GRANDEUR

The world is charged with the grandeur of God.
  It will flame out, like shining from shook foil;
  It gathers to a greatness, like the ooze of oil
Crushed. Why do men then now not reck his rod?
Generations have trod, have trod, have trod;
  And all is seared with trade; bleared, smeared with toil;
  And wears man's smudge and shares man's smell: the soil
Is bare now, nor can foot feel, being shod.

And for all this, nature is never spent;
  There lives the dearest freshness deep down things;
And though the last lights off the black West went
  Oh, morning, at the brown brink eastward, springs—
Because the Holy Ghost over the bent
  World broods with warm breast and with ah! bright
    wings.

GERARD MANLEY HOPKINS

PIED BEAUTY

Glory be to God for dappled things—
   For skies of couple-colour as a brinded cow;
      For rose-moles all in stipple upon trout that swim;
Fresh-firecoal chestnut-falls; finches' wings;
   Landscape plotted and pieced—fold, fallow, and plough;
      And áll trádes, their gear and tackle and trim.

All things counter, original, spare, strange;
   Whatever is fickle, freckled (who knows how?)
      With swift, slow; sweet, sour; adazzle, dim;
He fathers-forth whose beauty is past change:
                       Praise him.

GERARD MANLEY HOPKINS

THE PERFUME / OF FLOWERS! . . .

The perfume
of flowers! A haw

drops such odour
it stops me

in the wall
of its fall. Love

arrests

Lime-trees
saturate

the night. We walk
in it

On a path jonquils
fill

the air. Love
is a scent

CHARLES OLSON

GRAPPA IN SEPTEMBER

The mornings run their course, clear and deserted
along the river's banks, which at dawn turn foggy,
darkening their green, while they wait for the sun.
In the last house, still damp, at the field's edge,
they sell tobacco, which is blackish in color
and tastes of sugar: it gives off a bluish haze.
They also have grappa* there, the color of water.

There comes a moment when everything is still
and ripens. The trees in the distance are quiet
and their darkness deepens, concealing fruit so ripe
it would drop at a touch. The occasional clouds
are swollen and ripe. Far away, in city streets,
every house is mellowing in the mild air.

This early, you see only women. The women don't smoke,
or drink. All they know is standing in the sun,
letting it warm their bodies, as though they were fruit.
The air, raw with fog, has to be swallowed in sips,
like grappa. Everything here distills its own fragrance.
Even the water in the river has absorbed the banks,
steeping them to their depths in the soft air. The streets
are like the women. They ripen by standing still.

This is the time when every man should stand
still in the street and see how everything ripens.
There is even a breeze, which does not move the clouds
but somehow succeeds in maneuvering the bluish haze
without scattering it. The smell drifting by is a new smell.
The tobacco is tinged with grappa. So it seems
the women are not alone in enjoying the morning.

* grappa: *an almost pure-alcohol*
spirit distilled from brandy.

CÉSAR PAVESE
translated by William Arrowsmith

ODE TO MY SOCKS

Maru Mori brought me
a pair
of socks
which she knitted herself
with her sheep-herder's hands,
two socks as soft
as rabbits.
I slipped my feet
into them
as though into
two
cases
knitted
with threads of
twilight
and goatskin.
Violent socks,
my feet were
two fish made
of wool,
two long sharks
seablue, shot
through
by one golden thread,
two immense blackbirds,
two cannons,
my feet
were honored
in this way
by
these
heavenly
socks.
They were

so handsome
for the first time
my feet seemed to me
unacceptable
like two decrepit
firemen, firemen
unworthy
of that woven
fire,
of those glowing
socks.

Nevertheless
I resisted
the sharp temptation
to save them somewhere
as students
keep
fireflies,
as learned men
collect
sacred texts,
I resisted
the mad impulse
to put them
in a golden
cage
and each day give them
birdseed
and pieces of pink melon.
Like explorers
in the jungle who hand
over the very rare
green deer
to the spit
and eat it

with remorse,
I stretched out
my feet
and pulled on
the
magnificent
socks
and
then my shoes.

The moral
of my ode is this:
beauty is twice
beauty
and what is good is doubly
good
when it is a matter of two socks
made of wool
in winter.

PABLO NERUDA
translated by R.B.

THE DELIGHTS OF THE DOOR

Kings don't touch doors.

They don't know this joy: to push affectionately or fiercely before us one of those huge panels we know so well, then to turn back in order to replace it—holding a door in our arms.

The pleasure of grabbing one of those tall barriers to a room abdominally, by its porcelain knot; of this swift fighting, body-to-body, when, the forward motion for an instant halted, the eye opens and the whole body adjusts to its new surroundings.

But the body still keeps one friendly hand on the door, holding it open, then decisively pushes the door away, closing itself in—which the click of the powerful but well-oiled spring pleasantly confirms.

FRANCIS PONGE
translated by R.B.

THE BREAD OF THIS WORLD;
PRAISES III

On the Christmaswhite plains of the floured and flowering
  kitchen table
The holy loaves of bread are slowly being born:
Rising like low hills in the steepled pastures of light—
Lifting the prairie farmhouse afternoon on their arching
  backs.

It must be Friday, the bread tells us as it climbs
Out of itself like a poor man climbing up on a cross
Toward transfiguration.

                        And it is a Mystery, surely,
If we think that this bread rises only out of the enigma
That leavens the Apocalypse of yeast, or ascends on the
  beards and beads
Of a rosary and priesthood of barley those Friday heavens
Lofting . . .

        But we who will eat the bread when we come in
Out of the cold and dark know it is a deeper mystery
That brings the bread to rise:
                        it is the love and faith
Of large and lonely women, moving like floury clouds
In farmhouse kitchens, that rounds the loaves and the lives
Of those around them . . .
                    just as we know it is hunger—
Our own and others'—that gives all salt and savor to bread.

But that is a workaday story and this is the end of the week.

                              THOMAS MCGRATH

BREASTS

I love breasts, hard
Full breasts, guarded
By a button.

They come in the night.
The bestiaries of the ancients
Which include the unicorn
Have kept them out.

Pearly, like the east
An hour before sunrise,
Two ovens of the only
Philosopher's stone
Worth bothering about.

They bring on their nipples
Beads of inaudible sighs,
Vowels of delicious clarity
For the little red schoolhouse of our mouths.

Elsewhere, solitude
Makes another gloomy entry
In its ledger, misery
Borrows another cup of rice.

They draw nearer: Animal
Presence. In the barn
The milk shivers in the pail.

I like to come up to them
From underneath, like a kid
Who climbs on a chair
To reach a jar of forbidden jam.

Gently, with my lips,
Loosen the button.
Have them slip into my hands
Like two freshly poured beer-mugs.

I spit on fools who fail to include
Breasts in their metaphysics,
Star-gazers who have not enumerated them
Among the moons of the earth . . .

They give each finger
Its true shape, its joy:
Virgin soap, foam
On which our hands are cleansed.

And how the tongue honors
These two sour buns,
For the tongue is a feather
Dipped in egg-yolk.

I insist that a girl
Stripped to the waist
Is the first and last miracle,

That the old janitor on his deathbed
Who demands to see the breasts of his wife
For one last time
Is the greatest poet who ever lived.

O my sweet, my wistful bagpipes.
Look, everyone is asleep on the earth.
Now, in the absolute immobility
Of time, drawing the waist
Of the one I love to mine,

I will tip each breast
Like a dark heavy grape
Into the hive
Of my drowsy mouth.

CHARLES SIMIC

WILDERNESS

There is a wolf in me . . . fangs pointed for tearing gashes . . . a red tongue for raw meat . . . and the hot lapping of blood—I keep the wolf because the wilderness gave it to me and the wilderness will not let it go.

There is a fox in me . . . a silver-gray fox . . . I sniff and guess . . . I pick things out of the wind and air . . . I nose in the dark night . . . take sleepers and eat them and hide the feathers . . . I circle a loop and double-cross.

There is a hog in me . . . a snout and a belly . . . a machinery for eating and grunting . . . a machinery for sleeping satisfied in the sun—I got this too from the wilderness and the wilderness will not let it go.

There is a fish in me . . . I know I came from salt-blue water-gates . . . I scurried with shoals of herring . . . I blew water-spouts with porpoises . . . before land was . . . before the water went down . . . before Noah . . . before the first chapter of Genesis.

There is a baboon in me . . . clambering-clawed . . . dog-faced . . . yawping a galoot's hunger . . . hairy under the arm-pits . . . here are the hawk-eyed hankering men . . . here are the blonde and blue-eyed women . . . here they hide curled asleep waiting . . . ready to snarl and kill . . . ready to sing and give milk . . . waiting—I keep the baboon because the wilderness says so.

There is an eagle in me and a mockingbird . . . and the eagle flies among the Rocky Mountains of my dreams and fights among the Sierra crags of what I want . . . and the mock-ingbird warbles in the early forenoon before the dew is gone, warbles in the underbrush of my Chattanoogas of hope, gushes over the blue Ozark foothills of my wishes —And I got the eagle and the mockingbird from the wilderness.

O, I got a zoo, I got a menagerie, inside my ribs, under my bony head, under my red-valve heart—and I got something else: it is a man-child heart, a woman-child heart: it is a father and mother and lover: it came from God-Knows-Where: it is going to God-Knows-Where—For I am the keeper of the zoo: I say yes and no: I sing and kill and work: I am a pal of the world: I came from the wilderness.

CARL SANDBURG

O SWEET
SPONTANEOUS

O sweet spontaneous
earth how often have
the
doting

        fingers of
prurient philosophers pinched
and
poked

thee
, has the naughty thumb
of science prodded
thy

       beauty . how
often have religions taken
thee upon their scraggy knees
squeezing and

buffeting thee that thou mightest conceive
gods
     (but
true

to the incomparable
couch of death thy

rhythmic
lover

thou answerest

them only with

spring)

E. E. CUMMINGS

"West Wall" (W. S. Merwin) and "Ripening" (Wendell Berry) merge love for a person with love for the world; both ripen together.

WEST WALL

In the unmade light I can see the world
as the leaves brighten I see the air
the shadows melt and the apricots appear
now that the branches vanish I see the apricots
from a thousand trees ripening in the air
they are ripening in the sun along the west wall
apricots beyond number are ripening in the daylight.

Whatever was there
I never saw those apricots swaying in the light
I might have stood in orchards forever
without beholding the day in the apricots
or knowing the ripeness of the lucid air
or touching the apricots in your skin
or tasting in your mouth the sun in the apricots

W. S. MERWIN

RIPENING

The longer we are together
the larger death grows around us.
How many we know by now
who are dead! We, who were young,
now count the cost of having been.
And yet as we know the dead
we grow familiar with the world.
We, who were young and loved each other
ignorantly, now come to know
each other in love, married
by what we have done, as much
as by what we intend. Our hair
turns white with our ripening
as though to fly away in some
coming wind, bearing the seed
of what we know. It was bitter to learn
that we come to death as we come
to love, bitter to face
the just and solving welcome
that death prepares. But that is bitter
only to the ignorant, who pray
it will not happen. Having come
the bitter way to better prayer, we have
the sweetness of ripening. How sweet
to know you by the signs of this world!

WENDELL BERRY

Again, that concatenation of shared natural world and intimate personal feeling, bringing an organic contentment like vegetation receiving rain.

THE RAIN

All night the sound had
come back again,
and again falls
this quiet, persistent rain.

What am I to myself
that must be remembered,
insisted upon
so often? Is it

that never the ease,
even the hardness,
of rain falling
will have for me

something other than this,
something not so insistent—
am I to be locked in this
final uneasiness.

Love, if you love me,
lie next to me.
Be for me, like rain,
the getting out

of the tiredness, the fatuousness, the semi-
lust of intentional indifference.
Be wet
with a decent happiness.

ROBERT CREELEY

Loving the World Anyway
495

Three brief images—one Chippewa, one Turkish, and one West African—move the focus of a man's attention from self to world.

SOMETIMES I GO ABOUT PITYING MYSELF

Sometimes I go about pitying myself,
and all the time
I am being carried on great winds across the sky.

Chippewa music
adapted from the translation by Frances Densmore

UNITY

The horse's mind
Blends
So swiftly
Into the hay's mind

FAZIL HÜSNÜ DAĞLARCA
translated by Talat Sait Halman

OLD SONG

Do not seek too much fame,
but do not seek obscurity.
Be proud.
But do not remind the world of your deeds.
Excel when you must,
but do not excel the world.
Many heroes are not yet born,
many have already died.
To be alive to hear this song is a victory.

Traditional, West Africa

MUSÉE DES BEAUX ARTS

About suffering they were never wrong,
The Old Masters: how well they understood
Its human position; how it takes place
While someone else is eating or opening a window or just
    walking dully along;
How, when the aged are reverently, passionately waiting
For the miraculous birth, there always must be
Children who did not specially want it to happen, skating
On a pond at the edge of the wood:
They never forgot
That even the dreadful martyrdom must run its course
Anyhow in a corner, some untidy spot
Where the dogs go on with their doggy life and the
    torturer's horse
Scratches its innocent behind on a tree.

In Brueghel's *Icarus,* for instance: how everything turns away
Quite leisurely from the disaster; the ploughman may
Have heard the splash, the forsaken cry,
But for him it was not an important failure; the sun shone
As it had to on the white legs disappearing into the green
Water; and the expensive delicate ship that must have seen
Something amazing, a boy falling out of the sky,
Had somewhere to get to and sailed calmly on.

W. H. AUDEN

THE EARTHWORM

Who really respects the earthworm,
the farmworker far under the grass in the soil.
He keeps the earth always changing.
He works entirely full of soil,
speechless with soil, and blind.

He is the underneath farmer, the underground one,
where the fields are getting on their harvest clothes.
Who really respects him,
this deep and calm earth-worker,
this deathless, gray, tiny farmer in the planet's soil.

HARRY MARTINSON
translated by R.B.

Robert Frost's poem moves through four dimensions at once: from youth to age; from love to death; from air to earth; from sweet to salt and bitter. Though his love craves "the stain / Of tears," pain and hurt are not enough —perhaps they are too self-absorbed. And so he longs for the plain rough reality of the world as it is.

TO EARTHWARD

Love at the lips was touch
As sweet as I could bear;
And once that seemed too much;
I lived on air

That crossed me from sweet things,
The flow of—was it musk
From hidden grapevine springs
Downhill at dusk?

I had the swirl and ache
From sprays of honeysuckle
That when they're gathered shake
Dew on the knuckle.

I craved strong sweets, but those
Seemed strong when I was young;
The petal of the rose
It was that stung.

Now no joy but lacks salt,
That is not dashed with pain
And weariness and fault;
I crave the stain

Of tears, the aftermark
Of almost too much love,

The sweet of bitter bark
and burning clove.

When stiff and sore and scarred
I take away my hand
From leaning on it hard
In grass and sand,

The hurt is not enough:
I long for weight and strength
To feel the earth as rough
To all my length.

ROBERT FROST

THE GROUNDHOG

In June, amid the golden fields,
I saw the groundhog lying dead.
Dead lay he; my senses shook,
And mind outshot our naked frailty.
There lowly in the vigorous summer
His form began its senseless change,
And made my senses waver dim
Seeing nature ferocious in him.
Inspecting close his maggots' might
And seething cauldron of his being,
Half with loathing, half with a strange love,
I poked him with an angry stick.
The fever rose, became a flame
And Vigour circumscribed the skies,
Immense energy in the sun,
And through my frame a sunless trembling.
My stick had done nor good nor harm.
Then stood I silent in the day
Watching the object, as before;
And kept my reverence for knowledge
Trying for control, to be still,
To quell the passion of the blood;
Until I had bent down on my knees
Praying for joy in the sight of decay.
And so I left; and I returned
In Autumn strict of eye, to see
The sap gone out of the groundhog,
But the bony sodden hulk remained.
But the year had lost its meaning,
And in intellectual chains
I lost both love and loathing,
Mured up in the wall of wisdom.
Another summer took the fields again
Massive and burning, full of life,

Loving the World Anyway
503

But when I chanced upon the spot
There was only a little hair left,
And bones bleaching in the sunlight
Beautiful as architecture;
I watched them like a geometer,
And cut a walking stick from a birch.
It has been three years, now.
There is no sign of the groundhog.
I stood there in the whirling summer,
My hand capped a withered heart,
And thought of China and of Greece,
Of Alexander in his tent;
Of Montaigne in his tower,
Of Saint Theresa in her wild lament.

RICHARD EBERHART

from
A DIALOGUE OF SELF AND SOUL

MY SELF: A living man is blind and drinks his drop.
What matter if the ditches are impure?
What matter if I live it all once more?
Endure that toil of growing up;
The ignominy of boyhood; the distress
of boyhood changing into man;
The unfinished man and his pain
Brought face to face with his own clumsiness;

The finished man among his enemies?—
How in the name of Heaven can he escape
That defiling and disfigured shape
The mirror of malicious eyes
Casts upon his eye until at last
He thinks that shape must be his shape?
And what's the good of an escape
If honour find him in the wintry blast?

I am content to live it all again
And yet again, if it be life to pitch
Into the frog-spawn of a blind man's ditch,
A blind man battering blind men;
Or into that most fecund ditch of all,
The folly that man does
Or must suffer, if he woos
A proud woman not kindred of his soul.

I am content to follow to its source
Every event in action or in thought;
Measure the lot; forgive myself the lot!
When such as I cast out remorse

So great a sweetness flows into the breast
We must laugh and we must sing,
We are blest by every thing,
Every thing we look upon is blest.

WILLIAM BUTLER YEATS

from
VACILLATION

My fiftieth year had come and gone,
I sat, a solitary man,
In a crowded London shop,
An open book and empty cup
On the marble table-top.

While on the shop and street I gazed
My body of a sudden blazed;
And twenty minutes more or less
It seemed, so great my happiness,
That I was blessèd and could bless.

WILLIAM BUTLER YEATS

Index of Poets

Index of Poets

Index of First Lines

TWO: *Fathers' Prayers for Sons and Daughters*

THREE: *War*

FOUR: *I Know the Earth, and I Am Sad*

FIVE: *The House of Fathers and Titans*

"Those Winter Sundays" by Robert Hayden. Reprinted from *Angle of Ascent: New and Selected Poems* by Robert Hayden. By permission of Liveright Publishing Corporation. Copyright © 1975, 1972, 1970, 1966 by Robert Hayden.

"My Father Went to Funerals" by Howard Nelson. Copyright © 1992 by Howard Nelson. The poem first appeared in "Heroism: An Exhibition of Visual Art and Poetry," Peconic Gallery, Suffolk Community College, Riverhead, NY.

"Offering" by Thomas McGrath. From *Selected Poems 1938–1988* by Thomas McGrath. Copyright © 1988 by Thomas McGrath. Reprinted with permission of Copper Canyon Press, P.O. Box 271, Port Townsend, WA 98368.

"The Distant Footsteps" by César Vallejo, translated by James Wright and John Knoepfle. From *Neruda and Vallejo: Selected Poems*, edited and translated by Robert Bly, John Knoepfle, and James Wright. Beacon Press. Copyright © 1971 by Robert Bly.

"Yesterday" by W. S. Merwin. From *Opening the Hand*. Copyright © 1983 by W. S. Merwin. Reprinted by permission of Georges Borchardt, Inc.

From "Memories of My Father" by Galway Kinnell. From *When One Has Lived a Long Time Alone* by Galway Kinnell. Copyright © 1990 by Galway Kinnell. Reprinted by permission of Alfred A. Knopf, Inc.

"The Race" by Sharon Olds. Reprinted by permission; copyright © 1985 Sharon Olds. Originally in *The New Yorker*.

"The Irish Cliffs of Moher" by Wallace Stevens. From *Collected Poems* by Wallace Stevens. Copyright 1952 by Wallace Stevens. Reprinted by permission of Alfred A. Knopf, Inc.

SIX: *Language: Speaking Well and Speaking Out*

"Magic Words," "The Mind," and "Songs Are Thoughts." From *Technicians of the Sacred*, edited by Jerome Rothenberg. Copyright © 1969 by Jerome Rothenberg. Reprinted by permission of Sterling Lord Literistic, Inc.

From "Gargantua" by François Rabelais, translated by J. M. Cohen (Penguin Classics, 1955), copyright © J. M. Cohen, 1955.

From "The Havana Lectures." Translation of "Havana Lectures" by Federico García Lorca, copyright © 1981 by Herederos de Federico García and Stella Rodriques. Original Spanish work from *Obras Completas* (Aguillar, 1986 edition), copyright © 1986 by Herederos de Federico García Lorca. All rights reserved. For information regarding rights and permissions for works by Federico García Lorca, please contact William Peter Kosmas, Esq., 25 Howitt Road, London NW3 4LT.

"Poetry Is a Destructive Force" by Wallace Stevens. From *Collected Poems* by Wallace Stevens. Copyright 1942 by Wallace Stevens and renewed 1970 by Holly Stevens. Reprinted by permission of Alfred A. Knopf, Inc.

"In My Craft or Sullen Art." Dylan Thomas: *Poems of Dylan Thomas*. Copyright 1946 by New Directions Publishing Corporation. Reprinted by permission of New Directions Publishing Corporation and David Higham Associates.

"On the Words in Poetry." Dylan Thomas: *Early Prose Writings*. Copyright © 1964 by New Directions Publishing Corporation. Reprinted by permission of New Directions Publishing Corporation and David Higham Associates.

"Sound-Posture" by Robert Frost. From *Interviews with Robert Frost,* edited by Edward Connery Lathem. Copyright © 1966 by Holt, Rinehart and Winston. Originally published by Boston Evening Transcript. Henry Holt and Company, Inc., and from *Selected Letters of Robert Frost,* edited by Lawrance Thompson.

SEVEN: *Making a Hole in Denial*

Copyright Acknowledgments

TEN: *The Second Layer: Anger, Hatred, Outrage*

TWELVE: *The Cultivated Heart*

THIRTEEN: *Mother and Great Mother*

FOURTEEN: *The Spindrift Gaze Toward Paradise*

FIFTEEN: *Zaniness*

SIXTEEN: *Loving the World Anyway*

About the Editors

Robert Bly is the author, editor, and translator of numerous collections of poetry. Among his recent books are *American Poetry: Wildness and Domesticity* (a book of essays), *Iron John: A Book About Men*, and his collected prose poems, *What Have I Ever Lost by Dying?* He lives in Minneapolis, Minnesota.

James Hillman is a psychologist, scholar, and lecturer. Among his many books are *Re-Visioning Psychology*, *A Blue Fire*, and, most recently, *We've Had a Hundred Years of Psychotherapy and the World's Getting Worse* (with Michael Ventura). He lives in northeastern Connecticut.

Michael Meade is an accomplished scholar of the myths and rituals of traditional societies. As a lecturer and performer, he is known for weaving a rhythm through stories, poems, and tribal lore. He is the author of *Men and the Water of Life*, a book on initiation and culture. Meade lives on Vashon Island in Washington state.